Public Dollars,
Private Stadiums

PUBLIC DOLLARS,

PRIVATE STADIUMS

THE BATTLE OVER BUILDING
SPORTS STADIUMS

Kevin J. Delaney

and

Rick Eckstein

RUTGERS UNIVERSITY PRESS
New Brunswick, New Jersey, and London

Library of Congress Cataloging-in-Publication Data

Delaney, Kevin J., 1960–
Public dollars, private stadiums : the battle over building sports stadiums /
Kevin J. Delaney and Rick Eckstein.
p.   cm.
Includes bibliographical references and index.
ISBN 0-8135-3342-2 (hardcover : alk. paper) — ISBN 0-8135-3343-0 (pbk. :
alk. paper)
1. Stadiums—United States—Finance—Case studies.
2. Stadiums—United States—Planning—Case studies.   3. Finance,
Public—United States—Case studies.   I. Eckstein, Rick, 1960–
II. Title.

GV413.D45 2003   796'.06'8—dc21   2003005673

British Cataloging-in-Publication information is available from the
British Library.

Third paperback printing, 2006

The publication program of Rutgers University Press is supported by the
Board of Governors of Rutgers, The State University of New Jersey.

Manufactured in the United States of America

To our families—you know who you are!

Contents

Acknowledgments

We have been working on this book since 1998 and have benefited from innumerable formal and informal conversations with family, friends, students, and colleagues as the project grew from conception to its final form. Probably the most enduring support was from our many undergraduate and graduate students, who seemed very interested in the topic whenever we discussed it in class and kept pestering us to finish the book. There were also many kind comments from colleagues during and after conference presentations, suggesting that we weren't the only two people excited by these issues.

Other individuals were more directly responsible for the actual labor that went into this project. Brian Duffy, Katie Krackenberger, Mary Martin, Joelle Sano, and Donovan Wydner spent countless hours keeping us up to date on the nine cities we studied in the book and about eleven others we didn't study. Megan Kasimatis and Kerry Whittemore helped enormously with the research on Cincinnati and San Diego, respectively. Scott Edmond and Pat Cummens helped us to understand the Twin Cities as well as provided a place to stay. Our understanding of Hartford greatly benefited from discussions with Brendan Walsh, and we got some photographic help from Liz Douglas and Sarah Bergfeld. Terry Mambu helped us tie together all of the loose ends, and our friends at the Grassroots Policy Project (Sandra Hinson and Richard Healey) have been supporting us in one way or another since the beginning. Lee Clarke of Rutgers University offered extraordinarily good suggestions for improving our initial manuscript. Cheryl Cole read other pieces of our work and always provided excellent comments and encouragement. Michael Leeds and Andrew Zimbalist answered e-mail questions about sports economics with great patience. Indispensable financial support was provided by the sociology departments at Villanova University and Temple University as well as the

College of Arts and Sciences at Villanova. David Myers, Kristi Long, and Adi Hovav at Rutgers University Press and copyeditor Dawn Potter never lost faith in this book; and we hope this faith has been rewarded.

Most important, we would like to thank all of the individuals who took the time to talk with us about the process of building sports stadiums in their cities. All of those we interviewed were frank and passionate about their positions. We would not have been able to write this book without their candor.

Other friends and colleagues have provided less direct but no less important support during the past four years. On Kevin Delaney's list, many thanks to Patrick Shannon; Rich Gisonny; Doreen and all the Delaneys; Jay, Buzz, and all the Kormans; Gretchen Condran; David Elesh; Magali Sarfatti Larson; Julia Ericksen; Bill Yancey; Sherri Grasmuck; Maria Rosario; David Bouchier; Vincent Louis; Kelly Feighan; Mitch Telsey; Steve Mosley; Roy Tickle; Chris Zuech; and the crew from the Morrisville Tavern. On Rick Eckstein's list, heartfelt appreciation goes to Villanova's Center for Peace and Justice Education, Bill Werpehowski, Tom Arvanites, Bill Waegel, Fr. Kail Ellis, Lance Hannon, Bob DeFina, Carol Anthony, Dorothy Lairdieson, Joyce Zavarich, Abby Kiesa, Sarah Brino, Dave Boyer, Sara Shute, Larry Burnett, Tom Gibbons, Leslie Fenton, Ed Royce, Jon Gombola, Charlotte Vent, Jim Cugliari, the McCarron and Russell families (for child support), and the Friday afternoon regulars at Roache and O'Brien's.

Our families have been rock solid in supporting us during this seemingly endless project. Our youngest children, Kate and Carolyn, have yet to see their dads not working on this stadium book; and we hope they will still recognize us now that it is done. Older children Connor, Jack, and Emma did know their dads in a different time but have shown great patience in waiting for us to finish "just one more section" before we headed to the park or made breakfast. Finally, Susan Korman and Monica Nicosia never let our optimism waver, even when finishing the book seemed impossible. In addition to emotional support, they provided occasional editing and technical support (always pro bono) and dealt with leaky hot-water heaters, cold furnaces, ice storms, overflowing toilets, and ear infections while we were on the road doing fieldwork. Thank you all!

Public Dollars, Private Stadiums

Introduction

"There will be no plan B," promised Pittsburgh mayor Tom Murphy, just hours before the November 1997 general election. Residents in the eleven-county Pittsburgh area would soon be voting on plan A, a referendum to increase the region's sales tax to finance new stadiums for the Pittsburgh Steelers and Pittsburgh Pirates and expand the existing convention center. The referendum was crushed by an almost two-to-one margin, losing decidedly in every county. The public had spoken. Pittsburgh-area residents did not want to use public dollars for new stadiums. The message could not be clearer.

Clear or not, four years later the Pirates and Steelers were playing in two new stadiums paid for primarily with public tax dollars. Despite his election-day warning, Mayor Murphy organized a plan B working group immediately after the referendum, which quickly and successfully devised a strategy to finance these new stadiums publicly without a popular vote. The total price tag of these stadiums was more than $500 million, with most of the revenues accruing to the teams.

Eight years earlier, in 1989, Maricopa County, Arizona, voters soundly defeated a proposed stadium tax and, in addition, passed a law requiring public approval of any future sports or entertainment project in excess of $3 million. By 1994, however, the Arizona state government and the Maricopa County Board of Supervisors had devised a way to institute a $238 million stadium tax without going to the voters. This led to the 1998 completion of Bank One Ballpark in Phoenix, home of the expansion Arizona Diamondbacks' major league baseball team, a project that cost more than $400 million.

Meanwhile, in 1998, residents of San Diego County approved by a three-to-two margin a referendum that would publicly finance a large piece of the San Diego Padres' new ballpark. Four years after this strong showing of public and political support, construction had barely started, even though the ballpark was originally supposed to be

1

finished by opening day in 2002. Now even the projected 2004 completion looks far from certain, as does the estimated $410 million cost.

What is going on here? In two cities where residents opposed building new stadiums with public dollars, the stadiums were built anyway. In another city, where voters actually supported using public dollars, building the stadium has become a Sisyphean task. Clearly, there is no direct relationship between public sentiments and public policy. But if popular sovereignty, as reflected in these referendums, doesn't affect social policy, then what does? What are the implications of this inconsistency between democratic processes such as voting, and the actual policy decisions that affect people's lives? In this book, we hope to answer these and other equally disconcerting questions by examining how public dollars were used to build professional sports stadiums in nine U.S. cities.

There has been an explosion in new stadium construction since the 1990s, and several things make this current boom very different from any other period in history. First, the breadth of new construction across the country and the amount of public contribution is unprecedented. In the decade since the opening of Baltimore's Oriole Park at Camden Yards in the early 1990s, fourteen new baseball stadiums have been built and an additional three are under construction. When the three stadiums currently under construction are completed, seventeen of the thirty major league baseball teams will be playing in stadiums built since 1992. As for the National Football League, seventeen of thirty-two teams will be playing in stadiums built since 1992, once those currently under construction are completed. This is an unprecedented wave of stadium building, and one analyst has estimated that approximately $10 billion of public money has gone to all new sports stadiums since the mid-1980s (Keating 1999). Although these stadiums are almost always officially owned by quasi-governmental stadium authorities, the revenue streams from new stadiums increasingly flow toward private pockets. So our use of the term *private stadiums* refers less to the nominal ownership of these facilities and more to who benefits from their publicly financed construction and operation.

In this book, we focus on the processes behind these new stadium initiatives, not just their outcomes. This emphasis on process seemed imperative to us early on in our research as we quickly noticed how the outcomes in each of the nine cities we studied were in no way uniform and because previous studies on new sports stadiums could not account for these differences. Therefore, we designed a comparative framework to explain the distinctive elements of how each city built (or tried to build) new stadiums with public dollars. What is it about each of these cities that accounts for the variation? Are they completely different, thus making outcomes nothing more than random events? Or do certain recurring patterns almost help us predict what the outcome of a stadium initiative will be in a certain city?

Our comparative framework, which we develop in chapters 1 and 2, is built on two distinct but interrelated pillars. First, we identify the new stadium advocates in each of these cities. Who is leading the charge for publicly financed stadiums and how does that leadership, in and of itself, contribute to the relative success or failure of this charge (from the advocates' point of view)? In trying to identify the leaders of a stadium project, we immediately examine what we call a city's "local growth coalition." At heart, a growth coalition is an institutional alliance between the local corporate community and the local government, although the specific form of government involvement may vary. The local corporate community generally runs the growth coalition, which might include media, religious, and labor organizations (in supporting roles) but rarely includes a city's sports teams. Local growth coalitions have an inordinate influence over public policy and use that influence to serve their parochial interests, although they may claim they are pursuing the overall community good. Policies advocating public dollars for sports stadiums provide just one example of this bias.

As we show, however, not all cities have powerful local growth coalitions; and some may not have any growth coalition at all. Indeed, the existence and strength of these coalitions varies widely in the nine cities we study. We will show that the relative strength and coherence of the growth coalition has a significant effect on shaping the process of securing public money for new stadiums. The sports teams themselves, who usually have the most to gain organizationally from new publicly financed stadiums, often do not lead the battle to build them, particularly in strong growth coalition cities. In fact, these initiatives actually go more smoothly for advocates when the sports teams play only a supporting role because non-sports corporations can more easily obfuscate their vested interests in new stadiums and portray their advocacy as being in the best interest of the entire community. Only when a city has a weak growth coalition are sports teams (and other actors) forced to take a leading role in stadium projects.

The very existence and relative strength of a local growth coalition depends on the unique history and characteristics of that city. So while all of the cities covered in this book are responding to national trends, they are experiencing these forces at the local level. In other words, these are both national stories and unique city stories.

The second pillar of our analytical framework concerns the strategic choices made by local growth coalitions (or other advocates) to justify why a community should spend public dollars on new stadiums.

These strategies generally fall into two categories. The first claims that new stadiums will provide all sorts of tangible economic benefits to the local community. The second insists that new stadiums will benefi-cially augment the way in which a community views itself, how the community is perceived by others, and how community members get along with each other—what we call "community self-esteem" and "community collective conscience." Stadium advocates rely on both justifications and often use them simultaneously.

Nevertheless, there has lately been a noticeable shift away from economic promises and toward promises of social benefits. We believe this is not just random but reflects conscious strategic decisions by sta-dium proponents in each city. Proponents have realized that the path to publicly financed stadiums will be less problematic if they downplay the tangible economic benefits and accentuate the intangible social goods that might accompany stadiums. But like the existence and strength of local growth coalitions just discussed, these decisions are largely patterned by the unique structural landscape of each city. Sta-dium advocates certainly have some discretion about which strategies to employ, but certain cities lend themselves to making certain argu-ments about why it is in the community's best interest to build new sports stadiums with public dollars.

The first two chapters of the book elaborate the analytical frame-work we use to examine cities that have spent, or tried to spend, pub-lic dollars on new stadiums. Chapter 1 explores which individuals and organizations are most likely to champion publicly financed stadiums. Chapter 2 examines the shifting strategies employed by local growth coalitions (and other stadium proponents) to justify why all this tax money should be spent on new professional sports stadiums. This chapter includes a discussion of academic studies that challenge the alleged economic benefits of publicly subsidized stadiums.

The middle chapters apply this analytical framework to nine dif-ferent American cities that are part of this recent stadium construction boom. Chapter 3 examines Cincinnati, which exemplifies how a pow-erful local growth coalition manipulated notions of community self-esteem and community collective conscience to rather easily build two new stadiums with public money. The stadium deals in Cincinnati are among the most lucrative in the country—at least for the teams that play there. The focus of chapter 4 is Cleveland, where a local growth coalition experienced a tremendous comeback after growing mori-bund in the late 1970s. This comeback was centered on rebuilding Cleveland's downtown with, among other things, new stadiums.

Chapter 5 examines two cities with extremely weak local growth coalitions, and we show that this is an important reason why they have not been successful in building new stadiums with public money. In Minneapolis, a once-powerful coalition was largely responsible for building the Metrodome just twenty years ago; but today a shell of a coalition is having little success with new stadium plans. The remnants of Hartford's once relatively strong growth coalition recently tried luring the New England Patriots from Massachusetts by promising a new football stadium and all sorts of other amenities. This attempt was an embarrassing failure.

Chapter 6 heads west to explore the frontier cities of Denver, Phoenix, and San Diego. All of these cities have relatively weak local growth coalitions, yet all still managed to build new publicly financed stadiums. One reason is that these three cities, unlike the other six we study, are growing rather than contracting. Although this creates an entirely unique dynamic between the structure and strategy of building publicly financed stadiums, the road to publicly financed stadiums in these three cities has often passed over some very rough terrain.

In chapter 7, Pennsylvania's two largest cities offer a wonderful contrast in the importance of local growth coalitions and the strategies they choose for building publicly financed stadiums. In the late 1990s, the state promised huge financial support for building four brand-new stadiums, two each in Pittsburgh and Philadelphia. As of late 2002, both Pittsburgh teams are playing in their new stadiums. Meanwhile, in Philadelphia, the football stadium is still under construction; and ground has just been broken for the baseball stadium. This contrast provides strong evidence for how a growth coalition can shape the battle for public subsidies.

The concluding chapter reflects on the larger issues raised by the use of public dollars for new stadiums. Here, we argue that stadium battles are emblematic of much larger social and political processes in our society. These battles reveal how local power structures work within cities, and the processes we describe in this book say a great deal about our supposedly democratic institutions. *Public Dollars, Private Stadiums* is firmly rooted in sociologist C. Wright Mills's (1959) notion of the sociological imagination. Mills argued that sociological research should uncover the connections between private troubles and public issues. In other words, this research should help people understand that what personally troubles them is connected to more complex social forces. As we explore throughout this book, and take up as a central concern in the concluding chapter, policies that direct public dollars toward new stadiums may exacerbate rather than alleviate social problems such as poor schools, unemployment, poverty, and homelessness, even though proponents of these policies claim just the opposite.

1

Local Growth Coalitions and Publicly Funded Stadiums

During our first interview for this book, a Pittsburgh public official made it clear that the stadium tax's electoral defeat was, at best, a minor setback. He assured us that plan B would successfully steer public dollars to the two new stadiums anyway. When we asked if there would be any public referendum on this new plan, he smiled and said that was not part of the model. He told us that any possible city council opposition would be moot since it would not be voting on plan B either. Only three or four signatures would be needed, and he intimated that they wouldn't be hard to secure. What struck us more than his words was his demeanor in delivering them. This official seemed almost proud that plan B would circumvent popular approval achieved either directly by referendum or indirectly through city council. His wry smile suggested that he and other stadium supporters had figured out any potential problems and how to avoid them.

On the following day, we interviewed another public official, one who was a little less certain that plan B would actually fly. At one point, his computer started beeping incessantly, indicating an urgent e-mail message, which he politely ignored. Finally, the beeping stopped, but then the phone rang—an urgent call from the official we had interviewed the day before. The first thing our current interviewee said was "Yes, they are here with me now." He mostly listened for another minute and then hung up to continue the interview.

The interview itself yielded important information, but we learned even more from what appeared to be concern about our research. It shed new light on things we had been told the day before by a team executive who was gushing about the tireless advocacy of the many public officials and business leaders we were set to interview.

Everybody knew everybody, even though we had been unaware of this network when scheduling the interviews. So now, for the first time, we began envisioning a powerful coalition of individuals that was working to secure public dollars for private stadiums in Pittsburgh. We already knew that the stadium tax's electoral defeat was being ignored by Pittsburgh's powerful elite. But now we found ourselves actually in the middle of a plan created to disregard the popular referendum. Apparently, a well-organized coalition was determined to build two new publicly funded stadiums in Pittsburgh, regardless of public sentiment.

About a year later, we were in Minneapolis trying to understand why it was having such difficulty getting public subsidies for a new baseball stadium to replace the Metrodome. As in Pittsburgh, Minneapolis residents had continually opposed using tax dollars for a new Twins' stadium. In Minneapolis, however, there was no plan B. We learned about this difference during dinner with a prominent local businessperson at the private, exclusive Minneapolis Club. Our wide-ranging discussion kept returning to the theme that "Minneapolis lacked leadership." This man contended that the once-powerful, local business community (what he called "leadership") had largely disappeared from the Twin Cities. He waxed nostalgic for the days when John Cowles, Jr., then the local publisher of the *Minneapolis Star* and *Tribune* newspapers, could bring together a handful of leading local corporate titans, including Ken Dayton of Dayton Hudson department stores, Pete Ankeny of First National Bank, John Morrison of Northwestern National Bank, and others. In the 1970s, they could all get together at the Minneapolis Club, decide that the city needed a stadium, help raise the money to buy the land, and sell bonds to pay for the stadium. The loss of the Pillsbury family, the sale of Dayton Hudson to Target stores, the absorption of the local paper into a conglomerate headquartered in California: all had created what this businessman called a lack of leadership on the stadium issue. Today, the Minnesota Twins baseball team is on the verge of losing its major league franchise (despite a very successful 2002 campaign), and still there is no movement toward building a new ballpark. Unlike officials in Pittsburgh, no one in Minneapolis seems able to put together a plan B.

We believe these stories about Pittsburgh and Minneapolis underscore the key role played in each city by local growth coalitions. In Pittsburgh, that coalition was powerful enough to overcome a negative public vote and the vociferous opposition of a maverick newspaper owner. In Minneapolis, however, a declining growth coalition has been unable to overcome public opposition to a new stadium (despite a very supportive newspaper publisher). In this chapter, we will begin to lay the foundation for understanding the similarities and differences in the battles over new stadiums in American cities. Our main contentions are twofold: first, that the quest to secure public dollars for private stadiums can best be understood by thoroughly examining social power in each city and particularly how this power is exercised by local growth coalitions; and second, that these battles are emblematic of much larger disagreements about how a community most benefits from the allocation of scarce social resources.

LOCAL GROWTH COALITIONS

In this book, we use the idea of local growth coalitions to explain how publicly financed stadiums continue to be built despite increased resistance and why some of these stadiums are easier to build (and publicly finance) than others are. This concept is an extension of sociologist Harvey Molotch's notion of the growth machine that normally controls urban communities.[1] These coalitions are rooted in an institutionalized relationship between headquartered local corporations and the local government. They articulate and implement social policies that will supposedly stimulate economic growth, at least as defined by their members. In essence, these machines or coalitions are arbiters of what economic growth should look like in a community.

Locally based financial corporations are often the driving force of these coalitions; and the more powerful the local corporate community, the more powerful the local growth coalition.[2] Local government is the other key player in these alliances because it implements policies that will facilitate the coalition's vision of economic growth, especially when tax dollars are contributing to that vision. Governments may play either a conspicuous or inconspicuous role, depending on varying social circumstances. While financial institutions are often at the helm of these coalitions, nonfinancial local corporations are not excluded from leadership. The powerful local growth coalition in Cincinnati, for instance, is steered by Proctor and Gamble and Chiquita Brands International. Smaller, locally based corporations or those without a local headquarters may also be involved in coalitions but rarely assume leading roles. In addition, the increasingly corporate-controlled media outlets in many cities are frequently involved with local growth coalitions. Even nonbusiness organizations such as religious groups and labor unions may be part of these alliances. Interestingly, although the professional sports teams are usually part of the coalitions, they often do not take a leading role in promulgating a coalition's position, especially on public funding for new sports stadiums.

Even though we talk about these coalitions as if they are tangible organizations, they don't have an office, meet on a regular basis, or issue position papers on official letterhead. But as we will show, the individuals and organizations involved in them do plan, discuss, and strategize with each other in some structured fashion; and they do try to influence policymakers and the general public. Elite, CEO-only business groups present in many U.S. cities offer one highly structured forum for these discussions.[3] These groups are the standard bearers of the local growth coalitions and often play a leading role in securing public dollars for private stadiums, even if they are largely unknown to the general public. We believe that the strength and influence of these coalitions is directly proportional to the strength and influence of corporate roundtables in the community. A stronger roundtable means a stronger local growth coalition, which makes it easier for cities to build publicly financed stadiums even in the face of skepticism and hostility. We argue, however, that these coalitions are more successful when they work quietly behind the scenes.

We prefer talking about growth coalitions rather than growth machines for two main reasons. First, a machine sounds much more omnipotent than a coalition does; and we want to clarify that these alliances, while extremely powerful, do not always get their own way. For example, in the early 1990s, the powerful Cincinnati growth coalition was badly defeated when it tried to revise the city charter (see chapter 3). On the issue of publicly funded stadiums, growth coalitions have also not gotten everything they want. For instance, as we discussed in the introduction, Pittsburgh's strong local growth coalition was unable to build support for the 1997 referendum. In the end, that defeat didn't matter; but the path to Pittsburgh's new stadiums would have been less troublesome had the referendum passed (see chapter 7).

We also prefer talking about coalitions instead of machines because the term allows for much more empirical variation in the strength and unity of the coalition. The machine metaphor suggests a monolithic, standardized entity that uniformly influences social policy. But we believe these local alliances do not all look the same, even though they share many similarities. Indeed, not all cities even have growth coalitions. Some have powerful coalitions, while others have weak ones. Some coalitions have been powerful for many years, while others have only recently become powerful. Sometimes a coalition dies off and stays dead; sometimes it dies and rises anew. Identifying the existence of a local growth coalition and its relative strength yields important insights into urban power structures (generally) and the efficacy of building new sports stadiums with public money (specifically).[4]

LOCAL GROWTH COALITIONS AND SOCIAL POWER

Understanding how and why local growth coalitions exercise power is the key to unlocking the complex processes that direct public money to new sports stadiums. Unequal social power is especially important since there is clearly no preexisting, society-wide consensus about the propriety of such policies. If anything, skepticism and resistance to stadium subsidies have increased among the general public, academics who study the topic, and even some policymakers. Still, the stadiums keep getting built; and the public continues to foot the bill at most of these new ballparks because the people, organizations, and ideas that support this use of public dollars are more powerful than those that oppose it.

Sociologist Steven Lukes (1974) has developed one of the most interesting and useful models for understanding social power, and our idea of local growth coalitions is rooted in it. Lukes believes that power operates in three distinct (although overlapping) dimensions.[5] The first dimension of power refers to those normal, easily observable political arenas in which elected officials and nonelected citizens debate and discuss policy matters. These debates supposedly represent a wide range of perspectives, and the political process fairly (and without bias) decides which are best for the community as a whole. Decisions coming from these first-dimensional arenas have a certain legitimacy because they are equated with a democratic process. In terms of building new publicly financed stadiums, a first-dimensional analysis would concentrate on public referendums and other open processes such as city council meetings, all of which are part of the ordinary political process. The analysis would conclude that most new publicly financed stadiums have resulted from a fair democratic process. Given the approach's insistence on a level political playing field, local growth coalitions are not important to a strictly first-dimensional analysis.[6]

The second dimension of power refers to power exercised behind the scenes rather than in the more visible political arenas; it has sometimes been called *extraordinary politics*.[7] Local growth coalitions become more important in the second dimension, which acknowledges vast power differentials between and among individuals and organizations. Lobbyists often operate in this realm when they try to influence social policy without allowing widespread public knowledge of their activities. Sports teams and other businesses might try to influence stadium debates by inviting politicians to ballpark luxury boxes, contributing to political campaigns, financially supporting certain policy initiatives, helping draft legislation, and promising to enter (or threatening to exit) a community if certain policies are in place. This second-dimensional view challenges the fairness of political processes because not all citizens have an equal ability to play extraordinary politics.

In the third dimension of power, local growth coalitions influence public policy (and benefit from it) in more subtle ways. At this level, policy decisions seem automatically to serve the interests of the coalition as a whole, even when the coalition is not involved in the decision-making process and certain members of the coalition (individual or organizational) do not noticeably benefit. Lukes believes that two reasons explain why powerful social actors (such as growth coalitions) benefit from policy decisions even when they do not participate in making them. The first explanation concerns a society's dominant ideology: the taken-for-granted assumptions about what is correct or desirable in a society. The interests of the local growth coalition are served by the dominant ideology in different ways. For example, "proper" economic growth has become equated with large, visible projects funded by public dollars but planned and operated by private, usually corporate, interests. Other versions of economic growth, such as investment in basic work force training, small business development, or education, are seen as less proper. The local growth coalition may or may not participate in the creation of this dominant belief, even though it is a beneficiary of it.

More important in the case of new stadiums, the prominent place of sports within the dominant ideology also serves the interests of the local growth coalitions. Sports are bigger than life. In schools, at home, in the media, and within government, sports often carry more prestige than other cultural activities do.[8] There are no high school pep rallies urging the chess team to victory; we do not talk about model U.N. moms shuttling their kids from meeting to meeting; there are no twenty-four-hour web sites allowing us to watch schools getting built. Big-time college and professional sports boost this cultural importance to an even higher level. Athletes have become celebrities; their posters line the walls of millions of children (and many adults), who dream of slam dunks and grand slams. In the stadium battles we discuss in this book, the "bigger is better" growth ideology combines with the glorification of professional sports in a powerful and intoxicating brew. Local growth coalitions benefit from this dominant ideology as they pursue new publicly financed stadiums. Opposing these stadiums, then, becomes a nearly insurmountable task because it requires combating what most individuals and organizations accept and assume to be correct. Lukes (1974) explains:

> Is it not the supreme and most insidious exercise of power to pre-
> vent people, to whatever degree, from having grievances by shap-
> ing their perceptions, cognitions, and preferences in such a way
> that they accept their role in the existing order of things, either be-
> cause they can see or imagine no alternative to it, or because they
> see it as natural? (24)

When pursuing publicly financed sports stadiums, local growth coalitions operate simultaneously in the second and third dimensions of power. (By definition they invalidate a strictly first-dimensional analysis.) For example, it obviously serves the interests of powerful team owners to use public dollars (rather than their own dollars) for new stadiums, whether or not they are directly involved in forging these policies. Less obviously, new stadiums serve non-sports members of the corporate community because they help these members recruit and retain executives. Just as important, however, is how these policies fortify the ideological climate, which more subtly serves these powerful social actors. Such actors benefit from spending public dollars on private stadiums because it legitimates a system of corporate liberalism, whereby government subsidies of large businesses become part of the dominant ideology and thus become an accepted way of doing things.[9] Today this corporate liberalism may take the form of a subsidized stadium; but tomorrow it could become tax abatements, new highways to serve company headquarters, or a law limiting liability in case of a nuclear reactor accident. As always, the dominant ideology reinforces the idea that such policies are in everybody's best interests, not just those of powerful people and organizations. This is third-dimensional power in action.

Local governments' important role in allocating public dollars for private stadiums also straddles the boundary between second- and third-dimensional power. The remarkable similarity of governmental policies in the nine cities we study suggests a systemic rather than episodic bias toward powerful social actors. As we will show, rather than occasionally responding to some identifiable influence or coercion from powerful entities, local governments seem to make these biased policies almost by default. The political actors in these cities are rarely the reluctant victims of special interests, as a strictly second-dimensional view would argue. Instead, they are predisposed to agree with a world view that serves powerful interests while publicly asserting that such policies are good for the whole community, even if the majority of the community disagrees.[10]

LOCAL GROWTH COALITIONS, GROWTH, AND OTHER ISSUES

There are many other sociological factors besides local growth coalitions affecting how and why public dollars are spent on private stadiums. In fact, many of these factors actually contribute greatly to the strength of a city's coalition and possibly its very existence. Furthermore, these secondary factors (together with their influence on growth coalitions) greatly constrain the strategies employed by those pursuing public dollars for private stadiums. In short, while the shape and form of local growth coalitions are the key to understanding publicly subsidized stadiums, they are thoroughly entwined with other structural factors that are largely beyond any individual or organizational control. Table 1 summarizes these interrelationships.

One important element influencing the morphology of local growth coalitions and how it intersects with securing public dollars for private stadiums is whether or not the local population is actually growing. The three rapidly growing cities we study (Denver, Phoenix, and San Diego), ironically perhaps, have weak or nonexistent growth coalitions. One explanation is that the newer, western, frontier cities do not really need these coalitions to articulate "appropriate" growth strategies (and battle with competing strategies for scarce resources) because the cities already have plenty of growth whether or not new stadiums are built. Another explanation is that these cities have not had time to develop entrenched power structures like those in some (but not all) of the older cities in the northeast and the midwest. This is especially true within the business communities of frontier cities, which are distinctly *not* led by large corporate entities and are thus unlikely players in a powerful local growth coalition or a corresponding CEO-only group.

Growth cities still build stadiums with public dollars, but they have more difficulty doing so compared with cities that have strong coalitions. The lack of a growth coalition creates a power vacuum requiring other individuals or organizations to step in and lead the way toward publicly financed stadiums. Sometimes teams and team owners fill that vacuum (as in Phoenix and San Diego). This, however, makes it harder to construct publicly financed stadiums because opponents can condemn the obvious self-interest of the sports teams. As we have mentioned, that is why exercising power in the second di-

Table 1. Social Characteristics of Cities Building New Publicly
Financed Stadiums

City	Local Growth Coalition, 2000	Local Growth Coalition, 1980	Population Growth, 1990– 2000 (%)	Population Growth, 1950– 2000 (%)	Downtown Residences
Cincinnati	very strong	very strong	−8	−33	few
Cleveland	strong	weak	−5	−46	few
Hartford	weak	strong	−11	−30	few
Minneapolis	weak	strong	+4	−27	many
Denver	moderate	moderate[a]	+19[b]	+33[b]	some
Phoenix	weak	weak	+34	+1,030	few
San Diego	weak	moderate	+10	+266	some
Pittsburgh	very strong	very strong	−9	−45	few
Philadelphia	weak	moderate	−4	−27	many

Sources: Authors' research of U.S. Census Bureau data; authors' ethnographic research.
[a]Denver's local growth coalition was temporarily strong in the late 1980s.
[b]Neighboring counties grew at a far higher rate.

mension (by the sports teams) is a less efficient way to influence social policy than is exercising power in the third dimension (by a supposedly altruistic growth coalition). In Denver, the power vacuum was filled by a makeshift, state-level growth coalition, which rather easily financed and constructed that city's two new stadiums

Declining cities often have powerful local growth coalitions for the same reasons that growth cities do not. First, they are older cities with more entrenched political and economic power structures, which are often reflected in the large number of local corporate headquarters. Second, because actual growth is a scarce resource, much is riding on policies that will supposedly generate growth or at least slow down economic decline. Due to their composition, corporate-driven growth coalitions often have more ideological legitimacy (that is, perceived expertise) about economic growth than do other social entities. So if a local growth coalition thinks a new publicly subsidized stadium will help a city, that group will influence policy and public opinion more than if, say, a sports economist thinks the stadium will not help the city.

As we will show, cities with powerful coalitions (Cincinnati, Cleveland, and Pittsburgh) have had significantly easier times building publicly financed stadiums than have those without powerful coalitions, but even here there is some variation. Cincinnati's journey to new stadiums was extremely smooth, Cleveland's efforts were a little more troublesome, and Pittsburgh's were somewhat problematic (if only temporarily).

The history of growth coalitions in these declining cities is also relevant to understanding new stadium dynamics. For example, Minneapolis and Hartford once had fairly powerful growth coalitions, which have since become shells of their former selves (see chapter 5). Philadelphia, meanwhile, despite being the fifth-largest city in the United States (and formerly the fourth-largest), has never had a strong, corporate-driven, local growth coalition. Thus, we are not surprised that Minneapolis and Hartford will not be home to any new stadiums soon and that Philadelphia's road to new stadiums was filled with obstacles.

BEYOND GROWTH COALITIONS AND GROWTH

Unique social circumstances in each city interact with growth coalitions and growth dynamics in all sorts of permutations and combinations. Really, no two cities are completely alike with respect to this multitude of causal components, although some cities are more similar than others. For instance, specific demographic patterns are also quite important. Yet even the seemingly similar population explosions in the three growth cities are very different from one another. Phoenix, especially, is unique because its growing population is much older than the growing populations of Denver and San Diego. Age also matters in Pennsylvania (with two declining cities): the state has the highest percentage in the country of people older than age sixty (although the rate is not increasing as fast as Phoenix's over-sixty population).

Serendipitous political and geographical factors also come to play in the process of building privately financed stadiums. For instance, the pure size of a city matters, but it matters more or less given the city's relationship with surrounding counties. We will show that it does matter if populations and their taxes are leaving the urban core for the suburbs (as they are in all declining cities), the city and county are the same entity (Philadelphia and Denver), neighboring counties work harmoniously (Denver) or not (Cleveland), different cities within huge counties are growing differently (Phoenix and San Diego), or state governments are also located in the city (Denver and Hartford). Sometimes the importance and relationship of these political factors is even more random. For example, it is important if a city has a strong mayoral form of government (as in Pittsburgh, Philadelphia, and Cleveland); but this importance alters if a strong mayoral position is actually occupied by a strong, charismatic mayor (Philadelphia, in particular).

Each city's downtown personality also influences the stadium-building process. Some downtowns are strictly commuter destinations, while others are a vibrant mix of permanent residences and businesses open beyond banking hours. It may or may not be a coincidence that the three cities with very strong local growth coalitions (Cincinnati, Cleveland, and Pittsburgh) have sterile downtown areas that basically close when commuters leave for the day. Of the nine cities we studied, only Philadelphia (to a great degree) and Denver (to a lesser degree) had downtowns that were active for more than forty hours a week. As we will discuss in chapter 2, this difference can have a staggering impact on how new stadium advocates (be they strong growth coalitions or not) and opponents strategize for their respective success and then package the idea of using public money for private stadiums.

Opposition to publicly financed stadiums in each city, then, is linked with downtown vibrancy and other social circumstances. The composition of a city's downtown, especially if a new stadium is planned nearby, greatly affects the form and influence of any opposition. Planning a new ballpark in a decrepit warehouse and parking district (Cleveland) or an industrial site (Hartford) is different from planning it in a gentrifying middle-class neighborhood (Philadelphia) or a gentrifying warehouse district being transformed into a residential community (San Diego). It is no wonder that grass-roots opposition to new stadiums has been strongest in these latter two cities because most people prefer to go to the ballpark in someone else's neighborhood. Of course, if the local residential neighborhood is predominately poor (Phoenix), it can mitigate the effectiveness of potential neighborhood opposition.

Demographic characteristics also affect new stadium opposition. In Phoenix, the primary opposition came from groups representing elderly retirees, who opposed using public monies for ballparks and almost everything else. Their anti-tax focus prevented these groups from forming alliances with opponents who might have been less universally opposed to increasing local taxes so long as that money did not fund new stadiums. In contrast, residents near (although not adjacent to) Denver's downtown baseball stadium are mostly young, single men, a group that consistently shows strong support for new sports stadiums. This certainly contributed to the almost complete lack of organized opposition to Coors Field.

Stadium opposition can also be assisted by local mass media that investigate the hidden processes leading to the building of private stadiums with public dollars. Only one of the nine cities we studied (Pittsburgh), however, had a major media outlet that was systematically critical of the new stadium deals—a stand that created all sorts of havoc for ballpark advocates (see chapter 7). For the most part, local newspapers, television, and radio were editorial sycophants for proponents of new publicly subsidized stadiums and ridiculed opponents as shortsighted and selfish. This is not surprising: local media are increasingly owned and controlled by corporate conglomerates that are often part of the power structure in each city and usually agree with the definition of growth outlined by the local growth coalition. Nevertheless, this editorial bias did not always translate into journalistic bias, at least within the print media (which we were able to track in each city). Many newspaper columnists continually excoriated stadium proponents and their plans, while reporters wrote about all sorts of negative issues such as cost overruns and backroom deals. One reporter actually told us that she and her colleagues were being pressured by the publisher to stop writing negative stories about a city's new stadiums. In the end, these negative stories did not generally derail public subsidies; but if certain social characteristics had been differently aligned, they might have.

Finally, we can't overlook the impact of pure luck, although it is hard to classify luck as sociological. Sometimes things just happen at the right time—or the wrong time, depending on your point of view. In Cincinnati, for instance, a referendum on two new stadiums took place just ten days after the Cleveland Browns left Ohio to become the Baltimore Ravens, catching everybody in Cincinnati with their pants down. If the referendum had preceded the Browns' move, it probably would have had a very different outcome. San Diego's stadium initiative just happened to take place while the Padres were making a totally unexpected run to the World Series. Also in San Diego, the NFL Chargers started making unexpected new stadium demands at an inopportune time for the Padres' stadium dreams. Timing may not be everything, but we will show that it sure is something.

STRUCTURE AND AGENCY

A number of structural and historical factors combine to influence who leads a city's charge toward new publicly financed sports stadiums, including the past and present form of local growth coalitions, the characteristics of local economic growth, subtle social circumstances, and good or bad fortune. Together, these factors produce a framework for studying the stadium battles in the nine cities discussed in this book (and any other city with such a battle). These are structural issues because they are largely immune to any individual manipulation (even by powerful individuals.) The outcomes of stadium battles vary by city because the specific expression of historical and structural elements vary by city, although there are some identifiable patterns between and among them. For instance, we know that powerful local growth coalitions make it easier to build stadiums; but these coalitions are neither omnipotent nor immune from uncontrollable factors such as the age of the local population or a sports team that reneges on a promise to move to a particular city.

But human agency and personal idiosyncrasies also play important roles in understanding the different outcomes of these stadium initiatives. Within the framework of structural conditions, actual people are making actual decisions. These decisions are important in and of themselves, as are the people making them; but these people and their decisions cannot be divorced from a larger structural context. This context in each city creates and constrains the various choices available to individuals and organizations in the city, whether they support or oppose using public dollars for private stadiums. Certain structural combinations create one menu of alternatives, while other combinations lead to other menus. People are making choices, and these choices are important; but they are being made under circumstances not always of individuals' own choosing. This situation illustrates a fundamental friction between structure and agency: people are neither structurally determined puppets nor complete masters of their fate.

In chapter 2, we focus on agency—the actual decisions made and the strategies employed by the people and organizations who want to use public dollars for private stadiums. One of their most important decisions is how to justify such policies in the first place and deal with resistance. For instance, new stadium advocates can generally promise either all sorts of economic benefits or less tangible ones, such as how a new stadium will turn the community into a world-class city and give the entire community something to be proud of—what we call manipulating community self-esteem and community collective conscience.

But these strategic decisions are certainly constrained by the structural situation in each city. Sometimes stadium advocates might not want to link the new stadium with economic benefits but have little choice since largely uncontrollable circumstances have made the ballpark part of a grand downtown redevelopment project. Advocates in other cities might recognize the efficacy of manipulating community self-esteem and community collective conscience but find themselves unable to pursue that strategy because of the city's personality. Thus, as we explore these strategic decisions in chapter 2, we always keep in mind that they are being made in a structurally constraining environment.[11]

2

Strategies for Building Private Stadiums with Public Dollars

According to a Hartford business executive we spoke with, a proposed publicly subsidized football stadium that would lure the New England Patriots to the city would help "put feet on the street," leading to a major economic revival for Hartford. A public official in Pittsburgh argued that new football and baseball stadiums in the city would "put heads in beds" in the new hotels that would follow the new stadiums. Both of these influential people were perpetuating the "if you build it, they will come" brand of professional sports boosterism. Supporters in Pittsburgh believed the new stadiums would make the city a hot new tourist destination. The Hartford executive hoped an NFL stadium would anchor an entire development strategy, complete with retail shopping and entertainment that would draw people off Interstate 91 to spend time and money in Connecticut's capital city.

In Minneapolis, however, most of the people we interviewed insisted that a new subsidized ballpark would *not* spur economic development in the Twin Cities. Members of its weak growth coalition argued instead that a new baseball stadium was important because it would keep the city one of a handful of those with teams in all four major sports leagues. To them, this was a vital part of being a first-rate city.[1] Similarly, in Cincinnati, the entire campaign to publicly finance two new stadiums was framed around the slogan "Keep Cincinnati a Major League City." Growth coalition members completely eschewed any notion that the new stadiums would provide an economic shot in Cincinnati's arm.

These examples suggest that stadium advocates in each city select different strategies to justify using public dollars for private stadiums. Usually, justifications arise during referendum campaigns to convince an increasingly skeptical public that publicly financing these stadiums is good policy. Supporters of publicly financed stadiums must decide how they wish to frame this link between new ballparks and the public good. But like the existence and strength of local growth coalitions (discussed in chapter 1), these decisions are largely patterned by the unique structural landscape of each city. Stadium advocates certainly have some discretion about which strategies to employ, but certain cities lend (and do not lend) themselves to making particular arguments about why it is in the community's best interest to build private stadiums with public dollars. Still, such arguments are choices, although some choices seem to work out better than others.

Strategies to justify spending public dollars on private stadiums generally fall into two categories. The first claims that new stadiums will provide all sorts of tangible economic benefits to the local community. The second insists that new stadiums will benefit the way in which a community views itself and is perceived by others and improve how community members get along with each other—what we call community self-esteem and community collective conscience. Despite the particularities of individual cities, we have noticed certain patterns in these strategic choices. Generally, stadium advocates have been promising fewer links between new stadiums and economic development and more links between stadiums and community self-esteem and community collective conscience.

The first wave of the recent stadium movement (roughly 1990–94) relied primarily on promises of stadium-generated economic development. Justifications emphasizing community self-esteem and community collective conscience became more popular in the late 1990s and into the twenty-first century. We believe this is not a random shift but reflects conscious strategic decisions by stadium proponents in each city. They have realized, for a variety of reasons that we will discuss in this chapter, that the path to publicly financed stadiums will be smoother if they downplay tangible economic benefits and accentuate intangible social ones. There are, however, some important exceptions (for example, Philadelphia, San Diego, and Pittsburgh's plan A) in which structural conditions kept a new stadium strategy from focusing on community self-esteem and community collective conscience. In our view, this difference contributed greatly to the coalitions' relative difficulty in Philadelphia and San Diego and the need for plan B in Pittsburgh.

THE DECLINE OF ECONOMIC GROWTH STRATEGIES

In the recent past, the most common strategy for justifying the use of public dollars for private stadiums has included touting new stadiums as a way to generate local economic development. These strategies generally promise three main economic benefits. First, there will be many new jobs (albeit temporary) created just to construct the stadium. Second, the stadium's daily operation will create other, more permanent jobs that will enhance local tax revenues through increased ticket sales, concession sales, and income taxes from new employee wages. Third, and perhaps most important, the presence of a new stadium and the people it attracts will indirectly spawn ancillary development such as new restaurants and retail outlets. These new businesses will also provide hefty contributions to the public treasury. Sometimes these claims of economic windfall reach truly outlandish levels, as when a civic leader in Sacramento proclaimed, "The Raiders coming to Sacramento would be an event the magnitude of the Gold Rush."[2] If the Raiders had gone to Sacramento, they would have played just eight games each year there. In contrast, more than 300,000 people moved to California in the six years following the 1848 discovery of gold in Sacramento. It is doubtful that the Raiders would have caused such a massive migration.[3]

There are several reasons for the strategic decline in linking new stadiums with economic development. First, historical changes (which continue today) in professional sports have altered the relationship between and among teams, the local government, and city residents. These changing relationships have been accompanied by changing ideologies about the role sports should play in the local community. Second, there has been a dramatic increase in public skepticism concerning the sometimes spectacular claims made about the economic windfalls associated with new stadiums. This skepticism has been fueled, on the one hand, by local residents (and even some policymakers), who can see for themselves that recently built stadiums in their cities have not improved neighborhoods or public schools or ended poverty. It has also been fueled by a growing body of systematic academic research by sports economists and sociologists, which almost universally challenges the argument that new stadiums are an economic godsend. As these findings trickle down to the general public, they increase any initial skepticism based on personal experience. Many stadium advocates, whether or not organized in growth coalitions, have recognized this change and have tried to alter their strategic focus away from grandiose economic promises and toward "softer" community benefits. They have been mostly successful in this strategic shift (from their point of view) but, for one reason or another, not *completely* successful.

Professional Sports Grows Up

The history of sports and sports stadiums in the United States has contributed to the declining efficacy of grandiose promises concerning stadium-generated economic growth. Before World War II, most teams played in privately owned and financed stadiums. Any public contribution tended to be modest. After 1945, public commitment increased, but most teams paid substantial rent to use public stadiums (Quirk and Fort 1992, Rosentraub 1997). At this time, most football teams simply played in stadiums owned or controlled by baseball teams. Because so few games were played, most football team owners did not see the need, or perhaps did not have the revenues, to build stadiums that would be used infrequently.

With the advent and explosion of television coverage, professional sports became more lucrative and teams and leagues more powerful. Because professional sports leagues operate as a cartel, they can centrally control the existence and location of all teams in a sport. This means that leagues can artificially restrict the creation of a new team (or the relocation of an existing team) for whatever reason they want. In essence, the cartels can restrict supply regardless of consumer demand, which further increases the value of the restricted commodity. Eventually, the leagues began demanding that cities desiring a new expansion team would have to provide a new stadium for it. Throughout the 1960s and early 1970s, this demand produced a steady increase in the number of stadiums being built and financed by municipalities. Once existing teams saw that expansion teams were receiving publicly financed stadiums, they also wanted them. During this period, however, stadiums were almost always multipurpose, housing both football and baseball teams. New architecture in the 1960s and early 1970s featured flying saucer/doughnut stadiums (such as Three Rivers Stadium in Pittsburgh), while the late 1970s and 1980s featured more enclosed domes (such as the Metrodome in Minneapolis).

This shift in stadium ownership and financing has been accompanied by a shift in professional sports' labor-management relationships. The growth of free agency and unionization among professional athletes has contributed to a nearly uncontrollable bidding war for even midlevel players. The rapid escalation in athletes' salaries has led owners to vigorously seek new sources of revenues, and all fear that their brethren will be more creative in getting money from their home city.

As a result, owners are in a race to get more tax dollars out of their city in order to purchase higher-priced talent.

Combined, these factors have placed unprecedented pressure on cities to build new stadiums to retain their teams and on teams to look elsewhere for new forms of revenue. Today, each team wants its own facility; they are no longer willing to share. Baseball teams prefer smaller, more intimate parks that seat about 40,000 people, while football teams want much larger seating capacities because they have only eight to ten opportunities to sell tickets each year. Baseball teams have learned that larger, dual-purpose stadiums ignore the aesthetic intimacy that is part of the sport's cultural lore. Teams have also complained about the difficulty of growing grass in a dual-purpose stadium, and most dislike artificial turf substitutes.

Just as important, however, have been the tens of thousands of empty seats at baseball games played in large, dual-purpose stadiums. No baseball team has been able consistently to sell out a 65,000-seat stadium except for the 1993–94 Colorado Rockies (see chapter 6), which has left the public with the impression that one can always get a ticket to a baseball game. But the newer, smaller stadiums, at least initially, have been able to create a sense of urgent demand. Cleveland's Jacobs Field is an excellent example of this phenomenon. When 40,000 people attended a game at the old, cavernous Municipal Stadium, it still looked half empty. The same 40,000 fills Jacobs Field to the rafters and creates an image that something desirable (and scarcely available) is going on there.

At current prices, two stadiums are likely to cost close to $1 billion, with the public typically paying between 30 and 60 percent of that total—a public expenditure of as much as $600 million. But one of the less recognized changes in this building boom is the simultaneous diverting of more and more of the revenue streams created by new stadiums toward private interests and away from municipalities. Whether new stadiums are actually municipally controlled or privately controlled makes much less of a difference today than it once did because much more stadium revenue now flows toward the teams. This change has had a huge impact on how municipalities are able to fund their portion of stadium costs. Today, teams typically pay little or no rent, are given most or all parking revenues and naming rights to the stadium, are sometimes granted development rights for parcels of land around the stadium, and are in a few cases given ticket sale guarantees by cities. This means that very little revenue accrues to the municipality and is one of the reasons that cities have not been using general obligation bonds to fund new stadium construction as they did in the mini-boom of the 1960s and 1970s. There are simply not enough revenue streams in new stadium leases to cover the bond payments (see Danielson 1997). Thus, cities must now turn toward new taxes (with or without public approval) or divert existing taxes that were once used for other social goods. Alternately, they can bank on risky tax-increment financing schemes that rest on the promise that stadiums will create enough spin-off development to ensure that the increase in overall tax revenues coming into the city's general fund in future years will be enough to offset the costs of the stadium. Given the findings of the economic research that we will discuss in this chapter, this is clearly a dangerous strategy.

At the risk of stating the obvious, we recognize that team owners have a great incentive to convince the public that it should subsidize a stadium. Some economists have estimated that a new stadium or arena can add $10–40 million to a team's annual earnings and double the value of a franchise ("The Stadium Game" 1996, 26). Moreover, league rules sometimes make a new stadium the best way to gain an advantage over the competition. For example, NFL teams must share among themselves 100 percent of their television, licensing, and marketing revenues. Thus, no team can gain a competitive advantage over another team by, say, securing a lucrative contract with a company that will manufacture shot glasses bearing the team logo. In contrast, most stadium-generated revenues are not shared among teams (Zimbalist 1998, 18). Therefore, with the exception of winning the Super Bowl (which only one team can do), a new publicly funded stadium is a football team's surest route to increasing its value rapidly and providing the owner with a massive windfall.[4]

In short, the demands of teams on cities have increased dramatically in the past twenty years. As we discussed in chapter 1, it is not always necessary for stadium advocates to pressure the local government to spend public dollars on private stadiums. More and more often, local governments simply accept the necessity of building a new publicly financed stadium, even without threats from teams or a powerful local growth coalition. But as cities require more public dollars to pay for these stadiums, they find it much harder to justify them as beneficial to the entire community. It's one thing to argue that spending $160 million of public money on a ballpark (the approximate public share of Coors Field) is worthwhile because it will be a catalyst for local economic development. It is another thing to argue that spending more than a half-billion dollars on two new stadiums (the approximate public share in Cincinnati) is worthwhile because they will create a commensurate increase in local economic activity. That's a lot of economic activity from two stadiums that are open for a total of ninety days a year.

Anecdotal and Systematic Challenges to Economic Growth Strategies

The public's increasing disbelief in the "stadium equals economic growth" strategy has been buttressed by the specific reality of recently built, publicly financed stadiums. People living in or near cities with new ballparks can see for themselves that they have not been catalysts for neighborhood (or citywide) revitalization. Our fieldwork in cities with new ballparks yields the same conclusion. In cities with two new stadiums that had some lag time between their construction, the first stadium was rationalized with economic growth arguments, while the second was justified with noneconomic ones. This strategic shift was also evident in Pittsburgh, where plans A and B were presented very differently to the community. This shift suggests that proponents of publicly funded stadiums in these cities successfully reacted to a skeptical public that had no reason to believe another round of promises linking stadiums with economic nirvana.

Strategic decisions have also been influenced by the mounting body of rigorous academic research challenging the alleged economic benefits of building private stadiums with public dollars. The economists, sociologists, and political scientists who have systematically and scientifically studied this topic are almost unanimous in their conclusions: new stadiums do not stimulate local economic growth. Advocates of publicly financed stadiums have been forced to deal with this critical research, especially as it disseminates into the general public though media stories or when these scholars testify at public hearings about their findings. In tandem with people's firsthand experiences, this research has cast serious doubt on the once-effective argument that spending public dollars on private stadiums is in a community's best economic interest.

Substitution Effects and Ripple Effects

One way in which new stadiums are supposed to stimulate the local economy is by directly creating both temporary construction jobs and then more permanent jobs at the ballpark. When considering these latter jobs, however, stadium advocates often forget to consider the jobs "lost" at the old stadium. Of course, most workers will just move from the old stadium to the new, meaning that there will be a net increase in employment only if more people are hired—which presumably will occur if attendance rises at the new stadium. At first glance, this seems to be a reasonable assumption. Historically, new stadiums draw more fans than do the old ones they replace; and previous research suggests that such a honeymoon period lasts about ten years, after which a team's performance largely determines attendance (Baade 1996).

Very recent data, however, suggest that this honeymoon period is getting much shorter as more cities get new stadiums and the novelty effect wears off. Indeed, the new stadiums in Phoenix and Detroit showed precipitous attendance drops after only one year. In Pittsburgh, the 2001 inaugural season in PNC Park showed an average attendance of 30,000; but by the following year attendance had dropped to about 20,000 per game, paralleled by a 40 percent drop in season-ticket sales. Milwaukee's Miller Park showed a similar first- to second-year drop-off of 31,635 (in 2001) to 22,281 (in 2002), with season tickets falling by 23 percent (*New York Times*, May 7, 2002, D1). Even stalwarts such as Jacobs Field and Camden Yards, which were consistently sold out for five to six years, have seen more and more empty seats well before their tenth birthdays. It is increasingly clear that most teams should no longer expect huge attendance windfalls from new stadiums much past the first or second years.

Even without higher attendance, it is still possible that fans will spend more money at a new ballpark. The food might be better, the beer might be colder, and the tickets might be pricier. Moreover, at a new stadium with a new franchise, fans have a first-time chance to purchase team paraphernalia. But this increased spending will provide additional tax revenues to the city only if it represents spending that would not otherwise have occurred in the city. If fans are spending more at the new stadium but are simultaneously spending less at a local restaurant or a video store, the city has no net increase in tax revenues. This phenomenon is sometimes called the substitution effect, which assumes that individuals and families have relatively stable entertainment budgets that they split among different activities. If money is simply shifted from one activity (renting a few videos) to another (going to a ballgame), there is no net increase in city tax revenue, only a substitution of one purchase for another. There would be a net increase in tax revenues only if the stadium attracts dollars that would not otherwise be spent *in the city* and if there is no spending decline in other city venues. But if tourists or suburbanites come and spend money in your city *because* you have a new stadium, this does represent a real increase in local tax revenues for the city.

Nevertheless, thinking about total spending isn't enough. It is also important to consider how particular types of spending reverberate through a local economy—what is sometimes called the ripple effect. It might actually be worse for a city if revenues are spent at a ballpark rather than at local restaurants, movie theaters, and video stores. The reason is that a huge percentage of a team's expenses go into the salaries of players, the profits of owners, and the pockets of national food and beverage corporations (such as Coors). There is less chance that this money will be respent in the city than if it had gone to, say, the wages of a video store worker or a restaurant worker. Players and owners (although not low-wage stadium workers) are much more likely than video store employees to live outside the city limits and retire elsewhere eventually, taking their accumulated money with them. If the total salaries and profits of the team were instead spread across all the restaurants, video stores, movie theaters, bowling alleys, and bars in the city, then most of those dollars would likely go rippling through the local economy because they would be paid to working folks who live and spend in the city. So stadiums may provide what Ross Perot once called (in a different context) "that great big sucking sound" of dollars being drawn out of the local economy rather than reinfused into it.

Indirect Economic Development

Against new business opening

In addition to promises of direct economic gains from construction and job creation, advocates of publicly financed stadiums make even stronger promises about the indirect or ancillary economic development caused by these new ballparks. Previous research and our own analysis indicate that new stadium proponents almost always inflate the indirect benefits of stadiums on their surrounding neighborhoods. One form of this inflation is assuming that any new business near a stadium has opened as a direct result of the stadium. But the closing of existing businesses near the old stadium is never mentioned or subtracted from the calculation of value. It is equally possible that development around a stadium might have occurred in another part of the city. Similarly, there is never any accounting of businesses that do not wish to be near a stadium. In Phoenix, an expert in attracting new downtown businesses told us that a number of companies had expressed concern about locating themselves too close to Bank One Ballpark. They worried that their employees would have difficulty parking and getting to and from work during a game. If the stadium takes credit for any nearby business, it should also take the blame for any business that chooses to move away. Stadium proponents rarely offer this kind of balanced assessment of ancillary development.

Moreover, recent trends in stadium design may actually *reduce* potential ancillary development. The owners and architects of new stadiums have gotten much more clever about creating structures that try to channel all spending within the confines of stadiums themselves. This reduces the economic benefit available to businesses not connected with the team and its owners. In fact, expanded concessions within the new stadium provide a huge financial windfall for team owners at the expense of independently owned local businesses or franchises. Camden Yards in Baltimore was the model for this approach to concessions; and Bank One Ballpark in Phoenix, among others, has extended the concept. Now you can come to the ballpark a few hours early, stroll pedestrian walkways within the stadium, buy all kinds of food, play a video game, see how fast you can throw a pitch, and shop for souvenirs. Thus, with all this extra spending (beyond the ticket price) going on inside the stadium, it is less likely that any money will be spent outside the stadium.

Sports economists almost unanimously challenge the assertion that new stadiums will create waves of ancillary economic activity whose benefits will trickle down to the entire community. In fact, some studies have found that new stadiums have a negative impact on the local economy (Bernstein 1998, Coates and Humphreys 2000). In one study, Baade and Dye (1990) found that, in seven of the nine cities they examined, the city's share of regional income actually declined after adding a team or a new stadium. Baade (1994) looked at thirty-six metropolitan areas between 1958 and 1987 and found no cases in which a new stadium had a positive impact on a city's growth and three cases in which there was actually a negative one (Washington, D.C.; San Francisco/Oakland; and St. Louis). One carefully conducted study examined Indianapolis, which decided to use professional sports as the centerpiece of the city's economic development strategy. By most accounts, Indianapolis did this about as well as it could be done, yet "it seems fair to conclude there were no significant or substantial shifts in economic development" (Rosentraub et al. 1994, 236).

It is no surprise that new stadiums do not yield significant increases in private-sector development or public-sector revenues (taxes). Despite the incredible attention given to professional sports teams, they actually represent a very small part of a city's economy. As Mark Rosentraub (1996, 1997) demonstrates, the professional sports industry accounts for a tiny percentage of economic activity in a city or region, typically accounting for about 0.2 percent of total employment. Even when a generous assumption is made about ancillary spending around stadiums, professional sports still account for a small amount of total spending in American cities. Professional sports teams are not large businesses. In 1994, the average NFL team grossed $65 million and employed about 120 full-time workers and a few hundred seasonal, temporary, and part-time workers (Zimbalist 1998). Charles Euchner (1993) insists that a sports team has about the same local economic impact as a large supermarket.

STRATEGIES TO NEUTRALIZE ACADEMIC STUDIES

As these systematic challenges become more pervasive, they pose serious obstacles to supporters of using public dollars for private stadiums. Once-convincing arguments linking stadiums with economic development now run the risk of seeming anachronistic and totally unbelievable. In response, stadium proponents have developed a number of strategies intended to neutralize the implications of these challenges. Their strategies take a number of forms, depending on the people and organizations devising them and the structural characteristics of the city. New stadium proponents can ignore challenges, ridicule them, try to counter them with their own studies, or change the subject; and we were surprised by the intensity that some people displayed in formulating and implementing their chosen strategies. Clearly, as they see it, threats arising from these empirical challenges need to be taken seriously if publicly funded stadiums have a future.

Strategic Ignorance

One technique for neutralizing critical research is simply to ignore it. Even when directly challenged with contradictory findings, stadium advocates continue to insist that publicly financed stadiums will produce all sorts of economic windfalls for the community. Many declare that logical critiques such as the substitution effect are irrelevant to this particular stadium in this particular city. One team owner told us,

> Baseball stadiums are different. There is great economic power generated by drawing 3.5 million people. . . . That's an amazing, amazing thing. It's the synergy. . . . Economists, who are paid fees to take counter positions on many of these projects, have never been in the trenches. They look at numbers and then interpret what economic impact is all about. I am in the trenches. I see it, I feel it, and I know it because I have been there. I know how many business licenses have been taken out because of the developments that we are involved in. I know what kind of traffic [there is]; I know what kind of development. . . . When all is said, they are here because of what we have done.

This owner may have been in the trenches, but they were not the same trenches we examined (or that other academics have studied). For instance, many people we interviewed continually pointed to Cleveland, Baltimore, and Denver as glowing examples of how publicly financed stadiums can turn around a city's economy. According to another team executive,

> If you look at Cleveland and Baltimore ten years ago, they were dying industrial rust belts, and now they are [thriving]. If you ask people what was the number-one factor in turning your city around, I bet they would say Jacobs Field or Camden Yards.

This statement ignores reality. The neighborhood around Cleveland's new ballpark is not all that different from the way it was ten years ago, even though pro-stadium forces in other cities told us that the Flats, a trendy neighborhood, was created because of Jacobs Field. The Flats, however, isn't even within walking distance of the ballpark. Moreover, as we will see in chapter 4, the city certainly hasn't turned around for Cleveland's public school students, whose district was put into state receivership during the city's stadium binge in the 1990s.

In Baltimore, the robust Inner Harbor area was thriving for a decade before Camden Yards arrived—thanks mostly to the superb National Aquarium, which is open 280 days more each year than the ballpark is. In addition, one of Baltimore's poorest neighborhoods remains entrenched only a few blocks from the stadium, and the city's public school system has not improved. Denver's Coors Field is nominally located in the once-stagnant, now rejuvenated LoDo downtown area. But as we will show in chapter 6, the revitalization of LoDo began well before the stadium's arrival; and the stadium is relatively peripheral to the district's main action.

We discovered that the farther we were from the city in question, the greater the tendency to inflate a city's turnaround. This was especially true when we were talking to people who desperately wanted to build publicly funded stadiums in their own city. This is not particularly surprising if we think about this reaction as strategic deception rather than innocent ignorance. Few of the people we interviewed outside of Cleveland, for example, claimed to know about the scandals surrounding the building of Jacobs Field and Gund Arena, which we will describe in chapter 4. One person in Minneapolis spoke glowingly of visiting Cleveland to make a videotape touting the miracle of the ballpark there. The tape was then shown to civic leaders in Minneapolis to build support for a new stadium in the Twin Cities. When we mentioned the plethora of scandals that led to the removal of the very person featured on the promotional tape, the Minneapolis official said he had never heard of such things. Stadium proponents will strategically ignore empirical challenges to the alleged economic wonders of new stadiums. One ballpark supporter in Minneapolis seemed to think that if he wished hard enough, all these criticisms would go away:

I know you can't attribute [the entire $3 billion in downtown development] all to the Dome. But what if no stadium were built? If nothing happened, would this other stuff have happened? We can say it all happened, can't we?" (Weiner 2000, 73)

The Best Defense Is a Good Offense

Simply ignoring academic studies, however, is a limited and ultimately ineffective strategy. Typically, as debates heat up, anti-subsidy forces repeatedly point to this growing body of economic and sociological studies. We have found that opposition forces in many cities are growing more sophisticated in using academic studies to argue against stadium subsidies. Stadium opponents in one city are often connected with opponents from other cities through e-mail, listservs, and web sites. They constantly exchange information on the latest studies and discuss how they might best frame and disseminate them; grass-roots successes and failures are also shared. Sometimes the scholars who produce the studies are invited to testify publicly about their findings. As a result, systematic research very often becomes part of the discussion, even if subsidy advocates try to ignore it.

But when ignoring the studies does not work, subsidy advocates often use another approach: they ridicule the methodology or the findings. One of our own experiences overtly illustrated this strategy, although in other cases we saw it work more subtly. While we were interviewing the vice-president of a major league baseball team, he pulled out a letter forwarded to him by the president of the city council (and later the mayor of that city). The council member had received from a constituent a well-informed letter summarizing economist Robert Baade's critical research about the benefits of spending public dollars for private stadiums. The constituent had even attached one of Baade's scholarly articles. What was most interesting, however, was the handwritten note from the council president to the team executive, which read, "What do I say to a constituent who makes this argument against a new stadium?" The note did not ask whether Baade's argument was correct. Instead, it requested a strategy for responding to it. Clearly, the team executive and the politician were both searching for an effective tactic to counter possible community resistance that was supported by the findings of this study. When we asked the team executive how he had responded to the city council president's query, he replied that he had read the article and discovered that Baade was only reporting on stadiums built before the late 1980s. He then asserted, with absolutely no evidence, that stadiums built since 1989 were different.[5]

This response goes beyond merely ignoring the academic research, instead trying to counter it with a contrary intellectual argument. Of course, these counter-arguments are not based on any systematic research. A public subsidy supporter in Cleveland was equally imaginative with his more accurate "study" and even suggested that scientific studies were not a good replacement for having no studies at all.

> So it seems pretty obvious to me that if you put up a ballpark and arena and bring 4.5 million people into a concentrated area, you are going to spur some economic development. You aren't going to change the economy of . . . northeast Ohio since all the sports activity in the area is only 1.5 percent of the local economy. But if you concentrate this activity into twenty-eight acres, then you can do it, right? It was not studied. I just knew it. I would not waste $100,000 for someone to study this. It's the right place to build [the ballpark]. These things belong in downtown, and it was a weird-shaped site, and we could nestle it into the city, and the city can grow to it, and the project will grow to the city. It will work, assuming you design it right and don't surround it with a sea of surface parking.

Whether this site has worked in Cleveland is a matter of debate. This developer told us that there were thirty-six new retail establishments within two blocks of second base. A mayoral aide in Cleveland reported twenty new businesses. We couldn't reconcile the two numbers and never found all twenty businesses, unless we should have counted the sea of surface parking that still surrounds the ballpark. Nevertheless, these unsubstantiated economic claims give new stadium supporters a way to contradict the growing list of critical academic studies.

Advocacy Studies and Fantasy Documents

In some cities, subsidy proponents have taken these neutralization strategies a step farther and have produced their own "systematic" studies to demonstrate the positive economic impact of new stadium construction. These advocacy studies, as we like to call them, are usually performed by hired consulting firms (often large public accounting and financial firms) and are quite unlike academic studies. First, the methodologies are usually very different. The academic studies usually look at macroeconomic data in a city or region, such as overall economic growth, tax revenue growth, or employment growth. The advocacy studies rely on data gathered through surveys and questionnaires in which people self-report on current and future economic behavior. Such data are not inherently inferior to macro data, but they are especially susceptible to sloppy methodology.

Many of the team representatives and growth coalition members we spoke with provided us with advocacy studies that claimed to show the tremendous economic impact of a new stadium in their particular city. Often these studies contain flawed assumptions or methodologies that lead to overinflation of a team's economic impact. For example, Arthur Andersen produced a study showing the great economic benefits of building a new baseball stadium in center-city Philadelphia. The study attempted to show the different economic impacts of a new downtown ballpark versus one built near the current Veterans Stadium a few miles south of the central business district. As is typical of these studies, the authors tried to estimate the amount of money spent outside the ballpark and attribute this amount of spending to the presence of the team. As part of this analysis, the consulting firm conducted a survey of fans to estimate out-of-stadium spending before and after attendance at a Phillies' game. They administered the survey during five home games and gathered 1,652 responses. These respondents were asked about where they lived; where they worked; how they got to the game; and where and how much they spent on food, drink, and entertainment before and after the ballgame. The study reports that, based on this survey, attendees spent an average of $23.32 outside of Veterans Stadium (this includes those who reported spending nothing; it does not include the amount spent on parking fees). This figure was then multiplied by the average in-park attendance for the year (1,980,000 fans) for an estimated impact for out-of-stadium spending of $46,200,000.

There are several problems with this supposedly scientific study. First, there is the sampling procedure. The people that returned the survey were likely not to be a representative sample of the total population attending the game. There are, unfortunately, few details in the report about sampling procedure, despite its centrality to the entire study. Our best guess is that fans were handed the survey on their way into the stadium. Some probably threw it away; others filled it out and returned it. It is very possible that people with certain characteristics are more likely to respond than others are. Tourists, especially, might be more likely to show interest in the survey than local fans are. If true, this would lead to an overrepresentation of a group that certainly spends more money outside the stadium than local fans do, who can eat lunch and dinner at home if they want to. We are not implying that this overrepresentation of tourists actually happened. But the possibility that it might have happened and surveyors' lack of concern about it challenge the legitimacy of the study.

There is a strong possibility, however, that this study committed a more egregious error by undersampling one important group: children. Although, again, the report makes no mention of it, we assume that children did not fill out the survey because the questions about location of work indicate that it wasn't designed for children. Thus, heads of households were significantly overrepresented as reflections of "typical" ballpark visitors. This sampling problem would be even more severe at weekend or summer afternoon games, when the percentage of children in attendance is likely to be much higher.

So when heads of households fill out the survey, they are reporting out-of-stadium spending by the entire family, not just by themselves. For example, if adults attending the game with children were asked how much they had spent before coming to the game, they would probably include the lunch bill for the whole family rather than break out their own personal portion of the bill. After all, if they bought lunch for the kids, they did indeed spend all of that money. Thus, it is extremely inaccurate to multiply the $23.12 by the entire fan base since, in effect, that figure counts the children twice. This error can significantly inflate spending estimates.

Seemingly small errors involving a few dollars can become quite large errors in the final spending estimates. If a significant proportion of the 1,980,000 fans each year at a Phillies' game are children, then this proportion must be removed from the total before multiplying it by the average spending per fan. For example, if children are as many as 20 percent of the fans at Phillies' games, then the spending of $23.32 should not be multiplied by 1,980,000 fans but only by the adult fans (about 1,584,000), yielding not $46.2 million but $36.9 million, a difference of $9.3 million. Because this spending figure is then doubled (to supposedly account for the ripple effect), the magnitude of the error is also doubled to $18.3 million.

In addition to possible sampling errors, this survey also ignores the substitution effect. Many respondents probably include spending they would have done anyway, whether or not they went to the ball game. If you get pizza for the family's dinner on the way home from the game, is that spending attributable solely to the existence of the Phillies? If you hadn't gone to the game that day, would you have spent some or all of that money on other things? If so, then there may be very little or even no net increase in peoples' spending and no net increase in tax revenues for the city. Claiming credit for all of this spending, as advocacy studies almost always do, would be like a small business owner asking workers how much they spent on breakfast before work and dinner after work and then claiming that all of that spending was due to the fact that he or she had a business in the city. The owner could then ask that a new publicly financed office be built for the business because it was generating so much ancillary spending. Similar logic could be used by homeowners, who could simply tally all of their spending and then argue that if they don't get a new home built for them by their town government, then they will take all their spending elsewhere.

Sociologist Lee Clarke (1999) would say these advocacy studies are good examples of "fantasy documents," supposedly neutral and objective reports that really obfuscate more parochial individual, organizational, and political interests. In this case, new stadium boosters strategically produce fantasy documents to counter the critical academic studies. They rely on methodologies that inflate the value of a team to the region and inflate the economic impact of new stadiums. But these fantasy documents are couched in the language of objectivity and neutrality, often boasting that reasonable or even conservative economic assumptions are being made, while ducking much larger issues such as the substitution effect. Many of the people we interviewed skillfully tossed around findings from these fantasy documents, usually when we raised questions about the critical academic research. Apparently, their strategy is to challenge the very legitimacy of these academic studies and their contradictory conclusions. One team owner, citing a fantasy document said,

> Don't hold me to exact numbers, but this is close. The construction of the facility itself had about a $300 million economic impact, it was the equivalent of 3,000 full-time jobs, about $13 million in new sales taxes generated from the construction. On an annual basis, the economic impact is about $250 million; about 2,500 full-time jobs. . . . That kind of economic benefit is measurable. These are not dollars that would be used elsewhere, which is what the economists say. What's the word they use? [Substitution effect?] "Yes, these are not new dollars," they say! That's bull.

Teams, growth coalitions, and local governments could commission less problematic studies of a ballpark's economic impact. But this assumes that they are searching for truth rather than developing strategies to continue funding private stadiums with public dollars, despite the growing chorus of people skeptical about such policies. Even if these advocacy studies and fantasy documents do not destroy the legitimacy of academic research, they rationalize continuing to pursue questionable social policies. At the very least, they help to call into question that the academic studies that conclude just the opposite are not the final word on the matter; that there is scientific disagreement. For example, two separate studies on the annual impact of the Colts football team on the Baltimore economy found that it was either $30 million or $200,000—a 150-fold difference (Zimbalist 1998, 22). If skeptical community members

decide that the issues are really too complicated to reach definitive conclusions, then this particular neutralization strategy has been successful;
and there will be fewer potential problems on the road to securing public dollars for private stadiums.

NEW STRATEGIES TO JUSTIFY PUBLIC DOLLARS FOR PRIVATE STADIUMS

In addition to neutralization strategies, new stadium proponents are
starting to take an entirely different tack in justifying the building of
new stadiums with tax dollars. This new strategic approach insists that
tangible economic impact isn't really the issue after all. Instead, building private stadiums with public dollars is good policy because it will
provide all kinds of intangible social benefits to the community. These
benefits might include publicity and notoriety for the city, a sense of
community accomplishment, and a unifying focal point for all city residents to overcome the divisions so common in the urban United States.
There may be unexpected economic windfalls from such a strategy, and
stadium proponents do not downplay this possibility. But such economic benefits, they argue, are secondary to the social benefits that, ad-
mittedly, are difficult to measure. As one sports team executive put it:

> I know economists like to count, but it is not possible to quantify
> the benefits of a new ballpark in a downtown location. And even if
> they could be counted, the benefits you count are only a small part
> of the total value.

We call this new strategic focus the social construction of community self-esteem and community collective conscience. Although we
believe that both are important to cities, we wonder about their relationship to new publicly funded stadiums. We also wonder whether
local growth coalitions (or other stadium supporters) have a truly altruistic interest in these community values when they equate advocacy
for new stadiums with "wearing their civic hat." As we will argue
briefly here (and more expansively in chapters 3 through 8), powerful
individuals and organizations—which are often local growth coalitions—in fact consciously manipulate ideas of community self-esteem
and community collective conscience as a strategy to continue building private stadiums with public dollars.[6]

Manipulating Community Self-Esteem

Our idea of community self-esteem has two separate but related threads.
One concerns how people within a community perceive that commu-

nity. The other concerns how the community is perceived by those outside it. Do people, both in and outside the community, think a city is
"minor league" or "major league"? And how do new publicly financed
stadiums contribute to this perception? Originally, we made no distinction between these two components of community self-esteem.
But it became clear during our research that local growth coalition
members and other stadium boosters made this distinction (even if not
explicitly) and that it influenced their tactics in garnering support for
publicly subsidized stadiums.

Those attempting to manipulate internal community self-esteem
usually warn local residents about the danger of slipping to the depths
of some nearby city, which has been socially constructed as inferior. A
community's decline to minor league status, they argue, will surely be
exacerbated by not building a new stadium, which would precipitate a
team's decision to leave the city. So in Cleveland we kept hearing that
having professional sports (especially in new stadiums) would keep the
city from becoming another Akron. In Cincinnati, the presence of professional sports would prevent the city from turning into Louisville.
Stadium proponents in both Minneapolis and Denver did not want to
become colder versions of Omaha. As we will see in chapter 3, Cincinnati's local growth coalition honed this message to a fine edge during
its campaign to raise taxes for two new stadiums; and exit polls
demonstrated that the strategy was extremely effective. Many voters
said they reluctantly supported the tax increase because they didn't
want the city to become another Dayton.

The external component of community self-esteem was also a
dominant theme in many of the nine cities we studied. Members of
local growth coalitions strongly believed that new stadiums (replete
with luxury boxes) would project a desirable image to outsiders.
At first, we thought this strategy was just a remake of the standard
economic argument about attracting tourists and their money.
But while that argument was certainly part of their reasoning, advocates had something more important on their minds. An executive
explained:

> What are you going to sell [to executives you are recruiting]? You
> sell the city's amenities. We have a great art museum, a great or-
> chestra, and major league sports. Nice suburbs? There are nice
> suburbs everywhere. So you have to sell a package of things, and
> that means something to these CEOs.

It turns out that executive recruitment was on the minds of many
business leaders, especially in cities with powerful local growth coalitions anchored in the large companies headquartered there. One executive commented that new stadiums (and their luxury boxes) are the

sort of amenity that corporations need to draw the "A players" to his midsized city.

This link between new stadiums and executive recruitment took us completely by surprise. We came to understand, however, that corporate members of the local growth coalition viewed stadiums as integral to their companies' interests in recruitment. Thus, nonsports organizations have a concrete reason to be interested in building private stadiums with public dollars: new stadiums function as a public subsidy of the companies' recruitment efforts. The situation is an example of the corporate liberalism ideology discussed in chapter 1. Growth coalition members in these cities obfuscate their own vested interests by tying a subsidized stadium to the notion of community self-esteem. This manipulation often likens publicly financed stadiums to other pieces of the city's publicly financed infrastructure, such as libraries, parks, and museums—the cultural perks that make up a first-class city. But among all these entities, only the stadium is a privately owned, for-profit business that can be sold for a huge private windfall after it is built. Nonetheless, the manipulation of community self-esteem has been a successful and increasingly popular strategy for justifying why new stadiums should be financed by a skeptical public.

Manipulating Community Collective Conscience

Nineteenth-century sociologist Emile Durkheim (1933) coined the term *collective conscience* in referring to the shared values, beliefs, and experiences that bind together members of a society. We have added *community* to the term because, unlike Durkheim, who was discussing societies and nation-states, we are talking about smaller units (usually cities) within a nation-state. According to Durkheim, modern industrial societies have little collective conscience because their members are highly atomized and alienated from each other, unlike preindustrial societies, in which people constantly interacted and depended on each other for survival. Without shared everyday experiences that generate shared values and beliefs and without a single dominant religion, modern societies must find their social glue elsewhere.[7]

As they abandon their traditional emphasis on economic benefits, advocates of publicly subsidized stadiums have begun talking more about how sports—especially professional sports—can provide this missing cohesion in our modern alienated society. Sports teams, growth coalition members, and politicians may all argue that a city's professional sports are capable of doing what religion cannot: bringing disparate people together around a shared urban identity. A baseball team executive told us,

> I think sports can bring people together across social and economic lines. Those lines are obliterated. You can have a CEO of a major corporation sitting next to a homeless person, and they both are there for a baseball game; they are both there for the same reason. They can afford to be there. So it has tremendous social value. . . . I make the argument that it's good for the quality of life of the community and it is good for the soul of the community. It's good to be able to go to a place to yell at the umpire. In sports, people get out their feelings. It's a great thing for the soul.

In addition, some people justify using public dollars on private stadiums because a winning sports team (which apparently becomes more possible in a new stadium) will solve a host of social ills. Another team owner said:

> I don't want to overlook this quality of life issue and what impact baseball has on families. With the disintegration of families in our country, to me this is an important issue because one of the most enjoyable things I had last year was watching families, the little kids with parents and grandparents, and all of them enjoying [the game].

Of course, a mere claim that sports create community collective conscience is no proof that it does in fact provide this social glue. Ironically, although these new stadiums are purported to obliterate class and race differences, their attractiveness lies largely in greater numbers of luxury-level seats. Presumably, these seats are not available to all attendees, regardless of their social class.

Many of the powerful people we interviewed claimed that other intangible social bonanzas result from having a good team in a new stadium. People on the streets are friendlier to each other, domestic disputes decline, and city folks stop moving to the suburbs. But the benefits don't stop there. How could we argue with one piece of "evidence" used to justify public subsidy in Cleveland? The bike messengers around town were smiling more since Jacobs Field opened. This was the justification for spending half a billion dollars on a sports complex that wasn't creating an economic windfall.

STRATEGIES AND STRUCTURAL CHARACTERISTICS

In chapter 1, we argued that the existence and power of local growth coalitions are connected to the structural characteristics of a particular city. The same relationship exists when considering the strategies that justify building private stadiums with public dollars. New stadium advocates have a number of such strategies at their disposal, and they do their best to select the most effective ones. We think that strategies promising stadium-generated economic growth are becoming less effective, while those manipulating community self-esteem and community collective conscience are becoming more so. In the following chapters, we will show that, when new stadium supporters select this latter strategy, they can achieve their goals more easily.

But even though the second approach seems to be a better strategy for success, not all stadium supporters in all cities select it. While some plans can be attributed to bad decision making, it is also true that the structural characteristics of some cities simply do not lend themselves to the second strategic decision. Sometimes structural limitation is rooted in the personality of a city. For example, advocates in Philadelphia would have a hard time arguing that it would become another Harrisburg without two new publicly subsidized stadiums. Philadelphia's downtown is a thriving mix of residences, businesses, and cultural outlets that is increasingly popular even without a stadium around the corner. Similarly, in the rapidly growing western cities we examine in chapter 6, promoters would find it impossible to argue convincingly that new stadiums are necessary to attract people to the area. People are streaming into those areas anyway. As a result, stadium advocates are practically forced to use less effective strategies promising economic development. As we will see, this necessity has made it harder, although by no means impossible, for them to secure public dollars for private stadiums.

By integrating ideas from chapters 1 and 2, we have built a model for understanding the process of building private stadiums with public dollars in nine different cities. This model has two basic components. First, we closely examine the presence and efficacy of the local growth coalition in each city and which social characteristics contribute to its strength or weakness. Second, we explore the strategic choices made by local growth coalitions (or their proxies) as they justify why building private stadiums with public dollars is sound social policy. These choices, like the existence and strength of growth coalitions, are highly constrained by structural elements beyond the control of even the most powerful individuals and organizations. The easiest path to a new publicly subsidized stadium is to have a strong, clandestine, corporate-driven, local growth coalition that chooses to emphasize ways in which the stadium will enhance community self-esteem and community collective conscience. This combination of structure and strategy works best in a medium-sized city with a floundering economy, a weak mayoral form of city government, urban-to-suburban population migration, a commuter-oriented downtown, relatively few senior citizens, and no significant opposition. But even with all these ducks in order, plain luck still plays a part.

3

Cincinnati

QUEEN CITY OF LOCAL GROWTH COALITIONS

In August 2000, the Cincinnati Bengals played their first game in brand-new Paul Brown Stadium. Costing more than $400 million, the stadium was financed almost entirely by a sales-tax increase in Hamilton County, which includes Cincinnati, Ohio, and its surrounding suburbs. The Cincinnati Reds started playing in their new stadium, the Great American Ballpark, at the beginning of the 2003 season. The park's current price tag is approximately $400 million and will also be funded by the county sales tax. Both teams are making minor out-of-pocket payments for the stadiums. Their real contributions will come from future stadium-generated revenues such as seat licenses, naming rights, and parking fees. For example, the Great American Insurance Company paid $75 million for naming rights to the new Reds' stadium.

The stadium deals in Cincinnati are among the most generous in the recent wave of publicly financed stadiums. Certainly the Bengals' deal is the most generous of the agreements we discuss in this book. Yet at the beginning of the process, the local community voiced significant opposition to stadium building. Even immediately before the successful sales-tax referendum to fund these stadiums, most voters opposed the plan. What happened in Cincinnati that turned stadium antagonism into stadium support (and eventually back to antagonism again)?

The evolution of new publicly financed stadiums in Cincinnati was similar to the evolution of stadiums in other cities—at least on the surface. Since the early 1990s, the Bengals football team had been arguing with Cincinnati about the terms of its lease. Bengals general manager Mike Brown, son of the team's founder, Paul Brown (who had also founded the eponymous Cleveland Browns team many years before), felt that the city was according advantages to the Reds baseball team, with whom the Bengals shared Cinergy Field (formerly known as Riverfront Stadium). The Bengals believed this favoritism violated their lease, which guaranteed that the city would treat co-tenants equally. A lawsuit resulted and was settled in 1994, when the city agreed to pay the Bengals a certain amount each year ($2.75 million initially, with increases each year thereafter) and promised to build additional luxury suites and club seats at the stadium.[1]

Nevertheless, Mike Brown continued to announce publicly that the Bengals were being courted by at least four other cities, including Baltimore. Despite multimillion-dollar payments from the settlement, Brown claimed the Bengals could not compete with other NFL franchises. The only answer, of course, was a new stadium, which would generate enough revenues to let the Bengals acquire high-priced players, who would make the team better and bring a Super Bowl championship to Cincinnati. Other cities were willing to make that commitment, the Bengals argued, so now was the time for Cincinnati to step up and build new stadiums for its teams. Cincinnati chose to defer to Hamilton County for resolution of the issue: the county assumed ownership and control of Riverfront Stadium and also took responsibility for ironing out problems identified by the sports teams.

BUILDING A COALITION

In 1994, Cincinnati mayor Roxanne Qualls and Hamilton County commissioner Guy Guckenberger formed the Regional Stadium Task Force to explore options for new publicly financed stadiums. Supposedly, the task force used stadium initiatives in Denver and Arlington, Texas, as models for a regional effort. The following year, the task force concluded that $544 million would be required for all riverfront projects, of which $185 million would go toward the football stadium. The task force did not suggest a source for the money. At this point, according to the official story, a little-known county commissioner named Bob Bedinghaus stepped to the plate and proposed a plan to pay for the stadiums.

In January 1995, Bedinghaus had been appointed to fill a county commissioner vacancy. His prior political experience included a town clerk position (elected) and a stint as director of the Hamilton County Board of Elections (appointed). Although Bedinghaus was not particularly well known in the Hamilton County business world, he was working his way up the ladder in the local Republican party. Philosophically, he cast himself as a "no new taxes" politician, a popular stand in the conservative Cincinnati suburbs. But despite his claims to fiscal conservatism, Bedinghaus soon became chief spokesperson for a significant tax increase. This plan, known as Issue 1, was a half-percent sales-tax increase for Hamilton County. In March 1996, Issue 1 passed easily, receiving 61 percent of the overall vote in the county. The tax increase was supported in every precinct, although the margin of support was far greater in the suburbs than in the city.

With Bob Bedinghaus leading the charge, Hamilton County began discussions with both sports teams, although talks with the Bengals seemed to receive much greater priority, which Bengals' owner Mike Brown chalked up to his own quick action. But structural circumstances also made football a more important issue. First, Brown and the Bengals were threatening to move the team out of Cincinnati. Second, just ten days before the Issue 1 vote, the Cleveland Browns were lured from Ohio by the sweet sound of a new publicly financed stadium in Baltimore. Third, due to internal league rules, NFL teams are in general much more mobile than professional baseball teams are. Indeed, during the recent wave of publicly financed stadiums, not a single major league baseball team has moved, although many NFL teams have changed venues. Meanwhile, Bob Bedinghaus was on his way to being elected to a full term as Hamilton County commissioner. He had received 70 percent of the Republican primary vote and would soon garner well over 60 percent in the general election.

THE DEAL OF THE MILLENNIUM

After much haggling, the Bengals and Hamilton County signed a memorandum of understanding in September 1996, which laid out the general plan for a new football stadium. By the following May they had agreed on most of the details. But the city (primarily the city council) felt that the agreement was too generous to the team and was reluctant to transfer some important riverfront property to the county. The county tried to satisfy the city by fine-tuning the lease, upsetting Mike Brown, who renewed his threats to take the Bengals out of town— most likely to Cleveland of all places!

More important, the council also called for an increased ticket tax (rising from 3 to 8.85 percent) on all events at both stadiums, which would generate an estimated $100 million over twenty years for the Cincinnati public schools. The council argued that, during the sales-tax initiative, Issue 1 supporters had promised that these new stadiums would not be built at the expense of the city's dilapidated school system. The rough outline of this promise was that the city and the county would use stadium tax revenues to give a total of $10 million per year, for ten years, to the public schools. The city claimed that the Bengals' deal, as it now stood, would not generate enough money for the city to fulfill its $5 million commitment.

The Bengals opposed this plan, claiming that it would hurt ticket sales and therefore the team's ability to make money and compete for the all-important free agents. Most subsidy advocates argued that an admission tax hike was a bad idea because it might keep people from attending games.[2] After much negotiation, the plan was jettisoned. The parties agreed, however, to a twenty-five-cent ticket surcharge, which would go to the county. Presumably, some of that revenue would be used within city limits.

As conversations between the county and the Bengals continued, the deal became even more lucrative for the team. The proposed price tag for a football-only stadium had increased from an original estimate of $185 million to $270 million. According to the agreement, this latter figure was the guaranteed maximum contribution from the county. This amount still did not include costs for land acquisition, design fees, or practice fields. The Bengals' total up-front contribution would be about $47 million. This contribution, however, would not come out of Mike Brown's pocket but from future stadium-generated revenues: the team expected to cover almost all of its obligation using the twenty-five-cent surcharge, naming rights, and seat licensing sales. Officially, the county would own the stadium, and the Bengals would sign a lease to play there until 2026. The rent on this lease would be about $1.1 million per year for the first nine years and would then be dropped to nothing. Hamilton County would pay for stadium operations and maintenance; but the Bengals would receive all revenues from tickets, concessions, parking, and broadcast rights, not to mention half of the gate receipts for nonfootball events at the stadium and the right to present professional soccer there for ten years. Some of the parking revenues would be generated by a new 5,000-car parking structure funded by the state (paying 60 percent) and Hamilton County (paying 40 percent). Finally, if the team did not sell 50,000 general admission tickets at each of its first twenty home games, the county would make up the revenue difference. One sports executive familiar with the deal told us,

> The Bengals took the county to the cleaners as far as I'm concerned. The net present value of the Bengals deal is negative. The county is paying them to stay there. The county pays 100 percent of the maintenance, and the Bengals get 100 percent of the revenues. The county pays all the real estate and property taxes. It's a sweetheart deal, an unbelievable deal. [The county] just gave it to them.

There were clauses in the memorandum of understanding that said if a deal doesn't happen by some date, then [it] just goes away. That was [the Bengals'] trump card all the time.

THERE'S COST AND THERE'S *COST*

It soon became clear that the stadium's guaranteed $270 million price tag was, to coin a phrase, not even in the ballpark. By the time construction began in April 1998, the price of Paul Brown Stadium had soared to just over $400 million. Proponents argued that this price jump was in no way misleading: they had always maintained that neither of the earlier prices (including the original $185 million estimate) had purported to include the indirect costs of constructing parking garages, acquiring land, building practice fields (which alone cost $10 million), and designing the stadium.

As the August 1, 2000, completion date approached, new cost overruns brought the price to almost $450 million, a figure that did include some of the indirect costs just mentioned but not those associated with general infrastructural improvements to the stadium area, such as parking garages. Official county documents estimated those costs at $178 million (including $140 million just for parking garages). In addition, in the case of construction delays, the county would have to pay the Bengals $4 million for each game after August 1 not played in the new stadium.[3] Thus, the total cost of the football stadium alone (and certain shared elements such as garages) had surpassed the initial $544 million projection for *both* stadiums.

Meanwhile, as football was kicking off in new Paul Brown Stadium, construction on the Reds' baseball stadium was just beginning. By virtue of this second-fiddle position, the Reds would not be taking Hamilton County to the cleaners. Nevertheless, there was certainly no chance the team would wear dirty laundry. A sports team executive commented,

> The Bengals' deal was done, and they have their location; so [the Reds] sit down and say they want something similar. What's fair is fair. [The county] just laughed at them and said, "You're not getting the Bengals' deal. We'll give you a good baseball deal but not the Bengals' deal." So [the Reds] agreed to just get a good baseball deal. They could have argued that the "equal treatment" clause of their lease was violated, but what judge in [Hamilton County] would agree with that?

In 1998, the Reds did get a good deal, but it was not nearly so generous as the Bengals'. The differences lay mainly in extra guarantees that the county made for unsold seat compensation and nonbaseball revenues. Otherwise, the basic elements were the same: the county built, owned, and ran the ballpark; the Reds kept all revenues generated from ticket sales (minus the twenty-five-cent surcharge), parking, and concessions. The team agreed to pay $30 million toward building the stadium, which would be taken from future revenues. Supposedly, the guaranteed county contribution was $235 million; but once again, it did not include the indirect costs of design, parking, infrastructure, and (a new twist) demolishing thirty-year-old Cinergy Field (née Riverfront Stadium). These items might easily add more than $50 million to the county's contribution.

By early 2000, when construction was beginning, guaranteed costs to the county had risen to $280 million. One county administrator blamed this increase on simple, uncontrollable inflation, although he neglected to indicate why the county had to bear these costs alone. More important, the increase was accompanied by a growing public realization that the purported face value of public financing is far different from the actual amount of money that needs to be paid. The numbers tossed around (and voted on) always refer to the *principle* amount that a municipality wants to borrow (usually through bond sales) to build a stadium. But this face value does not include the *interest* costs of borrowing money. Anyone with a mortgage or an auto loan knows that you eventually pay your lender far more than the $100,000 price of a home or the $20,000 price of a new car.

By the middle of 2000, publicly discussed figures started to include the long-term principle and interest costs of building the two stadiums. Assuming that interest costs remain relatively stable and that bonds are not retired early, Hamilton County taxpayers will fork out almost $1.5 billion for these stadiums. The Bengals' and Reds' shares, however, will not increase over their official figures because their contributions require no borrowing.

Stadium supporters often defend this sort of discrepancy by using a home mortgage analogy: they tell the public the price of the principle, not the total cost of principle and interest over thirty years. But when you ask a bank for a $100,000 mortgage, that institution must, by law, estimate and inform you of your total costs over the life of the loan. The bank's approval and your agreement take into account your ability to pay back all the costs, not just the principle. Rating agencies (for example, Moody's) assess public bonds based on the partly objective, partly subjective assessment of a municipality's long-term ability to pay back all costs, not just the principle. It is interesting to speculate how the various stadium financing referenda would have fared if referendum language had included total costs.

TAKING THE FALL

Cincinnati residents who had opposed the stadium, and even many who had supported it, began to feel hoodwinked. One political official said,

> People are waking up [to find] that they got sold a bill of goods. Folks are a lot more [upset] than they were in 1995 because of the overruns [and total costs]. The slick [advertising campaign] really worked here for the vote; then people started seeing who was giving what. Everybody thought it was such a great thing; but you talk to the average citizen now, all the polls are thumbs-down. If it came up today, thumbs down. That's what the polls show.

Interestingly, this public realization occurred in San Diego at roughly the same time (see chapter 6); and the backlash from this deception (as defined by some members of the general public) is creating formidable obstacles to the construction of the Padres' new ballpark. In Cincinnati, however, the uproar from the deception (as some define it) did not seem to have any tangible effect on the stadiums. It did, however, have a tangible effect on the political career of Bob Bedinghaus.

For almost forty years, the Republican party controlled the Hamilton County government; not since 1964 had a Democrat even been elected to the three-member county commission. Basically, whoever won the Republican primary became the county commissioner. Despite this history, Bob Bedinghaus lost the 2000 general election to Democrat Todd Portune, a four-term member of the Cincinnati city council. Public opinion polls indicated that voters had boiled down the election to a single issue: stadiums. Ironically, Portune had supported Issue 1; but he believed that Bedinghaus and the county subsequently gave away the farm and mismanaged the stadium deals. Bedinghaus countered that stadium cost overruns were common everywhere and that the people of southwestern Ohio would feel good about these ballparks long after the hoopla over money had died down.

Maybe they will, but they didn't feel so good on election day in 2000. Portune took 48 percent of the vote, Bedinghaus 43 percent; and the margin would have been greater if Libertarian candidate Paul Naberhaus had not received 9 percent of the vote. Exit polls indicated that most of that 9 percent were anti-Bedinghaus voters who just couldn't pull the lever for a Democrat. As of 2002, two out of three Hamilton County commissioners were "anti-stadium." Stunned by Bedinghaus's defeat, Bengals owner Mike Brown said he thought that Bedinghaus had made the community better and compared him to Winston Churchill, who won World War II but then lost his next election.

BEHIND THE SCENES: THE POWERFUL LOCAL GROWTH COALITION

The rise and fall of Bob Bedinghaus symbolize the complex social processes that gave Cincinnati two new publicly financed stadiums in the face of significant, if not overwhelming, opposition. The official scenario shows a young, energetic Bedinghaus making tough decisions, bringing together warring factions, getting the job done, and taking it like a man when things went bad. But a closer look reveals that Bedinghaus, in fact, represented Cincinnati's powerful, well-oiled growth coalition. Although he was certainly a member of this coalition, he was not its leader. Instead, he was the public persona of a corporate community that chose, for good reason, to operate more covertly.

Cincinnati has a historically strong growth coalition. Despite a modest population of roughly 350,000, the city has six locally based, Fortune-500 companies, including three in the top one hundred.[4] Speaking about Cincinnati, a business leader said,

> The bankers are obviously very important. It's one of only a few communities where three of the four largest banks are locally owned. Name another community where that exists. It's part of the advantage of the size of Cincinnati. It's part of the way that things have always been here. Businesses are expected to do a lot . . . philanthropically. If you and your corporation don't give of your time and your treasure, then you are not a part of this community. It's part of the real fabric [of] this place.

These companies and the people who run them have been around for a long time and have created a highly organized, unified, and powerful corporate community. Organizationally, Cincinnati's local growth coalition is represented by the Cincinnati Business Committee (CBC) and the Greater Cincinnati Chamber of Commerce. The CBC consists of twenty-six CEOs from the city's largest corporations; the chamber has 6,700 members, mostly small and medium-sized businesses. These two groups are more closely aligned with one another than they are in any other city in our study. According to a leader of the business community, [the head of the chamber] sits on the CBC executive committee and the directors' committee of Downtown Cincinnati, Inc.[5] Their directors both sit on the chamber board. It is very incestuous. Every member of the CBC is a member of the chamber. More than 50 percent of them are (or were) officers of some sort. The chamber is the outreach arm that brings small businesses in. That's one of their secrets. Most cities have the elite group and the chamber at odds with each other. The CBC director and the chamber director are very close friends. They work together on the issues, so you're not screwing around with who takes the credit.

This unusual alliance within the business community contributes to the formidable power of Cincinnati's local growth coalition. In other cities with relatively powerful local growth coalitions (such as Cleveland and Pittsburgh), CEO-only groups are far more visible than the local chambers, at least on issues concerning stadium initiatives. In our view, the importance of the Cincinnati chamber lends extra authority to the corporate community and helps obfuscate any real or imagined differences between large corporations and smaller firms. Of course, there are real differences between the organizational needs of Proctor and Gamble and those of a small restaurant. But cooperation between the CBC and the chamber probably reduces potential friction among firms and increases the entire business community's influence on public policy. Perhaps most important, it creates a unified front for the media that, in this case, favors publicly funded stadiums. A corporate leader who supported the stadium initiative commented,

> Cincinnati is the thirty-third-largest market in the country, and it has the fourth largest chamber. Go figure. We have a business community, which is committed to the community; it makes a statement. Someone in a job like mine is given the privilege of shaping opinions from time to time. I can't do wonderful stuff; I'm not the genie. But every now and then you have the opportunity to tip the rock just enough and see what damage it will do. Those of us who are playing these roles, the influencers, have to sit and say, "Is [a stadium] the best way to spend [all these] millions?" The answer is probably no, but who else would [make these hard decisions] over the years? All [the business community] did was put up a million bucks. The nay sayers maybe had $40,000 in their campaign, certainly less than $100,000 going against our million.

Probably the biggest "rock tipper" in the local growth coalition has been Carl Lindner. In addition to being the majority owner of the Reds, he and his companies wield a great deal of economic and political clout in Cincinnati.[6] A business executive said,

The Reds are members of the chamber but not actually on the CBC. But one of [their] limited partners kind of runs it; he runs the business community here. Carl Lindner. He is the man. He runs the city. He owns American Financial Group, which is a publicly held insurance conglomerate; also Chiquita, Stokely–Van Camp, and Financial World.

In the closing weeks of the 2000 election campaign, Lindner quickly pumped $100,000 into the Hamilton County Republican party. Party officials acknowledged that almost all of this money was intended for Bedinghaus. The $100,000 complemented Lindner's previous $44,000 contribution to his campaign (*Cincinnati Enquirer*, October 27, 2000). Although a series of TV advertisements attacking Todd Portune appeared during the last few weeks of the campaign, exit polls suggested that those negative ads, along with web sites with titles such as "LiberalPortune.com," might have actually pushed fence sitters away from Bedinghaus. Clearly, even a powerful local growth coalition doesn't always gets its own way.

MODESTY AS STRATEGY

The deification of Bob Bedinghaus was only one of many strategies that helped ensure passage of the tax referendum and construction of the new stadiums. We do not have the proverbial smoking gun to prove that the corporate community was hiding behind Bob Bedinghaus; but based on numerous conversations with supporters and opponents of the stadiums, this seems to be a strong possibility. For instance, a local journalist who regularly covered the stadium story told us the business community had worked hard to make Bob Bedinghaus the official spokesperson for the initiative:

> Bob Bedinghaus tells the story about sitting around the kitchen table and coming up with the idea of the sales tax. However, many people are insisting that business leaders came up with the idea and presented it to him. But this was not really in his political nature. He was a clerk; then all of a sudden he was a star. Either way, he got out in front and has been "Mr. Stadium" for two years.

Another person deeply involved in the stadium campaign was also skeptical about the idea that Bedinghaus had masterminded the sales-tax initiative and that the local business community was just along for the ride:

> The kitchen table story is the most absurd thing I've ever heard. Bob Bedinghaus was a township clerk and head of the board of

elections. Not exactly big time politics. . . . I believe [the business community] said to Bob, "This is what we want to accomplish; you're our designated man to do it."

Members of the business community never said that they were pulling Bedinghaus's strings. It seems, however, that the decision to keep CBC members in the background was carefully thought out. A business leader told us,

> When we made a decision to get involved [on the tax issue], there were six or seven businesspeople, plus Bedinghaus. We finally came to the conclusion that we needed someone who had real expertise running this kind of campaign. [A consultant] out of Columbus came and was the brains behind things. So we had these six business leaders, each with their own ideas [about] who should be the spokesperson. . . . [We] didn't let ourselves get involved in a big ego hunt. We spent the next six to eight months working with the consultant, raising a million bucks so he had the resources to do what he needed to do, then being a sort of kitchen cabinet to advise. Until three days before the actual vote, you never saw a suit.

In hindsight, the business community's low-key strategy was extremely effective. Its reluctance to take center stage on the stadium initiative seemed to be rooted in a particularly painful recent experience. In the early 1990s, Cincinnati's local growth coalition had led the charge in a major effort to revamp the city's charter. Cincinnati has a weak mayoral/city manager form of government that arose in the early twentieth century after a notoriously corrupt mayor was involved in a serious scandal. Apparently, people in Cincinnati now have a real affinity for this type of government; and the Charter party, which orchestrated the initial changes in the 1920s, is still active in local affairs. Led by a highly visible CBC, the business community almost single-handedly championed a referendum to return to a strong mayoral government. The charter revision referendum was soundly defeated and generated considerable antipathy toward Cincinnati's corporate community. A business executive admitted that the campaign had been a disaster:

> It went down in absolute flames. There seemed to be a consensus [in the business community] that the form of city government needed to be changed. The [Charter party] was opposed. Community activists: real good people but . . . naïve. They have the same intense beliefs as, say, the enviromaniacs. So they are automatically opposed because it would replace the city manager, which is Satanism. The fact that the leaders of the business community supported this [so visibly] made the business community become the

issue. People rallied around that. The blacks and the Democratic party rallied against it, and it was dead.

So it was more than modest egos in the business community that gave Hamilton County a visible Bob Bedinghaus. Clearly, Cincinnati's local growth coalition had learned an important lesson from the charter campaign and strategically chose a lower profile for the sales-tax campaign. The willingness of Bedinghaus to take the lead on the initiative made it easier for the local growth coalition to remain discreet. In hindsight, this strategy seems to have been very effective.

COMMUNITY SELF-ESTEEM AS STRATEGY

"Keep Cincinnati a Major League City" adorned T-shirts, bumper stickers, and signs during the sales-tax campaign. This was *the* message, and well-organized stadium supporters stayed with it. Advocates rarely promised economic spin-off from the new stadiums, instead focusing almost all of their attention on promises of enhanced community self-esteem. As we mentioned in chapter 2, some cities (such as New York, San Francisco, and Philadelphia) find it hard to manipulate community self-esteem because those cities already possess many "major league" characteristics, in addition to sports stadiums. But in Cincinnati, the idea that Cincinnati could fall from the ranks of major league cities holds real resonance. According to one business leader,

> Sports do not operate on a rational basis. I sat there as [a business executive] and thought, intellectually, it probably doesn't pay in terms of dollars and cents. What kept it on my screen was the argument that [professional] sports will help give Cincinnati a major league future. So [stadium advocates] including the mayor [insisted] that it was not about rich ballplayers and owners; it's about Cincinnati; it's about the community. Do you want Cincinnati or do you want Memphis? Do you want Detroit?[7]

This portrayal of the stadium was a strategic decision by the local growth coalition, which seemed knowledgeable and savvy about the successes and failures of stadium initiatives in other cities. The community self-esteem strategy was effective because the area around Riverfront Stadium (a.k.a. Cinergy Field), although close to the central business district, has absolutely no ancillary economic development. A local reporter who has covered stadium stories for years told us that focusing on community self-esteem was a wise and well-calculated move:

For me, as someone who grew up in northern Kentucky, Cincinnati had always had a sort of superiority complex. The sales-tax campaign played off on those fears, which were already there. The thought was, what distinguishes us from these other towns is that we have two major league teams in such a small market. We need to hang on to this so we don't become another one of those podunk towns that doesn't have football. There was exit polling after the sales tax, when people said they voted for it but complained bitterly. [They] said these rich team owners don't deserve all this money; we're just working stiffs, so why should we pay more? But a lot of these people said, "I held my nose and voted yes because I don't want the city to turn into Dayton."

A local politician opposed to the sales-tax increase also thought these scare tactics about community self-esteem were extremely effective:

[The message was] if we don't do this, we'll lose both our sports teams, and we'll be a nobody town. You had a million-dollar slick campaign, and it worked. They rolled out the athletes in the greatest dog and pony show on earth. People don't spend billions in advertising because it doesn't work. Let's look at the Reds in particular. It's a great team with a great history, and its home is here. [Reds' owner] Marge Schott, in spite of herself, has always had a large following of supporters.[8] So a lot of people [were convinced] that a half-cent isn't so much. It will make us a world-class city, and people will live happily ever after.

Cincinnati itself was perfect for taking advantage of this strategy. Its downtown, like those in many other cities, empties out after 5 P.M., when the office workers head home. The city's lack of downtown vibrancy only grew worse in the 1990s. As one long-time resident noted,

Cincinnati took some big hits just before the sales-tax increase. McAlpin's shut down their downtown department store, which had been on Fourth Street for a long time. People came for generations to shop at McAlpin's downtown. Some of the other long established stores on Fourth Street also closed down and gave the impression that downtown was having severe problems. All of a sudden Indianapolis got a Nordstrom, and Cincinnati had wanted one forever. Then Cleveland started doing stuff on the lakefront. God . . . if Cleveland can do it, then what have we become?

Downtown Cincinnati lacks the permanent residential base that creates community self-esteem from the fabric of everyday life. In other cities with more vibrant downtowns and neighborhoods, identity can be built from a myriad of smaller interactions. In cities with downtowns that are heavily corporate and commercial, there is more fertile ground for manipulating angst about slipping to the depths of Louisville or Dayton if the sports teams leave town. Conversely, imagine stadium supporters in Los Angeles claiming that the old Dodger stadium is turning the city into Bakersfield near the ocean. But in Cincinnati, threatening community self-esteem was a strategy that worked.

EXTERNAL IMAGE AS STRATEGY

As we argued in chapter 2, the manipulation of community self-esteem is often complemented by an attempt to project a particular image of the city to outsiders. Especially in midsized cities such as Cincinnati, the local growth coalition needs to offer amenities to prospective upper-level managers and executives. Executives of major companies feel they need company skyboxes to be even considered by the A players in the labor market. An abundance of cheap stadium parking adjacent to downtown doesn't hurt much either. One executive said,

> What's the greatest single problem a business has today? Work force. If you interview fifty businesses at random, I'll bet forty-nine would say that my biggest problem is getting qualified workers. To get workers, you have to get people who want to be in your community because they love the community; it's got things to offer. As the incoming CEO of [one local] company said, I got eighty people making over $100,000 in this operation. Every one of them is young, aggressive, highly compensated people. They go to the best schools in the country; they can go anywhere they want; they are the A players in the business world. I need things that A players want.

Apparently, these A players are more interested in some amenities than others. For instance, mass transit does not seem to be a priority for new public financing or tax referendums. And while many people promised that the city schools would surely benefit from a major league Cincinnati, that promise has not materialized. A politician argued,

> I think the whole hypocrisy of this stadium stuff is that the schools have been in bankruptcy for six, seven, eight years. None of the sales tax is supposed to go to schools, just stadiums. The hypocrisy is you have all these business people who put a million dollars in. We know their kids do not go to the Cincinnati public schools. They don't live in the city. If the schools were the priority—and they should have been—then we should have taken care of the schools first and then worried about building the stadiums. But business

says, without the stadiums we can't bring in the kind of work force we want.

MEDIA CONTROL AS STRATEGY

Cincinnati's media outlets were an important part of the local growth coalition's drive toward stadiums. They provided a supportive mechanism for creating the illusion of modesty (and the short-lived veneration of Bob Bedinghaus) and for manipulating community self-esteem. An opponent of the sales tax commented,

> There were all these scare tactics. They would bring in the NFL commissioner to say something absurd that was completely not newsworthy [and] the *Enquirer* was a butt-kisser for these people. Did you see the front page last week when they dedicated the stadium? It was a shameless giving up of the front page. They have no shame . . . at the *Enquirer*. With all those resources, [pro-stadium people] could stage these events, which should have been on page 16.

These sorts of decisions are up to editors, not reporters. Many people we spoke with noted that reporters and managers at the *Enquirer* were not always in agreement on the stadiums generally or the tax referendum specifically. A business executive told us that referendum supporters knew that the *Enquirer* editorial board was very supportive but that the news side was always skeptical. We noted this pattern in several other cities as well. In Minneapolis, reporters threatened a walkout over the publisher's leading role in advocating a new stadium. In Philadelphia, there was a split between editorial policy (strongly pro-stadium) and reporters (who were neutral to skeptical).

There are two kinds of media bias at work here. The first is a subtle, third-dimensional bias (discussed in chapter 1) in which the editors (and sometimes the reporters) from the media agree from the get-go with the local growth coalition about what is or is not newsworthy; the agents of socialization have fomented similar ideological perspectives in seemingly different individuals and groups. This bias results in the uncritical reproduction of press releases from stadium advocates or fawning coverage of "dog and pony shows" such as the groundbreaking ceremonies just mentioned. One referendum opponent told us,

> Channel 9 had a report the other night where they got some new cost figure on the stadium and the headline was "cost figures meet budget." Sure, [it meets] the budget from a week before, but it's

twice the one you voted on in the referendum. The media people get handed a press release and just repeat it [instead of asking,] "What's going on? It was supposed to be $170 million, and now it's $400 million. How can you say it's on budget? We're not going to run this story." But they do anyway.

The other form of media bias is more overt: the media are usually owned and controlled by either agents of the local growth coalition or larger multinational corporations (such as Disney or Time-Warner). The intensity of this control varies greatly from city to city; there may even be a media wild card, as in Pittsburgh, where a wealthy growth coalition outsider owns his own newspaper. Apparently, however, Cincinnati's local growth coalition holds a tight reign.

> [Stadium supporters] also had all the talk-show hosts. [Major corporations] control almost all the radio here in town. . . . Their talk-show hosts were constantly pounding home the [pro-referendum] message. Day in and day out, they said we have to do this or Cincinnati will become another Dayton; we will slip to the next lower rung of cities. [So] speaking as one unified voice on these radio shows is not a coincidence. Some people on the radio did not support the tax, but it was made clear to them that they [should change their mind].

Opponents in many cities we studied, including Cincinnati, felt that, while local reporters tried to be balanced in their coverage of stadium issues, the editorial position of the local papers sounded the drum in support of stadiums. Often, newspaper publishers themselves played key roles in the growth coalitions supporting new stadiums, which suggests they share the vision of growth held by corporate members of the coalition: highly visible development projects designed to enhance community self-esteem and keep the home team in town.

POWER POLITICS AS STRATEGY

In addition to implementing these relatively subtle strategies, Cincinnati's local growth coalition played hardball. The most obvious illustration is the sheer magnitude of the funds used in the sales-tax campaign. Pro-stadium and pro-referendum forces had approximately $1 million to spend, most of it provided by the local growth coalition. This figure was 2.5 times greater than any funds ever spent on a ballot initiative in the Cincinnati area. In contrast, opponents of the tax increase had, depending on reports, between $30,000 and $100,000, mostly provided by small individual contributions or local labor unions.

This financial inequality also reflected the particular political-economic dynamic between the city of Cincinnati and Hamilton County. That relationship is very similar to the situation in Pittsburgh and Cleveland, two other midsized eastern cities with strong growth coalitions. As we mentioned in chapter 1, this city-county dynamic is an important component of the stadium-building process and seems to be highly interrelated with a local growth coalition's power.[9] One politician remarked,

> I think the county, especially after [it assumed control of] the stadium, has been given life to be a player. Before that, the papers never wrote about the county, and you never heard about the county government. Now the city is growing more African American, [but] urban resources are being used in ways that benefit white suburbia. They can come down to the arts center or to the game, and that's it. I don't think [stadiums] will bring one white person back to live in the city. The city also built a brand-new department store, which cost almost $100 million if you count the real estate. The plan is, if we build it, they will come. We'll see.

County politicians in several cities we visited expressed delight in their increasing power vis-à-vis city politicians. This probably reflects long-term enmities and a sense that county politicians are finally gaining respect and power. But something much more important than clashing political egos is at stake here. As counties that surround cities grow in both population and political strength, and cities concomitantly decline, priorities seem to shift. Quality-of-life issues important to city residents become increasingly underfunded, while there is increasing pressure on cities to provide entertainment (and other diversions) for suburbanites. This shift puts cities in a difficult position. To remain vibrant in the face of increasingly poor populations, they feel pressured to attract both tourists and suburbanites and their dollars. Creating those attractions costs a significant amount of money; and if the bet does not pan out (in this case, if the investment in stadiums does not produce the expected increase in tax revenue), then already strapped city budgets will tighten even further. A city official said,

> We are in a big fight now, where the county is trying to shove a jail down the throat of one neighborhood, and [the city is] trying to keep it out. The city is growing more African American. . . . It's an issue people don't want to talk about. They don't want to acknowledge it.

In Cincinnati, a further exercise in power politics concerned the actual construction of the tax increase and how it eventually appeared in the referendum to fund the stadiums. Ohio state law allows sales taxes to be raised only half a percentage point at a time (for instance, from 5.5 to 6 percent). To circumvent that law, county commissioners passed two separate half-percent resolutions. As envisioned, this tax increase would fund both new stadiums as well as other nonsports construction such as a new jail. But these kinds of tax increases cannot be imposed if, within thirty days of the resolution, a challenging petition is submitted with 26,000 valid signatures. A valid petition mandates a countywide referendum. Because there were actually two proposed tax increases, challengers had the difficult task of completing two valid petitions to force a referendum. A leader of the petition drive reflected,

> In July 1995, when the county first proposed the tax increases, a lot of people voiced opposition. [A petition drive] was never done before, so nobody knew how to do it. There was no example, so we said, "Good Lord, how are we going to pull this off with volunteers?" It was August. Terrible heat and rain. Our volunteers would go out and stand in front of Kroger's supermarkets [while the company itself was] being pro-tax. They would chase the volunteers away. It was hit-and-run. You would work at a supermarket for an hour until they shooed you away; then you would hit some others. It didn't take much to get signatures. In my neighborhood we used a schoolyard and had four tables set up. It was like a drive-in; they wouldn't even have to get out of their cars. We had cars lined up.

Within a month, 90,000 people signed each of the petitions, thereby forcing a referendum. By then, with opposition to the tax mounting, the governor convinced the county to scale back the tax increase to a single half-percent and dedicate it just to stadiums (Blair and Swindell 1997). The scaled-back referendum passed in every single voting ward of Hamilton County. Suburban voters were far more supportive, as were men and the relatively rich. Only two precincts showed an almost even split, both populated by University of Cincinnati professors and graduate students.

The final piece of Cincinnati power politics involved a concerted effort to split the city's African American vote from the labor vote. The pro-stadium consultant had concluded that the referendum could not possibly pass if it were opposed by significant swaths of blacks and union members. One supporter was very clear about the importance of the strategy intended to split this potential coalition against the new stadium tax:

> We had worked very hard to split labor and the African American community. [We spent] a night meeting with the African American leadership, some of them Baptist ministers. We cut a deal and convinced the black community that labor was no friend of theirs in terms of creating jobs. This was going to be the largest public works project ever, and we needed their support to get it done. So we split the African American community from the labor community. The labor community [said] it would only support [the referendum] if they had a contract agreement guaranteeing 100 percent union jobs for construction. We said, "No way." The African American community held. It took a lot of heat but held.

Stadium politics certainly produce some ironies. Here, a group of business leaders were pledging affirmative action efforts for a huge public project using new taxes. The local growth coalition used these arguments to win over some of the African American community's influential leaders. According to a referendum supporter who was central to the negotiations,

> [We convinced] them they were going to get the jobs. Nothing guaranteed but a commitment that there would hopefully be 15 percent of the total work done by African American firms. We initially suggested 10 percent, then realized we couldn't get the deal done for less than 15 percent, . . . and we did it. [Interestingly], with all the affirmative action changes now, the black community is having a difficult time [getting the] participation they want. It's an interesting twist.

After this meeting, African American clergy came out in support of the referendum.

Perhaps it is merely an interesting coincidence that less than 15 percent of the stadium construction has been done by African American–run companies. As is often the case, it remains unclear if this low percentage has resulted from a true lack of qualified minority-owned construction firms or a lack of effort in making construction opportunities available to such firms. Or perhaps, as one politician has concluded, the situation is just another in a long line of unfulfilled promises to the black community.

> They conned the African American community, which always gets conned. It is vulnerable because some of its leaders allow the community to be snookered. They got snookered again. They got promised jobs and business opportunities, and to this point none of it has materialized. They continue to say it's going to happen. But I wonder how, when you need people with training and skills to build these things. You can't just walk off the street corner and start building stadiums.

Just as important, perhaps, this same politician believes that sports stadiums don't bring people together across racial lines or help create community collective conscience:

> What we are beginning to see, not just here but nationally, is that second only to the churches, the most segregated place you're going to find on a given day will be the stadiums. [There is] a big conversation about the lack of blacks at the baseball games. Particularly now, the cost for games is prohibitive.

LUCK AS STRATEGY

Even with an extraordinarily powerful local growth coalition calling the shots, Hamilton County voters almost certainly would have defeated the sales-tax referendum if not for one chance occurrence: the Cleveland Browns' relocation to Baltimore in early 1996, only a few weeks before the referendum. Almost overnight, polls about the sales tax reversed from solid opposition to solid support. Many local residents never really believed that the Bengals might leave Cincinnati. But when the Browns left Ohio, it validated the argument that these things could happen.

Contributing to the impact of this chance event was another bit of luck: the actual timing of the election. A referendum opponent admitted that his side made, in hindsight, a very bad decision:

> You have to say on your petition which election day you want. We thought we would need the whole thirty days [after the tax resolution was announced] to get the 52,000 signatures. That thirtieth day fell beyond the cutoff point for having the issue on the November 1995 ballot. So we had to wait until March 1996. That was fatal. If we knew we would have had such an easy time getting the signatures, we would have done [the referendum in] November. We were so far ahead in the polls in November [that] the result would have been much different.

None of the pro-stadium people we spoke to put very much credence in the importance of timing, preferring instead to credit their own campaign for electoral success. They did admit that the Browns' move was important but said it was not the major cause of victory. The city's weak mayoral form of government also seemed to assist the powerful, well-established corporate community in achieving its goals.[10] Cincinnati is one small (and shrinking) part of Hamilton County, differing from, say, Philadelphia and Los Angeles, where city and county are geographically identical and there is no county government to generate possible city-county tension. Beyond geography alone, Hamilton County has the ability to levy and spend sales taxes, which makes it a formidable economic source.

Cincinnati is the exemplar city for crystallizing our ideas about how publicly financed stadiums get built even in the face of solid opposition. A combination of fortunate circumstances and a powerful local growth coalition generated one of the most stadium-friendly deals in the nation's recent wave of stadium games. The city's coalition generally eschewed arguments about direct economic spin-off and instead focused on community self-esteem and community collective conscience. It used a number of strategies, including the creation of a political champion, who received much of the credit and eventually much of the flak for the publicly financed stadiums. As in other cities, the point person for stadium deals sometimes ends up taking it on the chin, while the stadium still gets built and is ready for opening day.

The ramifications of these stadium battles are still being felt in Cincinnati. For example, the Bengals had apparently set aside certain premium seats for their large corporate fans (and also for Hamilton County), while publicly insisting that there would be a blind lottery for assigning all seats. More recently, the Internal Revenue Service has notified the Bengals that it may owe $14 million in back taxes on the seat license revenue. But an amendment to the lease between the Bengals and Hamilton County explicitly states that "the county alone shall be responsible to pay [and defend against] any claims or assessments for taxes relating to [the sale of seat licenses]." Advocates seem to have thought of everything.

4

Cleveland

THE COMEBACK GROWTH COALITION

L ike Cincinnati, Cleveland's identity as a major league city seems largely dependent on professional sports.[1] The obvious difference is that, in Cleveland, Akron and Toledo replace Dayton and Louisville as loathed minor league comparisons. A less visible similarity between Cleveland and Cincinnati is the presence of powerful local growth coalitions buttressed by strong, activist, corporate leaders. In both cities, these strong coalitions were instrumental in securing public dollars for private stadiums. This chapter tells the story of Cleveland's public financing of a new baseball stadium (Jacobs Field), an adjacent basketball arena (Gund Arena), and, most recently, a new football stadium (Browns Stadium).[2] We highlight the ways in which the local growth coalition orchestrated this effort and argue that, without this active role, the path to publicly financed stadiums in Cleveland would have been far rockier.

Cleveland has been hard hit in the latter part of the twentieth century, losing much of its manufacturing base and a significant amount of its people. Like people in Cincinnati, many in Cleveland seem to fear it will drop into the ranks of second- or third-class cities and that losing professional sports teams will symbolize a larger decline. In response, growth coalition members in Cleveland have decided to use sports stadiums to stem the loss and turn Cleveland into a tourist destination.

The real story in Cleveland is little known among people outside the city, who are quick to tout "the Cleveland miracle," unaware of the nasty events unfolding behind the scenes. So while this chapter is mainly intended to further our thesis that growth coalitions are critical for understanding the process of stadium financing and construction, it also contains important lessons for people in other cities who hope to re-create the "miracle" in their own communities.

SELLING THE CLEVELAND MIRACLE

In many of our early interviews for this book, we heard about the Cleveland miracle, supposedly generated through construction of a new baseball stadium (Jacobs Field, home of the Cleveland Indians) and a basketball arena (Gund Arena, home of the Cleveland Cavaliers). This combined project was usually referred to as "Gateway." Outside of Cleveland, politicians and businesspeople (including team executives) said they hoped to copy in their own city the transformative power of Gateway, especially the Jacobs Field component. The media in these cities stoked this view with editorials touting the widespread, drastic improvements in Cleveland after the Gateway project was completed. But if you look beyond the hype, the Cleveland story doesn't quite match its Cinderella tale. Make no mistake: the stadium is very nice; and fans have been supportive, with tickets selling out game after game (at least until recently). But this success came at a price. Not only did Jacobs Field (and Gund Arena) incur huge cost overruns; but it also generated a major scandal, lawsuits over unpaid bills, a countywide bailout of the project, and a deposed stadium czar. Moreover, the tangible economic benefits of the stadium continue to be hotly contested. While some studies have shown a modest benefit, others scoff at the idea that the public investment was worthwhile.

The story begins with Cleveland as an aging midwestern city desperate to hold onto its professional sports teams. During our interviews, a remarkable number of people in Cleveland spontaneously mentioned Johnny Carson's joke about Lake Erie catching fire—clearly a sore spot for residents of a city often ridiculed as "the mistake on the lake." Such defensiveness makes fertile ground for the belief that the departure of professional sports teams will hammer the final nail into the city's coffin. So when the Cleveland Browns moved to Baltimore in 1996, sports fans saw their worst nightmare come true.[3] But here we get ahead of the story. How, in this environment of despair, did pro-stadium forces come together to finance and build Jacobs Field, Gund Arena, and Browns Stadium? What was the role of Cleveland's local growth coalition in this process? After all, Cleveland was a city best known for failed projects. A 1984 referendum to increase countywide property taxes to fund two new stadiums had failed miserably by a 65 to 35 percent margin. How did Cleveland become "the comeback city?" In our view, the story is really about the comeback of a powerful local growth coalition.

CLEVELAND AS A CORPORATE TOWN

Cleveland has long been dominated by Fortune 500 corporations and the law firms that serve them. In all, ten such companies call Cleveland home, although none is in the top one hundred. A former city finance director explained,

> TRW, Eaton, and LTV Steel are all headquartered here. American [British Petroleum] is here but may be on the way to Texas. Republic Steel and U.S. Steel used to have a tremendous presence, although only LTV is left, and it goes in and out of bankruptcy. The two largest law firms pretty much run the place as surrogates for the corporate community, and their client lists look like a who's who of the local Fortune 500.

In 1977, the election of progressive mayor Dennis Kucinich challenged this corporate power. Kucinich, whose election was perceived by some as a backlash against business elites, attempted to arrest the age-old practice of giving large tax abatements to Cleveland businesses. He also tried to shift funding priorities from the downtown business center to the neighborhoods. One local journalist believes that Kucinich was a serious threat to Cleveland's corporate hegemony:

> [Kucinich] did some things that were nonproductive and undercut his support in the community, particularly the big law firms. We were about third in the number of Fortune 500 companies in the 1960s, and these lawyers were worried that nobody was coming here anymore. Kucinich embarrassed them nationally, and that's when in essence they took over. That is essentially when Cleveland Tomorrow comes into the picture.[4]

Cleveland Tomorrow (CT) emerged in the post-Kucinich era as an organization of CEOs from the city's major corporations. The organization was founded in 1981 by Ruben Mettler, chairman of TRW; E. Mandell de Windt, chairman of Eaton Corporation; Morton Mandel of Premier Industrial Corporation; and Thomas Vail, the publisher of the dominant local newspaper, the *Plain Dealer*. Similar in many ways to the CBC in Cincinnati, the continuing strength of CT indicates the continuing power of Cleveland's corporate presence. CT helps set the city's agenda, as evidenced by its leading role in creating Civic Vision 2000, a plan for Cleveland's physical infrastructural development. A business executive reflected on CT's origins:

> [It] started in the early 1980s, aimed broadly at economic development and economic growth of the region. It was an organization keyed up by a study done by [a consultant], who was contracted by

a group of four or five CEOs in town, who said, "We are Rust Belt; we are sliding; we need an assessment of where our big gaps are because of economic competitiveness." [The consultant] said that [Cleveland] really doesn't have a strategic, powerful, business-oriented organization to do this. These issues are not falling fully within the Chamber of Commerce; they are not fully public agency types of tasks. We need an organization with some clout to take on these strategies.

As a CEO-only organization, CT can easily focus on issues most important to the city's largest corporations. Each of the group's more than fifty CEOs pays dues that form the budget of the organization. CT does not release its operating budget, but a similar organization in Philadelphia runs on a budget of about $3 million; and Cleveland Tomorrow is probably not far off that mark. The organization acts as an alternative or adjunct to the Chamber of Commerce (called the Growth Association in Cleveland), which represents all businesses in town. CT has anchored the city's resurgent local growth coalition as it works to rebound from the Kucinich era and is a textbook example of how large corporations can band together to shape public policy.

A few years after its founding, Cleveland Tomorrow began showing interest in the city's physical infrastructure, which (in the view of members) should include new professional stadiums. As one growth coalition leader put it,

> [The] economic development initiative didn't pop up on the screen until the mid-eighties. [It materialized] at the urging of a couple of CEOs, particularly [one] who would become chairman of Gateway. So [these CEOs] said we have to play a role in the physical development of the core city. [It] is important to the whole region [and] a lot of our issues are regional-based. At that time one of the large challenges for downtown was, are we going to lose the Indians and do we need a new sports facility to keep them there? So we got involved with that. We are lucky that a lot of our CEOs are locally based people who drive to work and see this stuff [every day] rather than just on a monthly trip to Cleveland. It makes a difference, and a lot of them are homegrown Clevelanders.

LET THE STADIUM GAMES BEGIN

A central player in this drama was Tom Chema, a lawyer with a history of political connections among officials in Cleveland and Columbus. Chema was chair of the Ohio Public Utilities Commission in the mid- to late 1980s and had remained friendly with Richard Celeste, who was governor during that period. In a long, detailed interview, Chema told us about the origins and development of the Gateway project. Near the end of his term as governor, Celeste asked Chema how he could help Cleveland. Although it seems unclear who first made the suggestion, the idea was floated that something had to be done to keep the Indians in Cleveland. There was an effort in the early 1980s to construct a domed stadium to house both the Indians and the Browns, but it was solidly defeated at the ballot box. Another plan proposed convincing Cleveland State University to share a building with the professional teams. No one, however, could ever get the university and the professional team owners to envision common interests.

According to Chema, the governor asked him shortly after a dinner meeting to "pretend he was Henry Kissinger and go one on one to all these public officials and . . . try to convince them that they all had the idea to build this new stadium."[5] Chema began this work in the summer of 1989. He met with county commissioners; the new governor (George Voinovich); the crop of candidates then running for mayor; and eventually the owners of the Indians, the Browns, and the Cavaliers. Chema believed he had gained a general consensus about building a new baseball stadium to keep the Indians from leaving town, but few specific details had been worked out. He wanted to keep any word of this plan from reaching the media, knowing that once the stadium issue hit the news wire, opponents would begin lining up, questions would be asked about financing, and politicians might start running for cover. Chema was right. As he put it, "Once the news media got a hold of it, we were in the newspaper every day for the next six years."

Chema knew that there was not enough money in the city of Cleveland to fund the stadium that he and Indians' owner Dick Jacobs envisioned. He understood that he needed to build a countywide consensus around some form of funding mechanism. As in Cincinnati, this would exacerbate an important city-county tension that would constrain the options available to pro-stadium forces. Among other things, such a situation makes room for a new kind of politics in which the county jockeys with the city to take credit for new projects while not offending the other party too much. The city needs the county's larger tax base, while the county often needs city government approval on siting and zoning issues for new projects.

LET'S TAX THE POOR

According to Chema, Governor Celeste found some money to pay for focus group research, which determined there was scant countywide support for financing stadiums with increased sales taxes but moderate support for using a "sin tax" (on alcohol or cigarettes). Chema preferred to call it a luxury tax, presumably because of its populist connotation of soaking the rich. Of course, taxing cigarettes and liquor is the antithesis of soaking the rich; and the ultimate goal of the tax was to subsidize wealthy team owners. Despite Chema's semantic preference, the media generally used the moniker "sin tax."

Originally, Chema thought about a dual-purpose, baseball-football stadium but could never get Art Modell, the owner of the Browns, to agree. Modell had his own ideas about a $170 million renovation of old Municipal Stadium. As in many cities we studied, the owners of different professional teams often resent one another, usually believing the other team is getting a better deal. As we demonstrated in chapter 2, they often act like toddlers who have a hard time sharing. This attitude encourages, among other things, the movement toward single-purpose stadiums.

Meanwhile, Mike White was elected mayor of Cleveland. Stadium advocates knew it would be a challenge getting him to support a new stadium project. According to Chema, White wasn't a big sports fan; and since he had not campaigned on the issue of stadiums, he was reluctant to make them a major issue early in his administration. But he did leave an opening: he said that if Chema could convince him that stadiums were an economic development project, not simply a way to use public dollars for a new ballpark, he might be interested. Chema and a few allies decided that if they could combine a baseball stadium with a new basketball arena that could lure the Cleveland Cavaliers back from the suburbs, they might be able to demonstrate economic development. It might be hard to prove that a baseball stadium alone could be a major economic engine for the city. But an indoor arena (where the Cavs would play) could be used for concerts, wrestling, and tractor pulls—and maybe even for luring a hockey team to town. Chema's vision expanded to a side-by-side ballpark/arena complex that would function as a year-round venue. Of course, the price would be steep.

THE LOCAL GROWTH COALITION DEFINES THE ISSUE

According to Chema, during this period he was working with Richard Shatton, the executive director of Cleveland Tomorrow. A member of the business community told us that, at this time, new downtown sports facilities became CT's galvanizing issue. Although not all CEOs agreed that spending money for a sports stadium was the best use of funds, most eventually jumped on board. They tended to see stadium building as a way to spiff up the community's image, help companies recruit top-flight personnel, and (they hoped) provide some economic spin-off for their own corporations. As Chema put it,

> You're in Cleveland, Ohio, and you have twenty-three or twenty-four Fortune 500 companies headquartered here, and these guys are competing for the CFOs and COOs and all these key players with cities all over the world. They are trying to get the same talent as those in New York and Philadelphia and San Francisco and Los Angeles. And Cleveland is a town that is the brunt of Johnny Carson's jokes since the river caught fire and Dennis Kucinich took us into default. . . . [New stadiums] have a real impact on their abilities to sell key players on wanting to move to Cleveland.

But spending public dollars on large downtown projects is not always popular with average voters, and it is a particularly sensitive issue in Cleveland due to a long history of antagonism between the downtown (with its corporate citizens) and the neighborhoods outside of the business district. People in the neighborhoods might prefer the money to be spent on quality-of-life projects such as parks, sanitation, public safety, and improved public schools. The poor quality of the public schools was an especially important civic issue in Cleveland, and the school system eventually went into state receivership in the mid-1990s. According to some estimates, the schools were $150 million in debt; and only 8 percent of Cleveland residents would eventually earn a college degree.[6] Public education, however, was not on the radar screen of Cleveland's local growth coalition when it was building new stadiums. A business leader said,

> Some CEOs have absolutely no exposure to the Cleveland public schools. They could be a large company but only have one hundred employees here [in Cleveland] because they run companies across the country. They probably don't have a single person that ever went to the Cleveland public schools. CEOs have a lot of views about education, from the extreme free-market "blow up the public schools and go to charter schools" to the less extreme "blow up the schools" position!

There are two interesting points here. First, as we will also show in the Minneapolis case (see chapter 5), Cleveland corporations have "hollowed out" in that corporate headquarters, located in the city limits, may employ only a small number of highly-paid, highly educated, mobile individuals who did not grow up in Cleveland. Even those who did grow up in Cleveland probably did not attend the public schools. Only a few of Cleveland's large companies (for example, the local banks) need to worry that their employees cannot add or subtract or read at grade level. Other companies do not see basic education as an immediate concern. Second, many CEOs have a negative view of public education in general. Hypothetically, executives should understand the civic benefits of high-quality public education, even if it doesn't directly affect their organizations. But such a philosophical perspective is unusual.

In the mid- to late 1980s, it was probably impossible to generate consensus among Cleveland's CEOs on the importance of improving public education. Corporate elites were more willing to throw money at sports facilities than at schools because they were more likely to see tangible results from a new stadium. It is hard to argue that schools are more wasteful with public money than professional sports teams are. Nevertheless, if you were trying to recruit A players to your company, bringing them to watch a production of *Damn Yankees* at the newly modernized high school auditorium would probably not help you. But it might help recruitment to visit the company's luxury box at Jacobs Field and watch the Indians toil against those damn Yankees.

For all these reasons—self-interest, business interest, conviction, and political philosophy—the corporate community was a key, active supporter of what came to be known as Gateway. Chema said he continued to work closely with Cleveland Tomorrow and also with state government liaisons. He and his allies took the idea of both a baseball stadium and a basketball arena back to Mayor White, who became more enthusiastic about the project. Chema knew, however, that to raise enough public money to pay for the stadium and the arena, he would need a countywide tax, not just a tax in the city of Cleveland. So he had to gain the support of Cuyahoga County commissioners as well as the Cleveland city council.

Chema spent several months bringing commissioners around to the idea of a "luxury tax," which was finally placed on the ballot in 1990. As in Cincinnati, early polls showed significant opposition to the tax. But in the end, a well-run, well-financed campaign spearheaded by a reenergized local growth coalition turned the tide, and the tax passed by a narrow 1.2 percent margin. How did the turnaround occur?

THE GROWTH COALITION IN ACTION

As in Cincinnati, Cleveland's local growth coalition carried a big stick: money. The corporate community kicked in about $1 million for the pro-tax campaign. Tom Chema highlighted the strategy of securing these contributions:

By calling up CEOs and telling them to put money in. It was not a partisan campaign, so corporations could contribute to it. We put together a committee. The governor was very helpful. Dick [Jacobs, owner of the Indians] made calls; Hagan [the county commissioner] made calls. On the advisory committee, I had the chairman of the Republican party and the chairman of the Democratic party.

The opposition consisted of the United Auto Workers union, which represented many of the remaining industrial workers in the area (many of whom inhabited the deteriorating Cleveland neighborhoods); the tobacco and alcohol industries, which feared decreasing sales from a new tax; and a few local activists, including journalist Roldo Bartimole, who self-published *Point of View*, a well-distributed newsletter that was consistently critical of the sin tax specifically and the stadium project generally. While it is hard to get a handle on the resources of the opposition, nobody thinks they spent more than $100,000. Thus, as in the Cincinnati campaign, referendum opponents were outspent by at least a ten-to-one margin.

With the help of this well-financed campaign, the sin tax overcame initial resistance and passed by the narrowest of margins. Interestingly, the tax failed in twenty-one of twenty-two wards in the city of Cleveland (although in many of them the losing margin was close). Apparently, people living closest to the new stadium—presumably the main beneficiaries of promised economic development—were less than enthusiastic. But a solid yes vote in the Cuyahoga County suburbs carried the day.

According to Chema, the new sin tax would bring in an estimated $16 million in the first few years of implementation and decline over time, with the assumption that the higher tax and other societal trends might decrease alcohol and tobacco sales. The sin tax was a per-unit sales tax rather than a tax on the value of the sale. Therefore, increased prices on cigarettes and liquor would not by themselves lead to increased revenue because the tax was a flat fee levied on each unit sold, not a percentage of the price. The tax was set to go into effect in August 1990, with stadium construction to begin in early 1992. At election time, the price tag for the project was $344 million; but Chema admitted that the figure was a guess. Although he would have preferred not to name costs, the impending election forced him to provide some estimate of the total. Chema acknowledged,

It was stupid to say [a figure] because I didn't know. I didn't have a clue what this project was going to cost because we had no money, no organization, nothing. I didn't have a design. All I knew was that in Chicago and Baltimore, they were building stadiums for roughly *x* amount; they told me a certain number, and they lied. I knew a certain number of arenas had been built for "a number." So I take those numbers and ramp it up for inflation for a couple of years, and I take a look at labor costs in those cities versus Cleveland, and I put in a function for labor and throw in $20 million for property and . . . voila! I get $344 million. That wasn't a real number. I didn't want to say that number. I tried to avoid saying that number; but when you are in an election campaign, you have to put a number on it.

THERE'S COST AND THERE'S *COST* (REPRISE)

After the referendum passed, Chema and his now-official Gateway board had their money taken care of, or so they thought. Gateway would be a not-for-profit corporation jointly owned and controlled by the city and the county. Pat Parker, chairman of the Parker Hannafin Corporation, a Fortune 500 company and a leader of the local corporate community, was named the first chairman. Tom Chema was executive director.

As in every other city that built private stadiums with public dollars, Gateway's costs increased quickly. By the time it actually had designs for the stadium and the arena, the $344 million estimate had soared to $430 million. Eventually, a parking garage was added, making the project's final tally $462 million. So from the election number to the final cost, project expense increased by 35 percent. Chema argues that this comparison is unfair: the $344 million estimate did not include the garage and the walkways. But surely he and the designers realized that people would have to park somewhere and walk to the games.

Granted, part of the price increase was caused by the initial fantasy figure of $344 million. But these increases also resulted from the greed or business savvy (depending on your point of view) of the team owners. The Cavaliers were the primary (although not exclusive) force behind these overruns. The team had been happy in its relatively new home in Richfield (halfway between Cleveland and dreaded Akron) and was garnering healthy revenues from tickets, parking, and concessions. The Cavs' owners, the Gund brothers, argued that they would lose significant parking revenue by coming back to the city. Because political realities made the Cavs indispensable to the entire project, Chema knew who had the leverage.

According to him, the negotiations were long and hard and resulted in an agreement promising the Gunds, in what became an infamous phrase, "a first-class, state-of-the-art facility." Many of Chema's critics argue that he was naïve to allow such a phrase into a contract.

But Chema countered that he was not naïve at all and knew very well that it might prove troublesome. He said that representatives of the city and the county were well aware of the problems of this language and attempted to have it removed. The Gunds' position, however, was clear: without that guarantee, there was no deal. So public officials held their noses and signed.

The phrase would come back to haunt the project many times. The Gateway board preferred to define "first-class, state-of-the-art facility" like this: look around the country, find the best arena, and give the Gunds something similar or maybe even a little better. The Gunds had a different definition. What's the best scoreboard in the country? We would like one a little better. Who has the nicest coffee tables in the luxury boxes? We would like ones a little better. Who has the best elevators in their building? We would like those, too.

Also contributing to financial problems was the fact that the stadium/arena was treated as a fast-track project. This meant that the board and the teams never signed what are called "100 percent construction documents," which lock in the cost of certain items. Instead, change orders in mid-construction became routine. These two factors—the definition of *first class* and the fast-track schedule—often worked in tandem to increase the project's cost. Because no one ever signed off on the 100 percent construction documents, the "first-class" phrase was used to leverage many items in the new arena (Austrian and Rosentraub 1997, 363).

Another factor that increased the public cost of the project was the agreement that the Cavaliers would effectively pay no rent for their first few years in the new arena. The team actually started accruing rent *credit*. This phenomenon was rooted in the original negotiated agreement, which provided a host of rent offsets. One was a yearly $1.5 million credit for parking revenues the Cavaliers might lose by leaving Richfield Arena. Since nobody knew in advance if there would be greater or fewer cars at the Gateway complex, this was a win-win situation for the Cavs. They would keep all new parking revenues plus receive this sizable credit. In addition, the team was allowed to deduct from their "official" rent any capital repairs made to the arena. Other minor offsets included common area maintenance, security, and the like (Austrian and Rosentraub 1997, 364). Finally, even though the Cavs were exempt from paying the admission tax on each ticket sold, they still got to deduct the tax amount from their rent as if they were actually paying it. Ironically, when Cleveland later decided to raise this admissions tax from 6 to 8 percent to fund a new football stadium, the Cavs were able to deduct even more money from their rent payment.

ANOTHER CHURCHILL (OR KISSINGER)

Eventually, Gateway was unable to pay its bills. There simply was not enough sin tax revenue to cover the soaring cost of the project. Contractors were not getting paid; and many joined together in a lawsuit against Gateway, the city of Cleveland, and Cuyahoga County, alleging fraud because Gateway was approving expenditures when the board knew it was out of money. These and other embarrassing stories began to appear in the media, often first in Roldo Bartimole's *Point of View*. He ran stories about the cost overruns and allegations of a private luxury apartment hidden in the arena. (The Gunds argued it was an office.) Gateway began feeling more and more heat as news of cost overruns started hitting the mainstream press.

At this time, no one knew how much the total shortfall would be; but politicians in the city and the county began to worry they would be damaged by the scandal. Chema was spending much of his time working on a plan to pay the bills. To this day, he believes he had such a plan worked out. It entailed borrowing the money from Key Bank, with a guarantee from the Gunds, and then stretching out county bond repayments from thirty years to thirty-six or thirty-seven years. This plan, however, required the county to subordinate its repayments to the loan. In other words, the Key Bank loan would get paid before the county got paid. The county refused.

There are debates over exactly why the county refused. According to Chema, political enemies made during his tenure as head of the Ohio Public Utility Commission had grudges against him. He also implied to us that he had made enemies during the Gateway project, by either not hiring certain contractors who were favored by politicians or simply receiving too much credit for the project. Added to these skirmishes was the fact that Gateway itself was becoming a major political scandal. So if Chema had gotten too much of the credit for making the project happen, maybe he would also receive too much blame for the ensuing problems.

By early 1995, Chema's relationship with the city and the county was getting testy. In April, Craig Miller, an attorney with Ulmer and Berne LLP in Cleveland, was named the new Gateway board chairman. Miller was given the mandate of cleaning up the scandal and dealing with the contractors' lawsuit. He told us that his first job was to get a handle on the scope of the problem. He had seen the unpaid bills jump from $12 million to $18 million in just a few months. He began his own accounting and after six months concluded that the total amount of unpaid bills would be $30.6 million. About $6.5 million related to the stadium, and the remainder concerned the basketball arena. Miller admitted, "It is not that these bills could not just be paid right away. [It was that] there was no source of revenue to pay them at all. Not just right away, but at any time."

Miller's goal was to hold the contractors at bay, grasp the scope of the problem, and then figure out how to get additional revenue to pay the bills. Eventually, he was able to recover about $9 million from the Cavaliers. He did this by making clear to the public what had gone on in the new facility. He also hinted at an upcoming audit of the Indians to answer questions about past real estate taxes—this at a time when the Indians needed city approval to expand seating at the now-open stadium. Miller also parlayed a parcel of open land into some newly found money. One other important piece of land remained in the area of the stadium/arena. The teams claimed they held preferential development rights to it, but Miller interpreted this to mean that the teams had a preferential right against one another and that he could deal with a third party as long as it didn't favor either team. He put out a request for proposal and got a single bid from a small New Jersey hotel developer, who offered $2.5 million. The Indians balked, saying the deal violated the Gateway agreement. Miller made it clear he would take his chances and go with the bid. At the eleventh hour, the Indians offered $2.5 million with fewer contingencies; and their bid was accepted. The final transaction was never completed, however, because the city administration declined to approve it.

In the end, although Miller was able to find some of the money, he could not generate enough to cover the entire shortfall. So Cuyahoga County offered a "loan" to Gateway that many agree will never be paid back. This loan was made possible by an unconnected crisis occurring at the county level. As in Cincinnati, a stroke of luck, like a lightning bolt from the sky, created and eliminated options for the people and organizations making important decisions.

CITY-COUNTY DYNAMICS

In the mid-1980s, Cuyahoga County went through the "SAFE crisis," similar to the more famous financial crisis that later shook Orange County, California, and forced it into bankruptcy in 1994. According to a county official, local municipalities had pooled their money in a common investment fund, hoping the strategy might produce higher returns. The county had guaranteed the municipalities a 7 percent return but had made some risky investments itself to reach that goal. Although the situation had soured, the county felt obliged to honor the 7 percent guarantee; so it paid out the returns, thus creating its own enormous deficit. Problems mounted; and when SAFE losses surpassed $100 million, Cuyahoga County slashed its operating budget an astounding 11 percent across the board. In retrospect, the county only needed to cut about 9 percent to balance the books. But as fate would have it, an improving economy started generating huge budget surpluses for the now-austere county. This lucky money was eventually used to bail out Gateway. A county official explained,

> You are cutting 11 percent where you really needed 9 percent, and the tax revenues are now growing. What happened is, all the stars lined up right. People say, "Great planning." But a lot of it was sheer luck. The economy went bang and took off in '95, so the county caught a break. [It] had a lot of cash, and it just wrote a check. I won't say we didn't miss the $11.5 million, but the county was in a very good financial position.

Of course, that cash was public money garnered from increasing county tax revenues while simultaneously slashing services. But at this moment in the mid-1990s, the plan was convenient because it meant that county politicians did not have to raise any other taxes. Although the bailout has been officially termed a loan, most officials we talked to simply shrugged when asked if the loan would ever be repaid. What has happened is that the unpaid loan has been rolled into the next round of negotiations over the next set of projects. In other words, it has served as a bargaining chip for the county in negotiations over funding the new football stadium, which was just becoming an issue in the mid-nineties.

Technically, the city's Convention and Visitors Bureau was supposed to pay back part of the loan through extra tax revenues supposedly earned from increased hotel taxes caused by the presence of new stadiums. But a lengthy negotiation ensued over this issue, with the hoteliers arguing that they were not making any money from the new ballpark and arena, despite all the public pronouncements of economic windfall. Another part of the loan repayment was to come from the city of Cleveland, which instead rolled the obligation into negotiations over the new football stadium. We were explicitly told that the county did not expect to see the money again.

These confusing financial escapades make it very difficult to follow the money, as Deep Throat said about Watergate. As the convention center gets rolled into the baseball stadium, which gets rolled into the basketball arena, which gets rolled into the SAFE crisis, which gets rolled into the football stadium, the average citizen has little hope of following the trail. It becomes harder to say, "This particular money was paid to bail out this particular stadium," because the answer will be, "Oh no, that isn't true. This was a loan, and this money will be paid back." Maybe.

THE CLEVELAND MIRACLE?

Has the strategy to make Cleveland a first-class tourist destination worked? Have the new stadiums created great economic spin-off? Based on previous economic research augmented by our own field-work, we answer, "Probably not," to both questions. Certainly, the stadiums have generated a great deal of positive public relations for Cleveland. Few people outside of the city-county region have heard of the fiascoes described in this chapter, and belief in the Cleveland miracle is widespread and fervent. Indeed, almost all of the stadium proponents we spoke with in other cities gushed about Cleveland as the model for their own efforts. Some told us that we simply had to visit Cleveland and see for ourselves.

Quite honestly, Cleveland was not on our original list of target cities; but we thought it was important to explore a stadium-building process that had clearly beneficial civic outcomes. During our visit, however, we saw little evidence of Cleveland's downtown rejuvenation. The area containing Gateway has always been filled with old ware-houses, abandoned buildings, and many dirt-cheap surface parking lots for those willing to walk downtown to work. Since Gateway, some new retail businesses have sprung up around the stadium, particularly sports-themed restaurants and bars. Otherwise, the same sea of park-ing lots still exists, although they charge much more on game days (see fig. 1).

Our observations seem to match the findings of a carefully con-ducted study designed to assess the Cleveland miracle, which found decidedly mixed results—far short of a miracle (Austrian and Rosen-traub 1997). Total employment levels in the Gateway area actually in-creased at a higher pace (compared to surrounding areas) *before* the Gateway project, slowing down thereafter. Not counting direct sta-dium construction employment, slightly fewer than 1,800 jobs were created in the area in the years before Gateway was built (1989–92) but only 1,251 jobs in the three years after construction was initiated (1992–95). Austrian and Rosentraub (1997, 382) estimate that the cost per job created was an astonishing $231,000.

In the pre-Gateway years, fifty-four more businesses opened than closed in the area, while in the years after it opened, only fifty more businesses opened than closed. Thus, the data suggest that Gateway

Fig. 1. Cheap surface parking lots continue to be a major business around Jacobs Field.

has not led to a significantly different level of growth compared with the pre-Gateway years. Perhaps most interesting, however, is the shift in the pattern of industries surrounding Gateway. Not surprisingly, there was an increase in the number of restaurants and bars after Jacobs Field opened; but there was also an increase in the number of area retail stores that closed during those same years. This may reflect the fact that sports facilities create what you might call *game-day development* rather than true neighborhood development. In other words, stadiums foster the kind of economic development that directly supports activities during events (such as eating, drinking, and parking) but may lead to a decline in economic activities that support residential, neighborhood life. A large stadium provides exciting activities during games but desolation when it is empty.

WAGGING THE DOG

Since the opening of Jacobs Field and Gund Arena, Cleveland has gone on to build a new football stadium for the new Browns, the original Browns having left for Baltimore to become the Ravens. Revenues for the football stadium came primarily from extending the Gateway sin tax (voter-approved) and also from a new tax on city parking lots and garages.[7] The new football stadium was another piece of the downtown vision created by Cleveland Tomorrow and embodied in its Civic Vision 2000 report. The local government quickly and uncritically jumped on this corporate-led outline for Cleveland's future. A high-ranking city official made the corporate hegemony clear:

> [Cleveland Tomorrow] asked for the mayor's support on the endeavor in the first place, in part because they were dependent on funding from several major foundations—the Cleveland Foundation and the Gund Foundation; and these two foundations wanted to know that the mayor supported this effort. . . . The members of the Civic Vision and Beyond Committee were mostly identified by Cleveland Tomorrow, but they passed the list by us. We made a few suggestions for additions. . . . We are not formally represented on the group, but our staff has been invited to most of the major meetings. . . . The head of the group, Joe Gorman of TRW, has briefed the mayor on the work of the group.

This official did not think that such a process reflected a political community completely subservient to corporate interests:

> I want to be absolutely and totally clear on this point. Because a group of business leaders approach us with a concept that they

think is productive, and we did not turn them away or discourage them, should not be read by anybody that we are bound or locked into it. I could spend the rest of the evening talking about different groups, education, and everything else, but I'm kind of reacting pretty strongly to this point because there are folks, including the mayor's opponent in the last election, that criticized this administration for being focused on downtown development, and that is an inappropriate criticism because if you look at the actual record of this administration, there have been many more dollars and more effort put into neighborhood projects than into downtown projects. But a lot of people come downtown and look at the downtown project and write about those projects.

The political arm of Cleveland's local growth coalition still feels that it has had a relatively good experience in the use of public dollars for private stadiums. Several political officials we spoke with took the position that "our guys might be bad, but they're not as bad as the other cities' guys." They mentioned that Art Modell had received a brand-new stadium from the city of Baltimore without paying a cent and that Georgia Frontiere got a new stadium from St. Louis for moving the Rams from Los Angeles. They pointed out that "at least our guys put in *some* money." One official said,

> Cleveland is uniquely positioned in being able to focus on non-sports issues for the next fifteen to twenty years, while other communities . . . struggle to come up with financing packages. We don't have to worry about these issues for the foreseeable future.

In other words, at least Cleveland can move on. This sentiment is another example of third-dimensional power because the political players have completely internalized the ideology that "what's good for the corporate community is good for Cleveland." Direct coercion is not even necessary when ideological hegemony is this complete. Perhaps the best illustration of this relationship is a piece of art that stands just outside City Hall: a huge rubber stamp bearing the word FREE (see fig. 2). We assume this is supposed to have something to do with political freedom, but we couldn't help noticing that it is pointing directly at the nearby corporate towers. A metaphor for the ages.

Cleveland's local growth coalition, like Cincinnati's, was able to orchestrate the allocation of public dollars for private stadiums. The main players of this coalition were Cleveland Tomorrow, Tom Chema, and a city government in agreement with the corporate community's strategy. This strong local growth coalition was able to turn initial public sentiment against tax increases into a vote for tax increases. But

Fig. 2. This huge sculpture of a rubber stamp reading FREE rests just outside Cleveland City Hall. No one is quite sure what it means, but it sends an ominous message about the use of taxpayer money.

Cleveland's coalition, also like Cincinnati's, was not omnipotent: it made mistakes and barely won the vote. Still, it probably has earned the "comeback of the decade" award among the local growth coalitions we examine in this book.

One important difference between the coalitions in Cleveland and Cincinnati was the relative stress on tangible versus nontangible benefits alleged from new sports stadiums. In Cleveland, Gateway was sold primarily as economic development, which may have contributed to the close vote on financing it. Pro-subsidy forces tried to manipulate community self-esteem but not as a primary strategy. Probably the main reason Gateway was packaged as economic development came from the need to sell the idea first to a politician—Mayor White—who wanted to be seen as protecting the public purse strings. He was a dynamic individual in a strong mayoral system who set certain parameters on the stadium issue. A less dynamic individual or a different form of city government might not have generated the same constraints. Once again, chance mixes with observable behavior to produce a fascinating story.

Still, many people we spoke with insisted that economic growth was only one part of the Cleveland miracle. The fact that Clevelanders are allegedly feeling better about their city (as we learned in chapter 2, bike messengers are smiling more) was presented as evidence of a more esoteric kind of miracle. This shift was clearly reflected in the framing of the Browns' new publicly financed football stadium. With few economic miracles sprouting from Gateway, the football stadium was being linked much more with community self-esteem. As we argued in chapter 2 and demonstrated in chapter 3, these promises are difficult, if not impossible, to measure; and maybe that's the point. In our view, the real Cleveland miracle is that a formerly moribund local growth coalition could manage to direct hundreds of millions of public dollars toward a bunch of private new sports venues, thus giving its corporate members a powerful new recruitment tool. That and keeping the whole story behind the story a big secret.

5

Minneapolis and Hartford

DECLINING LOCAL GROWTH COALITIONS

In many ways, Hartford and Minneapolis are nothing alike. Hartford is a small city of 121,000 people that doesn't even make the top one hundred in U.S. urban population. Minneapolis is a much bigger city (380,000), particularly if you include its twin city, St. Paul (287,000). Hartford and the state of Connecticut have had no professional major league sports team since the 1997 departure of the Whalers hockey team, while Minneapolis–St. Paul has teams in all four leagues (baseball, football, basketball, and hockey). Although Hartford can be cold and snowy, it seems almost tropical compared to Minneapolis. Minneapolis is a lively intellectual center with major universities, while Hartford has been historically dependent on the insurance industry and struggles to overcome a reputation as a minor way station between New York and Boston.

But the two cities are alike in one important way: they have had tremendous difficulty in trying to build new stadiums for existing or desired teams. In the past decade, supporters have made five distinct and unsuccessful attempts to publicly finance a new baseball stadium for the Minnesota Twins. In 1999, the city of Hartford and the state of Connecticut made a desperate and unsuccessful bid to lure the New England Patriots away from Foxboro, Massachusetts, promising a brand-new stadium that would anchor an enormous redevelopment project and supposedly give downtown Hartford an economic and civic boost. Although the Patriots feigned interest, they eventually decided to stay in Massachusetts.

More important, Minneapolis and Hartford are alike because both have very weak local growth coalitions that used to be much stronger. These weak coalitions have been key to the cities' stadium troubles. In Hartford, civic leaders unsuccessfully attempted to recapture or replace an older coalition (known as the Bishops) that was strong when major insurance companies dominated the town. But corporate mergers and takeovers in the insurance industry have reduced the city's once-powerful growth coalition to a mere shadow of its former self. In Minneapolis, we heard many civic leaders bemoaning the decline of their formerly powerful local growth coalition, which led the effort in the 1970s and 1980s to build the Metrodome and cultural venues such as the Guthrie Theatre. Yet as corporations have left Minneapolis or been gobbled up by larger companies, the power of the local growth coalition has declined precipitously.

In terms of local growth coalitions, then, Minneapolis and Hartford are completely different from Cincinnati and Cleveland. New stadium proponents in Minnesota and Connecticut do not have the institutional alliances that can be decisive in turning public dollars into private stadiums. In this chapter, we will describe the decline of once-powerful growth coalitions in Minneapolis and Hartford. Without strong coalitions leading the charge, the process of building new stadiums has been far more difficult and far less successful.

MINNEAPOLIS'S DECLINING GROWTH COALITION

After the Minnesota Twins won the World Series in 1987 and 1991, the Twin Cities were on top of the world. Many felt that the Twins' success on the field proved that a small-market team could do well in major league baseball. Even at that time, however, both the Twins and the NFL Vikings were expressing unhappiness with the Hubert H. Humphrey Metrodome, where they played their games. The dome, which opened in 1982, is typical of the municipal stadium movement we described in chapter 2. Stadiums built during this period were usually multipurpose, no-frills (thus relatively inexpensive), and owned by quasi-public stadium authorities. By the late 1980s, the Twins and the Vikings both complained that the dome was not well suited to their needs, mentioning a lack of luxury suites, not enough signs for advertising, too few parking revenues (most went to the city), and a host of disagreements between the teams over revenue sharing. As other teams began to play in newer, fancier, single-purpose, publicly subsidized facilities with very generous lease terms, the alleged revenue gap expanded between Minnesota's teams and their competitors.

The stadium story in Minneapolis, however, is not just about two teams that have failed to share the dome or about small-market teams trying to survive in the oligopoly of professional sports. Although those stories are important, they are a backdrop for more vital issues. Our story focuses instead on how a once-strong local growth coalition, able to build the Metrodome in relatively short order, has evolved into a weak and fractured coalition that has failed in five attempts to build a new ballpark.[1] Without the type of coalition we observed in Cleveland and Cincinnati, team owners in Minneapolis have been forced to do the heavy lifting in their recent attempts to secure public money. As we discussed in chapter 1, such a situation creates a clear image of corporate welfare, making it easier for stadium opponents to fight the initiative successfully.

The Growth Coalition Builds the Metrodome

Understanding the Metrodome's origins requires a historical appreciation for its predecessor, Metropolitan Stadium (known as the Met). The Met was built in the 1950s in suburban Bloomington, Minnesota, and was seen as evidence that professional sports were becoming less urban and more suburban. This perception didn't sit well with the urban growth coalition, which was still powerful at that time in downtown Minneapolis. City leaders talked often about their desire to bring baseball back downtown. A key figure in those days was John Cowles, Jr., chairman and publisher of the *Minneapolis Star-Tribune*. At the time, he was generally regarded as the leading opinion maker in the city and the man who could galvanize the growth coalition (Weiner 2000).

It was no surprise that Cowles spearheaded the effort to build a downtown stadium and take baseball back from the suburbs. He was a close friend of Kenneth Dayton, powerful chairman of the Dayton Hudson Corporation, which owned Minneapolis's major department store. For obvious business reasons, Dayton worried about maintaining downtown vibrancy. Cowles saw suburbanization as an even bigger long-term threat to Minneapolis: "Even though [Bloomington] lacked skyscrapers at that time, [the growth of suburban Bloomington] was alarming for a metropolitan area our size. It was a prospect of a further decentralizing of the metro area and a scattering of its assets" (Weiner 2000, 69). By the 1960s, Prudential, General Mills, and 3M had all left the Twin Cities to relocate in the suburbs, and those interested in the future of the metro area decided that action was needed.

Cowles and Dayton wanted to form a cadre of corporate leaders to advocate for a new downtown stadium, and they had plenty of executive talent to choose from. They eventually selected Pete Ankeny, president of First National Bank of Minneapolis; Curt Carlson, CEO of the Carlson Companies; and Arley Bjell, CEO of the Lutheran Brotherhood Financial Services. Local businessman Harvey McKay, who had made his fortune in the envelope business, joined the other corporate executives in a concerted effort to build what would become the Metrodome. Although amassing this group of local business leaders was relatively easy because of Minneapolis's strong corporate community, it was harder to line up the political component of the local growth coalition, due more to the populism of Minnesota politics than to anything else. Skirmishes broke out over whether the stadium should be an indoor dome or a traditional outdoor stadium and later over the best location for the Metrodome. Anti-tax Republicans and social progressives sometimes lined up to block legislation at various points of the process of getting approval to sell bonds for the stadium (Weiner 2000, 79). Yet because of the dogged determination of a powerful growth coalition, the stadium bills were eventually passed. The process might have taken even longer if significant public revenue (such as a tax increase) had been required. Still, compared to current efforts to build a new ballpark with public money, constructing the dome was like a walk along the Mississippi.

When the dome was built, lots of promises were made about developing the parcels of land around the stadium; but it was never clear how strong those commitments really were (see fig. 3). Chuck Krusell, vice president of the Chamber of Commerce at the time, has since said, "You

Fig. 3. About the only development that has occurred around the Metrodome in Minneapolis is this small souvenir shop just down the block from the stadium.

got to remember, on our board we had big companies. They wouldn't be too interested in whether there was a restaurant nearby or not. The proximity of entertainment to the stadium was something we didn't consider when we picked a site. The question was whether we could get the land and whether it was relatively cheap" (Weiner 2000, 72). Notice that when business leaders are putting up money to buy the land, they look for cheaper land; perhaps only when the taxpayer is footing the bill must stadiums be on prime downtown real estate. Cowles also made it clear that he was looking after the interests of big business more than anything else: "I don't connect the dots to the neighborhood around the stadium. I connect them to the central business district" (Weiner 2000, 72).

More Than Greedy Owners

In contrast to the fairly swift building of the Metrodome, plans for a new baseball stadium have languished in the 1990s and early 2000s because there is no real counterpart today to John Cowles and Kenneth Dayton. Jay Weiner, a reporter for the *Star-Tribune* and the author of *Stadium Games* (2000, 76), a comprehensive study of the politics of sports stadiums in the Twin Cities, sums it up this way:

> A major player in the seventies that was missing in the 1990s was the business community. In the run-up to the Dome's political passage and financial creation, a cabal of Minneapolis's major business leaders determined that they would bring the Dome downtown, by hook or by crook. They didn't jump in at the very beginning. They jumped in when the political process turned a bit haywire. But when the business leaders decided to get involved, their involvement was deep and unswerving. They seriously put their money where their mouths were.

The city's older, more powerful, local growth coalition has all but disappeared. Several people we interviewed talked about how many of the homegrown corporations have been bought up by larger companies located elsewhere, leading to a vacuum in the business community. For example, by the 1990s, the *Minneapolis Star-Tribune* was no longer an independent entity run by a powerful local publisher like Cowles. Instead, the McClatchey Group of papers, a California company, had purchased it; and the new publisher, John Schueler, was not a homegrown Twin Cities guy. Schueler is a stark contrast to the powerful John Cowles, who shaped opinion in the city and brought together business leaders and politicians around large urban projects. Even Schueler himself recognized this change, as he told us:

> Most of us are hired guns. We don't own these companies; and therefore, many people were thinking about their business overseas, and

the global economy was forcing them to spend an inordinate amount of time out of this community. . . . What was nagging at us was that the people who made things happen in this community were family-owned businesses and very wealthy entrepreneurs and families that had been here for a very long time like the Pillsburys and the Daytons and so forth, and we felt we were kind of losing that kind of coalition of people who were looking out after the community.

Just as there is no counterpart to Cowles, there is no Kenneth Dayton to help lead the corporate-based, local growth coalition. The Dayton companies have become part of Target department stores, and only a tiny fraction of its total revenue comes from the Twin Cities. Corporate management is likely to be more national in its philanthropic giving and less concerned with the vibrancy of Minneapolis. Pillsbury was acquired by a British conglomerate, while Honeywell and ReliaStar both merged with other companies and moved their headquarters out of Minneapolis. The older civic leaders have retired, creating huge fractures within the city's once-powerful growth coalition.

Because of this fracturing, the Twins themselves have had to spearhead ongoing requests for a new publicly financed ballpark. A team executive described to us five different attempts made to secure public financing. The Twins cannot be accused of lack of creativity as they have tried just about everything: a nonbinding referendum (that never got on the ballot), a cigarette tax to raise money for a stadium, a special lottery, a plan to donate 49 percent of the ownership of the team to the state in exchange for money to build a new stadium, and a plan to donate the team to a charity. Each attempt was unsuccessful, with possibly supportive politicians running for cover as soon as they were framed as givers of corporate welfare to rich team owners. A Twins' executive admits that both team ownership and former governor Arne Carlson made mistakes in their efforts to secure public dollars. Another executive noted the importance of the now-weak local growth coalition:

> The corporations that are still big and still here are run by CEOs, and chances are pretty good that they didn't come from here and they aren't going to stay here either. So their job in the economy today is to increase the value of the stock of the company. . . . So it has changed a lot, an awful lot. They always talk about downtown movers and shakers. Well, we haven't got any. In fact, the opposite is true. The political power in Minneapolis is in the neighborhoods, not in the downtown.

Not surprisingly, subsidy advocates lament the days when those downtown movers and shakers could help get a major stadium project off the ground (see fig. 4). One executive sounded wistful as he described the story of funding the dome:

Fig. 4. This is the famed Minneapolis Club, where the formerly powerful local growth coalition met to "get things done" in the city.

Compare [today] to when the dome was done twenty to twenty-five years ago. . . . There was a downtown group of businessmen, maybe eight or nine guys who bought the land for this building. I don't know where they got the money. Then they donated the land to the sports commission so that this could be built. John Cowles was the head of it; Carl Pohlad, Harvey McKay, a couple others. Then they had to sell the bonds that had an interest rate limit of 7.5 percent. This was at a time when interest rates were going up very fast due to the oil crisis. They sold all the bonds to four banks—well, three banks and an insurance company—on a Sunday afternoon. They bought 'em all: $55 million. They just got together and said, "We'll buy them." They didn't have to go back and ask their board; they just did it.

Recently, some other stadium proponents have finally come to realize that the Twins' overt participation in the process has become a major problem. When we visited Minneapolis in June 2000, a brand-new effort was underway to garner public support for a scaled-down $150 million urban ballpark. Notably, John Schueler, the publisher of the paper and Jim Campbell, CEO of Norwest Bank, spearheaded the effort and made a conscious decision to keep the Twins out of it. When we asked Schueler about whether or not the Twins were involved, he answered enthusiastically,

Zero! Nada! They were the biggest part of the problem, we felt. . . . One of the things we learned is that this must be a community-based effort. So who is the community? Who carries the ball? We asked the politicians under what circumstances would they be able to go forward in a process with a plan for keeping major league baseball in town.

In the spring of 2000, Schueler and Campbell put together a working group excluding the Twins and began to try to develop a coalition around building a less expensive ballpark. They hoped to be able to build a park for $150–250 million without much public funding. Whether this was possible remained to be seen. There were skeptics, including the Twins, who had seen their brethren across the nation move into ballparks with price tags approaching $400 million. By late June, however, Schueler had resigned as co-chair of the committee pushing for a new stadium. Reporters at the *Star-Tribune* had become angry that the publisher was taking such a direct advocacy position on a contentious issue. In a meeting, the journalists convinced the publisher to pull out. He told us,

Well, the perception was that we have a conflict of interest. Our journalists were getting upset. My first obligation is to the newspaper and its integrity, not to a ballpark plan. So I am not going to be in the formal processes, but I am getting phone calls every day, from "How do you think we ought to do this?" to "Who do you think we ought to talk to?"

To proponents of the new ballpark, however, Schueler's move is merely symptomatic of the larger problem of a weakened growth coalition. Schueler, they argue, is the antithesis of Cowles, who was willing to risk his neck for the good of the entire corporate community. One key business leader, who laments the fracturing of the growth coalition in Minneapolis, reacted strongly when we told him of Schueler's decision:

> That's very bad news! It is also stupid. He was attacked by the help! It reminds me of a story. At the [*New York*] *Times* in 1970, when Bella [Abzug] was running in the Democratic primary, . . . the owner of the *Times* came into an editorial board meeting one day, and he said that he was sorry he was late but he was working on the Democratic primary endorsement editorial. And someone said, "That's okay; we've done it already; we decided to go with Bella," and he said, "I am sorry, gentlemen. If you want to determine editorial policy, go buy yourself a [expletive] newspaper." Who cares what the help thinks! . . . If the publisher is not going to provide leadership in the community and be among the important leaders in the community: . . . if not he, then whom?[2]

This same business leader talked at length and with great passion about the need for Minneapolis's CEOs to step up to the plate and put together a new stadium coalition, something he saw as an important part of the city's infrastructure and cultural life:

> I cannot imagine a CEO going to a shareholders' meeting and answering a question about this and saying, "My dear shareholder, my duty is to manage this company for you, and in order to do this, I have to have the best management personnel possible, and to attract them here, I need a whole community. I cannot do it with half a community. I can't do it with the Guthrie Theatre and the orchestra, very frankly. I have to have sports teams or they will not come. So it is an absolutely necessary investment of your company, and one that I am very proud of. It was a prudent thing to do." What can they say? "I disagree"? Well, congratulations. Let's call for the yeas and nays, and by the way, how are the proxies doing over there?!

Another business executive echoed these sentiments. He decried the lack of long-term CEOs with strong roots in the community:

You just go down the list of the major businesses in town twenty-five years ago and compare the leadership. It's night and day. The principal owners were the family; now it is all just professional help. . . . There has to be a real difference between Kenneth Dayton and that guy running Target now.

The head of a local business association sounded a similar theme:

We've lost a number of Fortune 500 corporations due to consolidations. The Daytons, who were enormous contributors to this city, at one time probably got 100 percent of their revenues from an intersection two blocks from here. Now I doubt if they get one-tenth of 1 percent of their revenues from that store because the universe of Target stores is so much bigger. Their responsibilities are to the shareholders, and the leadership is more nomadic. It comes through a community, and then it moves on. This has made it a lot harder.

What, then, was the key difference between the coalition's success with the Metrodome and the toils and tribulations of current stadium efforts? Many people blame the increasingly unpopular public persona of Twins' owner Carl Pohlad. But having a controversial or despised owner does not distinguish Minneapolis from many other American cities. A better explanation lies in the disappearance of the growth coalition in the years since the dome was built.

Politics and the Twin Cities

A weak mayoral system is another factor that makes creating a strong growth coalition difficult in Minneapolis. Unlike St. Paul, which has a strong mayoral system, the local government in Minneapolis often favors neighborhoods over downtown; and it is difficult for the mayor to set a direction on her own. As the head of a local business organization sees it, this situation factors into the difficulties the Twins have faced:

One thing that is different here is that we have two core cities with very different sorts of government. St. Paul has a strong mayor; so when Norm Coleman decides he wants hockey or baseball, he can set a direction for the city; and [even though] he may not always win [his attempt to win baseball away from Minneapolis was defeated], he has the ability to step out and coalesce public opinion. . . . Here [in Minneapolis], Sharon Sayles-Belton is in a weak mayor and a strong council system, and over the years there have been very strong neighborhoods who elect people who are extraordinarily good at protecting the neighborhoods. It's not quite Chicago, but it is a modified Chicago kind of system.

A similar sentiment was echoed by an executive of the Minnesota Twins, who lamented,

> The city council is a ward system with a weak mayor. So what happens is that the city council in their wards has an advisory group that is funded. So the center of power is dispersed into ten to twelve wards in the city and within these groups. So they come to the council meetings with that agenda. There are only one or two council members that represent the downtown area. Neighborhood people still have a lot to say. . . . It's a weak mayor system. Her heart's in the right place, but you can't get anything done.

Others spoke of the populism and liberal tradition of Minnesotans, which makes it difficult to give vast sums of money to wealthy team owners. But the powerful growth coalitions of the 1970s and 1980s managed to overcome a similarly strong populist tendency. Moreover, we have seen other cities in which liberal politics do not contradict (and sometimes strongly advocate) using public dollars for new stadiums. We have been surprised over and over again at the strange bedfellows involved in stadium politics. We conclude, then, that a strong growth coalition in Minneapolis might overcome both populism and a weak mayoral form of government and be able to champion a new stadium successfully by touting it as a civic contribution. As we argued in chapter 3, the weak mayoral system actually helped the growth coalition's efforts to build stadiums in Cincinnati. But without such a coalition in Minneapolis, and given the weak mayoral system, the team itself remains in charge of securing public money for a new ballpark. This is almost always a sure-fire recipe for disaster from the point of view of those who want public dollars for new stadiums.

HARTFORD: FILING CABINET OF THE NORTHEAST

Small cities sometimes wish they were bigger. Hartford, Connecticut, has long tried to shake its image as the "filing cabinet of the northeast," a moniker that Bostonians, in particular, like to apply to the city. Located between Boston and New York, Hartford has long struggled to establish its own identity and reestablish a local growth coalition that can implement major projects and revitalize the city. This hasn't been easy in the past few decades; so Hartford decided to mimic the approach of other small cities, such as Nashville, which are trying to become major league by acquiring a professional sports team. In both cases, the cities wanted football teams.[3]

Hartford, long the insurance capital of the nation, declined in the 1970s and early 1980s as three significant shocks rocked the city's economy. First, the downsizing of the defense industry led to reductions in staff at companies such as Pratt & Whitney in East Hartford, United Technologies, and a host of nearby companies such as Hamilton Standards, Sikorsky, and Electric Boat. Second, the banking industry was consolidating operations all over the country, and in Hartford this meant that almost all of the local banks were acquired by two mega-banks: Bank of Boston and Fleet, both headquartered in Boston. Finally, the insurance industry, long the heart and soul of Hartford, underwent drastic consolidation and change. Travelers merged with Primerica and became a more integral part of New York–based Citigroup. Phoenix Home Mutual merged with Home Life, also a New York company. In short, the main corporate components of the local growth coalition were either bought up or hollowed out. Related to the decline of Hartford's traditional industries has been the struggle to hold on to a dwindling population in the city proper as a rising tide of suburbanization strengthens the surrounding communities. All of these trends have exacerbated the problems of identity for Hartford as a city.

One long-time observer we interviewed compared the current corporate power vacuum in Hartford to the old days, when the Bishops would "get things done":

> They used to be called the Bishops. Eight or ten large corporate directors—the head of Travelers, the head of the Hartford Insurance Group, the head of Aetna, the head of Cigna: they would get together with the former president of the Hartford Chamber of Commerce, and they'd say, "You want to do this. Fine, I'm in for a million; you're in for a million," and it gets done, and the chairman did the work. They were eight or ten guys, all over six feet tall, all Anglo; they all ran major financial services institutions, and they were giants in the domestic economy. We are now in a global economy. A lot of those institutions no longer exist because they have merged or gone out of business, and we have a completely different environment now.

While there may be a bit of nostalgia in this summary of local politics, the person we interviewed describes a tight-knit corporate growth coalition that once had the will and the muscle to dictate much of went on in Hartford. The consolidation and downsizing in Hartford's three major industries eroded this coalition and consequently led to a decline in the commercial real estate industry as its firms also downsized, merged, and moved headquarters out of Hartford. In the midst of this corporate exodus, commercial office vacancy rates approached 25 percent, and many planned civic projects were abandoned. Community self-esteem also took a blow in 1997, when the town's only professional sports team, the NHL Whalers, moved to North Carolina, a larger media market with no local hockey tradition.

Feet on the Street

What was left of the growth coalition in Hartford kept trying to turn things around. Attempts to lure an NFL team to Hartford had their origins back in 1995. A group of local architects approached executives at Phoenix Home Mutual Life Insurance Company about three acres of parking lots outside the Phoenix building. Only Interstate 91 lay closer to the nearby Connecticut River. Since the highway was built, Hartford's downtown has been largely cut off from the river; and some people in town thought it would help the city to "recapture the river." Business leaders (such as they were) seemed to envision something akin to Baltimore's Inner Harbor. A nonprofit group, Riverfront Recapture, spearheaded an effort to build pedestrian bridges across 91 to allow some access to the riverfront. Developers saw the three acres of surface parking lots as an opportunity to create some kind of major development that might, in the long run, entice local workers into living downtown rather than commuting from the suburbs.

Reflecting their positive impression of Baltimore, members of Riverfront Recapture imagined a local version of the Inner Harbor marketplace, with entertainment, restaurants, and retail stores. Bob Fiondella of Phoenix agreed to fund an initiative to look at possible development of the land. A planning group was formed that included executives from Phoenix, CTG Resources, and the Travelers Group, all of whom owned land at the site. Eventually, the group arrived at a plan, which later came to be called Concept I. It called for 3,000 square feet of retail and entertainment space plus a midsized hotel on the site of the old parking lots. Hartford's economy, however, was in poor shape during the mid-nineties; and retail vacancies were already high without adding more shopping outlets. Although the planning group considered abandoning Concept I, it decided instead to make it bigger and grander. They discussed adding a convention center and a conference hotel to draw more nonresidents to Hartford. In the recent past, Hartford had not had much luck in developing a convention center. Nevertheless, what eventually emerged as Concept II included a convention center, a conference hotel, entertainment, retail, and an apartment complex. The entire development project soon became known as Adriaen's Landing, named after Adriaen Block, a Dutch explorer who had supposedly landed on this spot now covered with parking lots.

Like many other cities we visited, Hartford has struggled to maintain and improve its downtown personality. There are probably no more than 1,500 high-quality rental units in the downtown area. A few lively neighborhoods lie adjacent to downtown, but most local office workers commute from the suburbs. As we have mentioned, Hartford itself has slightly more than 120,000 residents, although the greater Hartford metropolitan area has about 1.2 million people, making it a medium-sized urban area. This also means, however, that ten times more people live in Hartford's surrounding suburbs than in its urban core, the highest proportion of any city we discuss in this book. Even Cleveland's greater metropolitan area, which officially includes Akron's 500,000 metro residents, is only six times larger than the city itself

But despite its small size, the local growth coalition in Hartford has always competed with Boston and New York; and with both the coalition and the city in decline, recent strategies for survival have become more desperate. Thus, when planners couldn't make the smaller Concept I work, they tried, as one business leader told us, to "upscale it." This more complex plan set two goals for Adriaen's Landing. First, it hoped to make Hartford a destination for people living and traveling in the densely populated northeast corridor. Second, it wanted to attract and retain an eclectic variety of people, particularly young people, who hold the key to Hartford's long-term vibrancy and rejuvenation (*Adriaen's Landing Preliminary Master Plan* 1998, 1).

By the time Concept III was created, a football stadium for the University of Connecticut had been added to the project. The University of Connecticut, which had been exploring the possibility of moving up to division I-A football, knew that this change would require a bigger stadium and bigger crowds. UConn has been enormously successful in both men's and women's basketball, and many administrators thought this was the moment to add big-time college football. They debated the idea of putting the stadium in Storrs on the UConn campus but eventually decided that linking the stadium to Adriaen's Landing might be a better move. A key player here was Roger Gelfenbein, who worked at Anderson Consulting in Hartford and was chair of the UConn board of trustees. Gelfenbein was well connected with Bob Fiondella and Scott Noble at Phoenix Home Mutual Life as well as other members of the Adriaen's Landing planning team.

UConn's hometown, Storrs, is a somewhat isolated, semi-rural area about twenty-five miles from Hartford. Considering the university's location, school leaders were not sure that a new campus stadium would draw enough people to satisfy NCAA attendance requirements for a I-A football program, so they were interested in the idea of building something in Hartford. Meanwhile, those working on Adriaen's

Landing were excited about the possibility of bringing thousands of UConn students to Hartford as well as potential Huskies fans from the entire metropolitan area. Combining a stadium with a convention center, they thought, might support the retail space and make the overall project work.

Opportunity Knocks

About this time, Governor John Rowland appointed a task force to look into efforts at revitalizing Hartford. Bob Fiondella was appointed to the task force and was positioned to put the Adriaen's Landing development on the committee's front burner. By early 1998, the task force had created an agenda called "The Six Pillars of Progress for the City of Hartford." In early May 1998, the state legislature passed a bill that created a Capital City Economic Development Authority (CCEDA). This authority would provide the bonding for various projects related to the "Six Pillars" plan. On May 13, 1998, Concept III was formally presented to the city council of Hartford. The plan envisioned a domed, 35,000-seat stadium for UConn football, retail and entertainment, a convention center, and a hotel.

There is some debate about how the NFL Patriots came to be involved in the Adriaen's Landing project. The most plausible story seems to be that Bob Kraft, owner of the New England Patriots, made a phone call to Governor Rowland, telling him how impressed he was with the process that had led to Adriaen's Landing. He talked of his frustration at getting a new stadium built in Massachusetts and wondered aloud about whether the new stadium in Hartford could, or should, be factored into his future plans. In other words, Kraft seemed to suggest that the Patriots might consider moving to Hartford.

A key business leader involved with Adriaen's Landing told us that Kraft "was impressed by this large, mixed-use development, seemingly well planned and articulated; and that the state would be able to come up with $300 million of grant money to revitalize downtown and that some significant piece of it would be available for the development of this project." Other members of the Adriaen's Landing team and Governor Rowland seemed downright giddy at the prospect of Hartford becoming an NFL city. One central supporter told us,

> I have to admit a couple of times along the way, as I read about the travails of the Krafts [in Foxboro and Boston], I'd say to Bob [Fiondella], "You know, I wonder whether we ought to think about the Patriots?" and we said, "Naaaah, it's too big. This city has been there, done that." So we never really approached that subject. But then they came to us. And of course, John Rowland is a young

man, a football fan, and a big supporter of UConn. I think the response of all of us was "This is a two-fer. We can build a very expensive stadium, and instead of just having UConn games there, we can also have the New England Patriots."

State money for the project was to come from general obligation bonds. By this time, the Connecticut economy had improved in response to a rebound in the national economy and thanks, in no small part, to revenues being brought in by Foxwoods Casino, the largest single-floor casino in the country, located on Native American land in rural Connecticut. Governor Rowland and his executive staff were deeply involved in negotiations with Robert Kraft. This lent a certain legitimacy to the entire initiative: it was now bigger than Hartford; it was the whole state of Connecticut. Finally, on November 19, 1998, the state reached an agreement with Kraft to move the Patriots to a new stadium on the site of Adriaen's Landing. The local Hartford paper celebrated with the front-page headline TOUCHDOWN! above a photograph of Governor Rowland and Kraft taken during a celebratory press conference in the state capitol's Old Judiciary Room. At that event, Kraft, state politicians, and business leaders welcomed the arrival of the Patriots to Hartford. According to several spectators, many a tear was shed during the hoopla, celebrating an agreement that many saw as a major coup for "the filing cabinet of the northeast." Maybe Hartford was finally becoming a major league city.

Flies in the Ointment

Nevertheless, fitting an NFL stadium onto the Adriaen's Landing site would be no easy feat. The planned 68,000-seat professional football stadium would be twice the size of the original college stadium and would require at least 25,000 parking spaces. As the planning team moved toward Concept IV, which included the NFL stadium, it struggled with the logistics of fitting everything onto a rather constricted site. The only solution was to add a new parcel to the original site that would make room for the convention center. This would "merely" entail removing an office building, moving a gas company operations control center, and relocating the steam plant that heats and cools all downtown office space.

Even if these problematic removals and relocations were managed, there was still little room for parking on the site. Planners figured they could provide 6,000 parking spaces on the site of the stadium, only enough to serve fans with premium seats. The remaining 15,000 to 20,000 or more cars would have to park in existing lots spread around town, including East Hartford on the other side of the river. Those people would be bused to the stadium. Certainly, people without premium seats would see this as an inconvenience. But stadium advocates told us that fans would be happy to put their feet on the street and walk the short distance to the stadium because they would be enmeshed in the overall excitement of Adriaen's Landing. That excitement would become contagious and lead to the economic rejuvenation of the entire downtown.

Still, it was highly uncertain whether the necessary removals and relocations were even possible. There was a question about whether the area would pass an environmental assessment due to the current presence of the steam plant and the possibility that past occupants might have contaminated the soil. In addition, it was unclear who would pay for removals and relocations. The planning group hoped to apply for a section 108 loan of $8 million from the U.S. Department of Housing and Urban Development to move the facilities, arguing that the money would help preserve low- and moderate-income job opportunities by keeping the six hundred employees of the steam facility working in the city. Apparently, what didn't get mentioned was that the only reason those employees might be in danger of leaving the city was the group's own intention of replacing their place of employment with a football stadium.

Legislators planned for rapid movement. CCEDA had been granted what is referred to as "quick take condemnation authority," meaning it would be much easier for the group to take sites and pay owners for the land. "Quick take" authority would allow streamlined condemnation; any legal battle over the price of the land would not hold up the process. Planners hoped condemnation would be necessary for only a small portion of the total site. Nearly 96 percent of the land (other than the land controlled by the city) was owned by just five companies or individuals, all of whom were represented in the newly formed Adriaen's Land Company. The other major impediment might be environmental problems related to the site. The cost of any cleanup was likely to be borne by the public—most certainly not by the Patriots.

Cracks in the Weak Coalition

The coalition that supported the building of Adriaen's Landing was a fairly tight circle composed of the few corporations that owned the land. It seemed to be led by representatives of Phoenix Home Mutual Life in conjunction with Governor Rowland. Other members of Hartford's residual growth coalition were left out in the cold and did not always fully support the project. For example, the Hartford

Growth Council, an economic development organization whose main goal is to attract new businesses to Hartford, had been working on a wholly different agenda. At first unaware of the addition of the Patriots to the Adriaen's Landing project, the council had commissioned its own consultant, who had come up with a much different plan for Hartford's redevelopment. He had drawn up a plan envisioning Hartford as a "European" city with attractions scattered around town, which encouraged people to park and then walk through the city—a very different vision of rejuvenation. It presented a smaller-scale definition of development in which mixed-use neighborhood development was favored over massive projects designed to bring in tourists and centralize development in just one or two areas of the city. As a result, the council tended to be skeptical of the magnitude of the Adriaen's Landing project. As one business leader told us,

> The concentration of significant investment in one location as a solution to revitalizing the city was seen as a bad move. Now you can begin to see why there were some hackles raised over Adriaen's Landing. . . . We were all excited about that property along the river because it would be a nice complement to all the other things going on along the river. Where the rubber hit the road has been the magnitude of the concept. As it is proposed, it is two-and-a-half times bigger than Faneuil Hall [in Boston], South Street [in Philadelphia], or the Inner Harbor [in Baltimore] in terms of its retail and entertainment. . . . A big concern a lot of people expressed was the fear of the big sucking sound.

At the time of our visit to Hartford in January 1999, there was still much speculation that Robert Kraft might be using Hartford as a negotiating chip in his ongoing battles with Massachusetts over a new stadium in either Boston or Foxboro. People we chatted with around town seemed considerably more skeptical about whether or not the Patriots would actually leave Massachusetts for Hartford. When we raised this possibility with a supporter of the Adriaen's Landing project, he brushed it aside as an example of the pessimism that grows in a city that has been punched in the face one too many times. This advocate insisted that there was no manipulation involved, that the plans for Adriaen's Landing had simply impressed Kraft:

> Bob Kraft was dazzled. He was dazzled and taken by it. Now he is a very good salesman, and I am sure there was some showmanship in it, but I really think the vision that he had of building a new stadium and what he wanted to do in the Back Bay of Boston: I don't think he ever thought Hartford, Connecticut, would be the place

for it; but the more he thought about it as I described the region, he was very much taken by it.

Somehow the dazzle must have worn off. On April 30, 1999, just five months after the celebration in the Old Judicial Room, Robert Kraft announced that he was not coming to Hartford after all. Debates still rage over why Kraft changed his mind. The Patriots' official explanation concerns the ongoing uncertainties about the Adriaen's Landing site, particularly the environmental and infrastructural problems that might have delayed building a new stadium. Others believe the NFL intervened, fearful of losing a major market like Boston and thereby weakening the league's hand in upcoming television contract negotiations and hurting the pocketbooks of all team owners. Rumors also abound as to what the NFL gave to persuade Kraft to give up the Hartford deal. Many sports analysts agree that Kraft will be helped by a new NFL plan that will lend the team up to half of the money for the new stadium at no interest.

Many simply believe that Kraft pursued the age-old strategy of using Hartford as a bargaining chip to get what he wanted from Massachusetts. Hartford was desperate to gain status as a city on the move and banked a great deal on attracting an NFL team. The Patriots decided instead to build a new $275 million stadium in Foxboro adjacent to the old one. Massachusetts has authorized $70 million in what the state insists is only "infrastructure support" of the new stadium, not public subsidies. State politicians consistently call the stadium "privately funded" despite this $70 million in support. Foxboro residents seemed to welcome the new stadium and voted overwhelmingly for zoning changes necessary to create a new access road for premium seat customers. The town will receive about $1.8 million in rent from the team. Some opposition came from residents of a trailer park that will be moved, but these folks were little match for those planning to drive on this private road.

According to an article in the *Boston Globe* (February 5, 2000, 1), the NFL will pay the state of Connecticut $2.4 million to settle the claims the state has made against it concerning Kraft's allegedly disingenuous courtship of Hartford. Because the agreement between the Patriots and Connecticut prevented the team from conducting negotiations with any other state for a new stadium, Connecticut was attempting to gain information to prove that the Patriots had been simultaneously negotiating with Massachusetts. The NFL payment, however, settled all such claims. Rowland concluded at the time, "We all knew from day one that maybe we were being played against other states. But it was a risk worth taking." (*Boston Herald*, March 2, 2000, 1).

Brendan Fox, a legal counsel to Governor Rowland during the negotiations with the Patriots, simply said, "It was an experience. Let's leave it there." (*Hartford Courant*, November 20, 1999, B1).

Meanwhile, Boston and the state of Massachusetts have moved on to proposals to build a new baseball stadium for the Red Sox. Some estimate that public investment is likely to top $200 million in the new facility. Hartford did not find a professional team to remake its image and now plans to build a UConn football stadium not on the Adriaen's Landing site but across the Connecticut River in East Hartford. The Adriaen's Landing project has yet to get off the ground; and Hartford still seems to be searching for a new identity, a new way to get those feet on the street and resurrect its moribund local growth coalition.

The lessons of Minneapolis and Hartford are clear. When growth coalitions decline, they leave a power vacuum in the effort to get stadiums built with public money. This forces team owners themselves or a local politician to do the heavy lifting and suffer attendant criticisms. By requesting hundreds of millions of dollars in tax revenue while paying their players millions of dollars, team owners are quickly painted as greedy villains in search of corporate welfare. When politicians lead the charge, they prefer to frame stadiums as development tools to defend their use of public money as a "wise investment." Without local corporate leaders to reorient the campaign for public money around ideas of civic duty, the battle to secure public dollars for private stadiums is much harder to win.

6

Denver, Phoenix,
and San Diego

NASCENT GROWTH COALITIONS
ON THE FRONTIER

Chapters 3 through 5 examined cities with either very strong or very weak local growth coalitions. The relative strength of these coalitions was the driving force behind cities' success or failure in procuring public dollars for private stadiums. The three cities we study in this chapter are a bit more complicated. All have weak or invisible local growth coalitions, yet all have had some success in building new sports stadiums with public money.

Two reasons explain why the weak growth coalitions in Denver, Phoenix, and San Diego are different from those in Minneapolis and Hartford. First, Denver, Phoenix, and San Diego have *never* been controlled by a small, unified, corporate-driven alliance. Therefore, any semblance of a local growth coalition is now in a maturing stage, although that maturation is not always proceeding smoothly. In contrast, Minneapolis and Hartford once had very powerful growth coalitions. The remnants we found in those cities suggested a last gasp before extinction.

Second, Denver, Phoenix, and San Diego are actually growing in population, whereas Minneapolis and Hartford are contracting or barely staying even. The consistent growth of the three western cities, even during the economic recession of the early 1990s, seems metaphorically akin to frontier expansion. As we have already suggested, growing cities are under far less pressure to find the brass ring that can save the city from post-industrial decline. The frontier cities spend much less time battling over the "correct" model of stimulating economic growth or slowing economic decline. In these cities, growth is a given. It is everywhere. With or without a strong corporate presence, with or without new stadiums, the regions continue to grow. As large media outlets, Denver, Phoenix, and San Diego are all very attractive to major sports leagues and team owners. All would like to have a presence in the cities for many reasons, not least of which is the fact that these markets will make national media contracts more generous.

Without powerful local growth coalitions, however, the path to new stadiums has been bumpy. Even on the frontier, a connection exists between the strength of local growth coalitions and the relative ease of securing public dollars for private stadiums. Denver has the most developed growth coalition of the three cities, while Phoenix's and San Diego's are practically nonexistent. This difference has contributed to Denver's relative ease in building two new stadiums. In contrast, Phoenix had some trouble financing and building a new baseball stadium, and San Diego continues to have great difficulty in completing its publicly financed baseball stadium.

Therefore, understanding the dynamics of stadium battles on the frontier requires less emphasis on local growth coalitions and more on several sociological forces that have thus far been less central to our analysis. These forces include the institutional maturity of local or state governments, the existence of powerful or charismatic business leaders, urban demographic peculiarities, the structure and efficacy of stadium opponents, and particular local idiosyncrasies that play out differently in each city. While local growth coalitions are still important, they are notable for their absence or weakness rather than their presence. Because this absence creates a power vacuum, other political and economic organizations end up taking the lead in securing public dollars for private stadiums. Depending on individual social circumstances, different entities have filled the vacuum in each frontier city. This power vacuum can also elevate what would be minor problems in a place such as Cincinnati (with a strong growth coalition) into major headaches for a frontier city (with no growth coalition). It is by no means impossible to secure public dollars for private stadiums without a strong local growth coalition, it just requires different strategies.

DENVER: AN ADOLESCENT LOCAL GROWTH COALITION

The Colorado Rockies, created in 1993, opened their 1995 baseball campaign in spanking-new Coors Field after sharing Mile High Stadium with the NFL Broncos for two seasons. In 2001, the Broncos began playing in newly constructed Invesco Field at Mile High after a forty-year run in the original Mile High Stadium, which was built in 1948 for the Denver Bears, a minor league baseball team. Coors Field cost approximately $215 million and Invesco Field just over $400 million. Both were funded largely by a 0.1 percent sales tax increase (that is, one cent on every ten dollars) in the six-county Denver metro area. Public dollars accounted for about 75 percent of the costs at each of these private stadiums—a fairly average percentage among the recent wave of new stadiums.

Public dollars were approved by two separate votes in the six-county area. The baseball stadium was approved 54 to 46 percent in 1990, the football stadium 58 to 42 percent in 1998. The first tax increase expired in 2001, ten years earlier than expected, due to favorable interest rates and an exploding local population. The football stadium tax increase is set to expire in 2012. The leases between the city and the teams are in line with other recent stadium deals, with one important exception. The $60 million paid by Invesco Funds Group for twenty-year naming rights to the Bronco's stadium will offset the public share of construction, not the team owners' share. This was not the case with the $15 million that Coors paid for naming rights to the baseball park. Otherwise, the teams will pay no rent and receive the vast majority of revenues from tickets, parking, and concessions. They are responsible only for everyday operations and maintenance costs.

Baseball Was Only a Blip

The origin of Coors Field is entwined with the origins of Denver's adolescent local growth coalition. Denver does not have the equivalent of the Cincinnati Business Committee or Cleveland Tomorrow. A few powerful corporations have headquarters or regional offices in Denver, but there is no longstanding, CEO-only group that strongly influences public policy. For instance, Qwest Communications and United Airlines, which call Denver home, rank 102 and 125 on a recent Fortune 1,000 list. The next largest corporation is Coors at 603. Indeed, recently Denver actually lost some corporate financial power when locally based United Banks of Colorado was taken over by Minneapolis-based Norwest, which has since been devoured by California-based Wells Fargo.

Reflecting this moderately powerful corporate community was a moderately powerful corporate organization. The Greater Denver Corporation (GDC) was created in 1987 as the economic development arm of the Denver Metro Chamber of Commerce. The idea was that GDC would focus on large public-private policy initiatives while the chamber focused on traditional business services. Any company that contributed $1,000 or more could be part of GDC's investors' council, which, in the words of one chamber historian, "had quarterly meetings of those who had paid to play."[1] The low membership fee and lack of independence suggest that GDC was not in quite the same league as the Cincinnati Business Committee. Despite its modest organizational power, however, GDC still had significant influence on local policies— including the building and funding of a new baseball stadium.

But stadiums were nowhere near the top of GDC's priority list in the late 1980s. Higher on its agenda were a new international airport and a new downtown convention center. At its very first meeting, the GDC board pledged $700,000 to support the building of Denver International Airport. Some of this money was spent campaigning on the issue before the election in which voters would decide whether or not to annex land in Adams County for an airport. Annexation passed 56 to 44 percent. More money was spent in a subsequent election to publicly finance the airport. Early polls showed that voters were split on the issue; but the GDC-led campaign proved to be successful, and the referendum passed by a two-to-one margin.

United Airlines was the biggest beneficiary of the GDC plan because it stood to gain the most from a new publicly financed airport as opposed to one the airline itself might pay for. Denver is one of United's major hubs and accounts for 72 percent of airport traffic. United also stood to gain from a new convention center (passed by referendum as well), which presumably would bring many more people to Denver who were likely to be flying on United. Perhaps surprisingly, United executives were not among GDC's leaders; but the company's interests were certainly well represented: according to available minutes, issues important to United were often central in those meetings.[2]

Major league baseball became part of the GDC agenda in 1989. One impetus was a fantasy document produced by the chamber extolling the economic benefits of a new professional ballpark in downtown Denver (Silverstein n.d.). State government was a more important source of this growing interest: Governor Roy Romer asked GDC member Dick Robinson to put together a legitimate ownership group necessary to begin the franchise application process. At the very least, an ownership group (or an individual) would have to guarantee the $95 million franchise fee charged by Major League Baseball. Robinson, Romer's choice for the job, was an executive at Robinson Dairy, a second-tier business (in terms of sales) but with deep historical roots in the community. Nevertheless, he had considerable trouble finding people and companies interested in putting up the fee for a franchise that might never exist.

This was not Colorado's first try to bring major league baseball to Denver. Supporters had made numerous attempts since 1960, although none had been woven into plans to build a new publicly financed stadium. In some regards, new stadium proponents in Colorado were ahead of the public financing curve. Their preliminary discussions took place before the financing and construction of Baltimore's Camden Yards and Cleveland's Jacobs Field. The 1990 vote was really the first of its generation.

The GDC gave $75,000 to the state-created Metro Major League Baseball District, whose members were appointed by the governor and would represent the entire six-county metro area. The organization was, in essence, the local stadium authority for Coors Field. Officially, the GDC money was a loan supposed to be repaid if the tax referendum passed. During 1989, the district developed some preliminary designs and narrowed their preferences to five sites in the Denver area. Members were working with two interrelated goals in mind: first, to convince a seemingly indifferent Denver metro public to vote for the August 1990 stadium tax (which the state legislature easily agreed to put on the ballot); and second, to help convince Major League Baseball in September 1990 that Denver deserved a new franchise more than eleven other interested cities did. A former executive of the Rockies later said that a successful referendum was a tangible and public way to show baseball's gatekeepers that Denver was serious about having its own team. Of course, a strong ownership group, eager to spend money, also would help.

The Power Vacuum

New stadium proponents, including the GDC, poured about $500,000 into a campaign supporting the referendum. In hindsight, this kind of support, even from an adolescent growth coalition, was extremely important. There was token opposition to the referendum but no real organized or official resistance. Both the state government and the six county governments institutionally supported the tax increase, although a few elected individuals thought it was a bad idea. Governor Romer was a steady champion of bringing baseball and a new stadium to Colorado. The state's political apparatus was fairly well established and fairly powerful. It could fill the power vacuum often occupied in other cities by a strong, corporate-based growth coalition and blaze the trail to new publicly financed stadiums. The Denver city and county governments (largely identical) were also supportive; but the nature of the initiative, which included the entire six-county metro region, lent itself to state-level coordination. The situation was similar to

Hartford's, where state rather than city politicians spearheaded the drive to attract the Patriots, although Denver's campaign had a much different ending.

Surveys throughout 1990 showed that the public was pretty evenly split right up until the election. Exit polls suggested that the relatively close vote was, in part, due to the uncertainty that a team would even exist to play in the stadium. The absence of a definitive owner exacerbated this uncertainty. As usual, men were more likely than women to support the stadium tax. There was no great difference between suburban and urban voters. Relatively rural Adams County showed the weakest support, while more suburban Arapahoe County showed the strongest. Younger voters (who were underrepresented among total voters) were more inclined to support the tax than older voters were. The best stereotype of a stadium tax supporter was a single male under age thirty living in or near the city of Denver.

With no definite ownership group in place and the franchise application looming, Governor Romer personally stepped up efforts to lure investors. Taking into consideration GDC's earlier recruitment setbacks, the governor courted Ohioans John Antonucci and Mickey Monus, principal owners of the gigantic Phar-Mor pharmaceutical chain, who were involved in a variety of minor league sports operations. Antonucci and Monus agreed to put up 25 percent of the necessary money and become principal owners of the nascent franchise. They would be joined in the executive circle by potential CEO Steve Ehrhart, a local entrepreneur long interested in bringing major league baseball to Colorado. Antonucci and Monus soon became known as the "drugstore cowboys."

Giving Away the Farm (Reprise)

One month after the successful referendum, the Baseball District made its formal presentation to an expansion committee of Major League Baseball; and in July 1991, the National League awarded its newest franchise to Denver. In anticipation of this decision, the Rockies' ownership group started selling season tickets for the 1993 season, which would be played in Mile High Stadium. It also decided to accept approximately $15 million from Coors Brewery, a minority owner, for official naming rights to the new ballpark. Meanwhile, the Baseball District decided on a final location for the new ballpark: the supposedly resurging lower downtown (LoDo) area of Denver, about ten blocks from the central business district. Construction of the new stadium began in October 1992 and was targeted for completion on opening day, 1995.[3]

More important, the Rockies and the Baseball District had worked out a preliminary lease agreement four months before the franchise was officially awarded to Denver. This preliminary lease was munificent to the Rockies and is certainly comparable to the Cincinnati Bengals' lease in its generosity to the team (see chapter 3). The seventeen-year lease would give the team all revenues from tickets, concessions, parking, and advertising (including naming rights). In addition, there was a yearly management fee of 5 percent of gross revenues or $4 million (whichever was greater) paid directly to Antonucci, Monus, and Ehrhart. The team would pay only $3 million to $4 million annually for upkeep and operations. With stadium construction initially estimated at $150 million, the deal struck local critics as extremely unfair. People seemed especially upset because, during the sales tax campaign, the Baseball District and other proponents had said that private financing for the stadium might be as high as 50 percent. Appearances weren't improved when John McHale, former chair of the district and chief negotiator of the lease, resigned to take a management job with the Rockies. McHale claimed that he had never actively sought the position and that the timing was coincidental.

As we have argued throughout this book, it is overly simplistic to explain a sweetheart lease as merely a function of greedy owners or "captured" politicians. The situation involves a complex calculus of financial and social factors, making a one-sided lease the default arrangement. Much subtle pressure is instigated by the professional leagues, which are vague about what kinds of financial commitments (beyond the franchise fee itself) are required to make an application attractive to the owners responsible for picking a winner. The decision is driven by the collective self-interest of the league, not the interests of the community that will house the new team. This enormous pressure falls squarely on prospective owners (who are competing with one another) to prove that they can really make a deal beneficial not only for them but for the other owners in the league. The president of the National League, Bill White, made it clear in a letter to Rockies owners that the lucrative lease they had negotiated made a positive impression on the league. According to White, Denver probably would not have received the franchise without such a favorable agreement. Responding to growing local criticism of the deal, he intimated that the league might change its mind if the final lease agreement differed substantially from the one that had factored into the league's decision (*Denver Post*, October 17, 1991, 1A).

Because the requirements for getting a new team are not fully spelled out, those desiring one of these monopolized franchises try to gain every possible edge. Municipalities also want sports teams, so they join the effort to make the home team's application look better than anyone else's. As a result, team owners and public officials become almost indistinguishable. Thus, a Rockies' owner says that, without this kind of lease, there will be no baseball in Denver; and a Baseball District spokesperson wonders publicly if the lease's critics are agents of competing franchise applicants from St. Petersburg, Florida (*Denver Post*, October 4, 1991, 1A). The structural arrangement of the process to gain a new franchise, which resembles a very competitive auction for a limited and rare prize, often pressures municipal governments into acting in the interests of team ownership.

Perhaps because of negative publicity about the deal, the lease agreement was amended just before the Rockies started playing in 1993 to make it somewhat less generous to the team. The district will now receive 20 percent of game-day parking revenues and 80 percent of nonbaseball parking revenues. It will also receive twenty-five cents from each ticket sold after the first 2.25 million and a larger amount (up to a dollar) on each ticket sold after other attendance thresholds are reached. In addition to upkeep costs, the Rockies will kick in an extra $500,000 per year to fund large repair jobs on the stadium.

In part, the Rockies were amenable to these changes because they were trying to increase, by about 25 percent, the proposed size of the new stadium (from 40,000 to 50,000 seats). Much to the owners' surprise, the team appeared likely to sell out every game at 80,000-seat Mile High Stadium. Imagining that the same situation was possible for Coors Field, the Rockies decided that a bigger stadium would be better. The Baseball District agreed to the expansion if the Rockies paid for the added cost (about $60 million) and agreed to the just-mentioned changes in the final lease. With 810,000 more tickets available each year, the team happily agreed. The National League also made no objection.

Rockiesgate?

These lease changes were actually the secondary story during the two-year period between the preliminary and final stadium agreements. More interesting (and related to the lease changes) was a scandal involving the original majority owners of the Rockies. According to stories in the media, Antonucci and Monus had allegedly used their Phar-Mor–based financial power to leverage other team owners as well as certain outside vendors. Within the ownership circle, the most important target was Coors Brewery. According to allegations, as the official franchise application grew nearer, the principal owners requested more money from Coors. When the company objected, Monus apparently reminded Coors that Phar-Mor was one of its largest U.S. distributors. In addition, some outside vendors complained that they were pressured to contract their services with the new stadium. They alleged that, in return for a slightly higher fee, Antonucci and Monus promised them higher visibility and promotion for their products in all Phar-Mor locations (*Business Journal of the Five-County Region* [Youngstown, Ohio], October 15, 1992, 5; *Denver Post*, August 25, 1992, 1D).

This kind of pressure may not be unusual, but it has been largely absent from arguments about why teams want a single-purpose facility largely under their own control and how this desire blurs the line between private and public stadiums. According to an executive from another major league team, one problem with locating a team in a truly municipally run, multipurpose stadium is that the team is not able to subtly—or overtly—pressure its various concession vendors (such as the hot dog supplier or the beer and soda distributors) into buying luxury boxes. In a truly municipally controlled stadium, vendor contracts are usually awarded by the stadium authority and are open, in theory, to public scrutiny and accountability. Thus, vendors are better able to resist pressure to buy luxury boxes without fear of losing their concession contracts because the contracts have been made with the stadium authority, not the team. In a stadium where a team has control over marketing and selling luxury boxes and selecting concessionaires, that team can give a dazzling presentation about its new luxury-box lease packages to the vendor companies. Even without overt pressure, any good businessperson can see that leasing a luxury box or two might cement the business relationship and increase his or her chances of winning or retaining a concession contract. This is one reason why a team wants to control its own stadium. The cost to a vendor company of leasing a luxury box might account, in the end, for only a small portion of the extra money the public pays for a hot dog and a soda at the game; but it is an important contribution to the team's bottom line as it searches for a competitive edge over the other teams in the league. Team owners are a small group and often hear of advantages (real or imagined) that other owners have over them in their leases. Thus, they come to believe that if they, too, had similar advantages, their bottom line—and the team on the field—could be improved.

Even before the official franchise application, Monus relinquished his stake in the Rockies amid separate embezzlement charges in Ohio. His departure was not amicable, and negative publicity about the preliminary lease pressured state lawmakers into tinkering with the Baseball District's composition. Sensing a change in social sentiment, district chair Ray Baker said the group would not fight the legislature on any reorganization, even though the district had spent $12,000 during the previous year to lobby against this issue. By the middle of 1992, the ownership group had been completely revamped, relegating Antonucci and Ehrhart to subordinate financial and management roles (*Denver Post*, August 25, 1992, 1D).

It may or may not be a coincidence that the preliminary agreement with the Rockies was renegotiated just after this management purge. Critics of the preliminary agreement seemed to believe that the renegotiations could never have taken place with the original ownership-management trio in place. That claim is probably true. It also may be true that the new management's willingness to reconsider the agreement was rooted in an honest assessment of its fairness to the community. Nevertheless, even the amended agreement is extremely favorable to the team and its owners; and the new majority owners may have used renegotiation as a strategic move to assuage negative public and political opinions about the entire stadium project. The bottom line remains: the new stadium has been paid for mostly with public dollars, with revenues going almost entirely into private pockets.

Omaha Near the Mountains

Coors Field, along with Jacobs Field and Camden Yards, was a pioneer in the recent wave of using public dollars for private stadiums. In contrast to cities that focused on community self-esteem, proponents of these three stadiums usually stressed the economic benefits that would accrue from new publicly funded ballparks. Arguments about community self-esteem and community collective conscience were not completely absent, but they definitely took a back seat. Indeed, these three ballparks have become something of a holy trinity to the dwindling group of supporters who still exhort the economic advantages of using public dollars for private stadiums. For instance, new stadium advocates in Hartford and Philadelphia continually cited Denver, Baltimore, and Cleveland as models of stadium-driven downtown rejuvenation.

Denver provides an excellent illustration of a strategic focus on economic growth that does not completely ignore noneconomic issues. New stadium advocates in Colorado promised enormous economic spin-off and community revitalization from Coors Field while reminding people that, without a new ballpark, they might as well move Omaha to the mountains and call it Denver.[4] Several fantasy documents were created during and after the sales-tax campaign to demonstrate how the ballpark would transform the once-seedy LoDo section of Denver into a thriving urban paradise. Nine years after these promises were made, and four years after the ballpark was built, most have failed to materialize. This is especially interesting because Coors

Field itself has been a tremendous success. At one point, the Rockies sold out more than 230 consecutive home games. Attendance has dipped slightly in the past few years but remains extraordinary by major league standards.

The relationship between Coors Field and the surrounding neighborhood is much more complex than stadium proponents sometimes acknowledge. The LoDo area *has* seen a great deal of economic development in the 1990s and is now considered one of the trendier entertainment areas of Denver. That development, however, began well before Coors Field was built and before the Rockies were awarded a franchise. Stadium advocates have tried to take credit for this economic rejuvenation that was already present before the arrival of Coors Field. Indeed, development is concentrated in the part of LoDo farthest from Coors Field. LoDo comprises approximately twenty-four square blocks north and east of Denver's central business district. Coors Field occupies the far northeastern corner of this district, while retail and residential development has been centered in the district's southwestern quadrant. That area is anchored by the successful Sixteenth Street pedestrian mall that bisects both the business district and LoDo.

When we visited Denver in 1999, LoDo development seemed to be expanding between Thirteenth and Seventeenth streets, away from Coors Field, which is centered on Twenty-first Street (see fig. 5). Indeed, the closer we got to the ballpark, the greater the noticeable decline in retail and residential activity, with the exception of a series of restaurants near Union Station (Eighteenth and Nineteenth streets). Most of these restaurants opened before the arrival of Coors Field, when LoDo development took off in the late 1980s and early 1990s. We spoke with a manager at Morton's Steak House, two blocks from Coors Field, who said the company had opened the restaurant in 1993 because LoDo was becoming trendy. At that time, the ballpark was not an issue; and Morton's business is still not affected greatly when the Rockies are at home. Workers in less-upscale area restaurants told us that they preferred not to work on game days because their regular customers often stayed away.

Economic development is completely absent east of Twentieth Street and beyond the ballpark (moving away from central LoDo). In a two-block area adjacent to the stadium (still nominally in LoDo), we saw four pawnshops, a few active warehouses, and numerous surface parking lots. There were also many abandoned warehouses, empty lots, and transients. A thriving microbrewery is located at Twenty-second Street, just east of and across from Coors Field; but it opened before the ballpark did and has always been more of a beer producer

Fig. 5. In Denver, this is the renewal found near Coors Field.

than a retail establishment (and did not serve Coors beer). In all fairness, this microbrewery has expanded its restaurant service because of the nearby ballpark. Directly across from the park's main Twenty-first Street entrance is a beautifully restored warehouse occupied by a public storage facility. Due east of the stadium is the main parking area, which resembles a mammoth lot at Disney World. Interestingly, its primary entrance-exit does not face toward downtown but away from it— across the new Twenty-third Street viaduct and toward Interstate 25, providing easy access for commuters.

This viaduct was mentioned in the fantasy documents produced by the Downtown Ballpark Redevelopment Committee in June 1992. As far as we can tell, its construction was the only fulfilled promise in the neighborhood influence studies. Unfulfilled promises include a pedestrian overpass from near Union Station to the ballpark's plaza, new housing immediately adjacent to the stadium, and an international shopping district supposedly poised to emerge in the area still populated by pawnshops and warehouses. The report also called for tastefully landscaping the main parking lot and use of this lot for other activities. Seven years after the report, the lot is utterly barren. Even on a busy December Saturday night, with LoDo restaurants and parking lots crammed, the main stadium lot was totally empty. Finally, the document contained an artist's rendition of Twenty-first Street "streetscape improvements," which were guaranteed to accompany the new stadium. The new street would have shops and wide sidewalks leading from near downtown directly to the ballpark's main entrance. But in 1999 the area looked much the same as it had in 1992 (see fig. 6).

This development pattern suggests an interesting question that deserves further research: do ballparks really foster the kind of mixed-use development that benefits cities in the long run? Because of their size and scope, and because they are inactive for most days of the year, they may not be the best way to promote spin-off economic development in the immediate vicinity. Stadiums may play a role in further cementing an established area, as Coors Field has done in Denver; but in and of themselves they may not be enough to generate area development.

Strategic Shift

Unlike supporters of the baseball stadium, advocates of using public dollars for Denver's new football stadium were hesitant to promise economic miracles. Like the Gateway complex in Cleveland, Coors Field did not generate a tidal wave of new development in downtown Denver. Because this fact was readily apparent to local citizens, proponents of the Broncos' new stadium (like those of the Cleveland

Fig. 6. This vast Coors Field parking lot was supposed to be beautifully landscaped and central to LoDo's rejuvenation.

Browns' new stadium) were forced to emphasize community self-esteem and community collective conscience. With only eight regular-season home games per year in a football stadium, claiming economic miracles seemed patently ludicrous. This change in strategy has been reflected in an overall national shift (discussed in chapter 2) toward "softer" justifications for building private stadiums with public dollars.

During the football stadium tax campaign, supporters emphasized Denver's uniqueness in having four major league franchises within the city limits and frequently drew comparisons between Denver and other midwestern cities that were decidedly minor league. While Omaha still led this list, state capitals such as Des Moines and Topeka also made occasional appearances. Of course, people outside of Colorado (like those outside of Cleveland) were still susceptible to the rhetoric extolling the economic wonders of using public dollars for private stadiums. New stadium advocates in Phoenix frequently pointed to Denver as the trouble-free model for building a beautiful new stadium, attracting a major league franchise, improving the economic lot of local residents, and demonstrating that it is a city on the go.

PHOENIX: WEAK GROWTH COALITION
MEETS THE WILD WEST

As we mentioned in the book's introduction, Phoenix area voters in 1989 overwhelmingly rejected a proposed property tax increase to build a new baseball stadium. In addition, voters passed a referendum that would require a public vote for *any* future stadium proposal in excess of $3 million. This was probably the loudest community opposition in the recent history of funding private stadiums with public dollars, surpassing even the decisive 1997 anti-tax vote in Pittsburgh (see chapter 7). Amazingly, just five years later, without a public vote, the Maricopa County Board of Supervisors, acting as a stadium district, approved (three to one) a new $238 million sales tax to construct Bank One Ballpark, future home of the newly franchised Arizona Diamondbacks baseball team. A poll taken just before the supervisors' decision showed that 66 percent of county residents still opposed the sales tax. Public backlash was unambiguous. Of the three supervisors who voted for the tax, one was defeated for reelection, another lost a bid for state office, and the third was barely reelected—but not before she was shot in the buttocks by a deranged person shouting about the new stadium. Regardless, Bank One Ballpark opened in March 1998.

The agreement between the Diamondbacks and Maricopa County

is somewhat different from those examined elsewhere in this book. Compared with other deals, the Diamondbacks are paying a little more and the municipality a little less (as a percent of total costs). Significantly, the county's share was capped at $238 million, meaning that cost overruns would be paid by the team. The stadium was originally estimated to cost $280 million, with the team putting up the remaining $42 million not covered by the county sales tax. Because the Diamondbacks were responsible for cost overruns, they had to pay the difference when the final cost jumped to $370 million. The county owns the stadium; and the team pays $1 million per year in rent, which is supposed to go toward maintenance costs.

The county also receives some extra bonuses. First, it gets 5 percent of the initial licensing fees for premium and club seating at the ballpark—basically a one-time windfall on the fee (kept by the team) charged for the privilege of buying premium tickets. As in Denver, the county also receives a bonus (per ticket) after 2 million total tickets are sold each season. But while the deal sounds relatively great for the municipality, it is tempered by the fact that, to pay for their share of the stadium, the Diamondbacks were able to sell tax-free municipal bonds. Those bonds were sold through the Phoenix Industrial Development Authority (PIDA), the city's economic development agency. These municipal bonds are tax-free and low risk, so they offer a much lower interest rate for investors. This lower interest rate subsidized the Diamondback's borrowing costs. But more important, it also reduced PIDA's overall bonding capacity, meaning that the agency had fewer resources available for other urban redevelopment projects.

As is usual with stadium deals, most people outside of Phoenix and Maricopa County are unaware of the process behind the area's stadium initiative; they only know the outcome. Bank One Ballpark has been publicly heralded as the stadium that brought major league baseball to the desert. It was the first stadium with a fully retractable roof that takes just over four minutes to open or close.[5] An open roof lets in occasional monsoon rains and just enough sun to grow real grass but, when closed, keeps out the stifling Arizona heat. Apparently, during the ballpark's first year, people actually stood and cheered whenever the roof opened or closed. The stadium also features a swimming pool beyond the outfield fence that can be rented by people who want to catch fly balls while practicing the backstroke. Millions of TV-watching Americans saw the stadium in 2001, when the Diamondbacks marched to a World Series championship.

The story of Phoenix's Bank One Ballpark, affectionately known as the BOB, sounds somewhat like the plot of a Zane Gray western. Phoenix has many similarities to cities such as Denver and San Diego because of its tremendous growth during the past few decades. But it is also very different from those cities in population demographics, the composition of its political institutions, and the strength of its corporate community. In particular, the large number of retirees in Phoenix is an important element of the public's anti-tax opposition. Generally, however, Phoenix is more similar to Denver and San Diego than to the Rust Belt cities we examined in chapters 3 through 5. Those older cities are in desperate pursuit of publicly financed stadiums, which they hope will magically reverse their social and economic decline. In contrast, for Denver, Phoenix, and San Diego, the issue is not decline but growth. Nevertheless, in Phoenix, this growth did not translate easily into support for using public dollars for private stadiums—although in the end, that lack of support proved to be largely irrelevant.

Ignoring Public Sentiment

One year after the initial tax referendum was defeated, the Arizona state legislature's house majority whip, Chris Herstam, helped pass a bill that would allow for the creation of a special Stadium District with the authority to levy a tax without a public vote, so long as this tax was for a baseball-only stadium. The baseball-only provision was, in part, protection against using any more public money to help the Arizona Cardinals football team. The state had already put a great deal of money into rehabbing the Arizona State Sun Devils Stadium for the Cardinals, who had been wooed from St. Louis in 1988. Many state legislators from the East Valley towns of Scottsdale and Mesa feared that the team might be lured to Phoenix with a brand-new stadium.

Herstam's efforts seemed to be aimed at helping Martin Stone, owner of the minor league Phoenix Firebirds baseball team. As in Denver, however, Stone may also have been trying to show Major League Baseball that there would be funding for a new Phoenix ballpark if the league wanted to place a new team there. But Herstam still had to deal with the voters' requirement of a referendum for any sports- or entertainment-related spending above $3 million. He outmaneuvered this public decree by creating a short-term statute that allowed the board of supervisors to create the Stadium District with taxing authority. Herstam said, "You don't take every major issue, town-hall style, to a vote of the people. We were giving the county board the ability to hold public hearings, and they would be accountable to the public" (*Phoenix Gazette*, March 2, 1994, A1).

By the summer of 1993, Martin Stone and the Phoenix Firebirds were no longer central to the story. Instead, county supervisor Jim Bruner met with Joe Garagiola, Jr., a Phoenix lawyer and son of former major league catcher Joe Garagiola, Sr., to discuss the possibility of building a new baseball stadium in Phoenix and landing a major league franchise. Also invited to the meeting was powerful local businessman Jerry Colangelo. Colangelo had been general manager of the Phoenix Suns basketball team from 1967 to 1987 and became majority owner after 1987. He told us that initially he was uninterested in the idea; but once Bruner and Garagiola reminded him of the special tax provision, Colangelo saw an opportunity.[6] The tax provision meant that proponents of a new publicly funded stadium would not be forced to bring the issue before a clearly hostile community. He told us,

> There was a tax on the books, the tax was going to expire, baseball was thinking about an expansion, and there was a window. There wasn't time to build a lot of public support and take it to a vote. The window would have closed. Nor was I interested in going through that whole process. The only reason I felt I could move forward was that this mechanism was in place; the county supervisors gave me indications that they were prepared, under the right terms and conditions, to move ahead.

The board of supervisors appointed themselves to be the Stadium District and, as mentioned, voted for the new tax by a three-to-one margin. The tax never went to a public vote.

The new tax would be a one-quarter cent tax on all sales in Maricopa County and would remain in place until $238 million was raised. Any costs above that amount would not be covered publicly. In addition, the new franchise (if approved by Major League Baseball) would receive a $15 million loan from the county. The original construction estimates placed total stadium cost at $279 million, meaning that the team's contribution would be $41 million, or 14.7 percent. Eventually, as with all ballparks, the final costs were much higher. With these increases, team owners eventually contributed about $100 million of the stadium's total $338 million cost (about 30 percent). As we will show, however, even this calculation is tricky and politically charged.

The Power Vacuum

Since World War II, Maricopa County and the city of Phoenix have expanded phenomenally. With a population increase of 34 percent between 1990 and 2000, the region has been struggling with the pressures of massive population growth in what is little more than a barren desert. Phoenix is now the sixth-largest American city, a fact that seems to take many people by surprise, including those in Phoenix. This incredibly rapid overall growth has left little time for a corresponding growth in the powerful political and corporate institutions so common in more established American cities. Indeed, the most interesting sociological phenomenon in Phoenix is the complete absence of an entrenched, hierarchical, urban power structure.

In essence, compared to other U.S. cities, especially those in the east, there is a great void of institutionalized power in Phoenix. The city has no strong corporate community and no powerful political machine. Because of the region's very rapid growth, the political leadership in Phoenix is often not as experienced or sophisticated as the leadership in many older cities. The resulting power vacuum allows strong individuals and organizations to, quite literally, get things done. In Denver, that vacuum (although it was not as strong as Phoenix's) was filled by the well-oiled state political system that largely orchestrated the building of Coors Field and successfully attracted a major league franchise. Philadelphia, as we will see in chapter 7, also has a growth vacuum caused by a weak corporate community. But that vacuum was filled by the historically powerful city government, which took charge of securing public dollars for two new private stadiums. In Arizona, however, local and state political institutions could fill only some of this void with interventions, such as Herstam's special tax legislation.

Instead, one powerful individual, Jerry Colangelo, helped call the shots in Phoenix. Colangelo grew up outside of Chicago, where he was a well-recognized amateur athlete. After working briefly for the NBA Chicago Bulls, he left for Phoenix in 1967 to become the first general manager of the new NBA Phoenix Suns. His power and stature grew in Phoenix, where there was little entrenched corporate competition for power. After purchasing the Suns in 1987, Colangelo was recognized as the most powerful person in Arizona. A local magazine voted him the city's most influential person for several years in a row. Even when the magazine tried to spread its accolades by creating other categories, Colangelo kept turning up on the lists in one way or another. Former Phoenix mayor Terry Goddard acknowledged that "Jerry Colangelo is the primary arbiter of what goes on downtown. Jerry personally decides" (*Phoenix New Times*, March 26, 1998, 3). A Philadelphia business leader also recognized that Jerry Colangelo has been a key power broker in Phoenix (see chapter 7).

We were quite surprised to discover the extent of Phoenix's corporate nonpresence. Business executives we spoke with in Phoenix neither denied nor lamented their weak corporate community:

> [It] is limited. You have more Fortune 500 companies in most of the other major markets than we have here in Phoenix. This is more of a regional-based corporate community, but most of the

major decisions are made in Denver or Chicago or Los Angeles or
what have you.

Phoenix does have an elite business group, but it hardly compares
to powerful organizations such as the Cincinnati Business Committee,
Cleveland Tomorrow, and the Allegheny Conference (in Pittsburgh).
Phoenix simply doesn't have the corporate lineup to create such an organization. Phoenix Downtown Partnership was started in 1990 in
hopes of creating some kind of corporate presence, but it has been
largely unsuccessful; and the turnover of CEOs in town since that time
has been astounding, especially within the financial community.

For instance, three good-sized local banks (Arizona Bank, the Valley Bank, and First Interstate) worked together in the 1960s to finance
the Phoenix Suns arena. Since then, all have been consumed by banks
located outside of Phoenix. By the time the BOB was built, the three
major banks in Phoenix were Bank One, Wells Fargo, and Bank America—all based somewhere else. The lack of an established, corporate-
led, local growth coalition in Phoenix has created a situation in which
anyone interested (for whatever reason) in obtaining public dollars
for new sports stadiums would have to carry the burden him or herself. The absence of corporate headquarters in Phoenix vastly reduces
the role that new stadiums need to play in executive recruitment. Instead, corporate involvement is linked with less parochial organizational interests and with the influence of Jerry Colangelo. A business
leader explained,

> You mean recruiting employees? I don't think that's much of a mo-
> tivation. I don't think [a new stadium] is a perk or benefit to help
> employers [attract talent]. If anything, I think they play that down.
> I think . . . it's partly a community participation thing, a civic hat.
> And it's partially Jerry's ability to cultivate that sort of support.

The second main contributor to Phoenix's power vacuum is the
absence of an entrenched political apparatus (either local or state) to
coordinate stadium initiatives in lieu of a corporate-dominated, local
growth coalition. The state of Arizona is less than one hundred years
old, and Phoenix had only 100,000 residents just after World War II—
making it about the same size, at that time, as Jackson, Mississippi.
There simply hasn't been enough time to build the institutionalized political machines that dominate northern and eastern cities. Colangelo,
with experience in both Chicago and Phoenix, senses this political difference. He told us,

> I think it is easier to accomplish things in the west. . . . There
> are opportunities to establish oneself here, develop the kind of

relationships that are necessary over a period of time; and when ownership becomes ingrained in the community and becomes one of the leaders of a community, when the time comes to put a package together for an arena or for a ballpark, the pathway is much easier than in other places. . . . Things are more entrenched in the midwest and the east, in particular; things have been done a certain way for a longer period of time, so it's much more difficult to kind of crack that dam. The other thing I would say is that the political scene is much more structured back east than it is here. It's more of a kind of free-spirit here that I sense; people are more apt to take risks here than not. It takes leadership, of course. There is leadership in certain communities and not in others.

This distinction between the more open politics of the west and the more entrenched politics of the east and the midwest was a strong theme in many of our interviews in Phoenix. This political vacuum seems to help deals get made. Perhaps this sentiment was best summed up by the Diamondbacks' owner:

People say to me, "Isn't it unusual that someone involved in sports can be considered the leader, or one of the real leaders?" I say, "Well, that's my fault; I'm one of the few left standing. Everyone else has come and gone, turned over, or churned." So same people, same faces back east. They don't change as much.

Death and Taxes

It is hard to imagine a more anti-tax community than Phoenix and surrounding Maricopa County. The initial wave of post–World War II migrants to Arizona were retirees on fixed incomes, who much preferred to spend their money playing tennis or golf rather than building new public schools or publicly subsidizing sports stadiums. This demographic factor is extremely important for understanding the story of Bank One Ballpark and distinguishing among the three frontier towns explored in this chapter. In terms of taxes, Denver's local culture is almost the opposite of Phoenix's, mainly because the post–World War II migrants to Denver have been much younger. San Diego occupies something of a middle ground. The culture there is not particularly amenable to taxes, but the younger demographic composition makes tax resistance much less intense than it is in Phoenix.

Jerry Colangelo knew this anti-tax sentiment was a formidable obstacle to his major league dreams. He told us,

What I found to be very surprising is to what degree someone will go to voice their displeasure over a tax. I think in a marketplace where we have a number of retired people, and I'm generalizing when I say this, but many have the attitude that "I have paid my dues," and they'll vote against anything on the ballot that will increase their taxes one iota because they are on fixed incomes and they don't need new roads or new schools; or why would they want to [fund] a new stadium? So [the anti-tax groups] are definitely the most vociferous. . . . We didn't have environmentalist [opposition]; it was anti-tax [opposition].

We met with representatives of a Phoenix-area group called Citizens Right to Vote. The group tried unsuccessfully to establish a public referendum that would require an admissions tax on all tickets to Diamondbacks' games until the county was repaid the $238 million it had collected through the stadium sales tax. Based on our review of local papers, the group had a large following and seemed to touch a nerve in the general public.[7] Citizens Right to Vote was concerned not just with the outcome of the tax but, as its name implies, the entire process underlying the sales tax. Providing millions of public dollars to rich owners and players was bad enough; it was even more galling that the tax increase blatantly disregarded public sentiment.

Many local politicians played to this somewhat significant grass-roots opposition. Jan Brewer, for example, rode the wave of opposition and was elected to the county's board of supervisors in 1996. Shortly after her election, however, she became a stadium booster and was an honored guest at Bank One's christening. This did not please members of Citizens Right to Vote, some of whom started calling her "Judas Brewer."

The Phoenix anti-tax resistance has settled down, now that the stadium is up and running and the team was quickly successful. But waning grass-roots opposition to the BOB has not resulted in a totally smooth ride for Colangelo and the Diamondbacks. The team established an excellent fan base in its first year (about 3.6 million) but saw an unprecedented 30 percent drop-off in season-ticket sales in its second season, probably due to a 12 percent price hike. The team collected data on the situation, concluding that many season-ticket holders had decided that tickets to more than eighty games was too many so began sharing tickets in groups, thus cutting down on the total season-ticket base (see fig. 7).

The team responded with a spending spree to acquire talent, including star pitchers Randy Johnson and Curt Schilling. Colangelo told us that the drop-off in season-ticket renewals prompted him to immediately spend money on free agents rather than let the farm system develop young talent. In a city with a largely transplant population, citizens have no historical investment in a new team, making on-the-field success important in drawing fans. Colangelo's move seems to have

Fig. 7. Drop-offs in season-ticket renewals led to reduced parking prices around Bank One Ballpark in Phoenix after the inaugural season.

paid off. In only their fourth year of existence, the Diamondbacks beat the New York Yankees in the 2001 World Series, winning the deciding game in their final at-bat. Off the field, however, things are less clear.

Without a large corporate base to purchase luxury boxes, the wealth of the Diamondbacks is directly tied to general attendance. But this factor may be inherently problematic in the desert southwest. Phoenix's weather is simply too hot for people to come to eighty baseball games each year, even in a fancy stadium with a built-in pool and lots of air conditioning. Phoenix's dry climate means that participatory outdoor activities often take place before and after the height of summer, which may also cut into ballpark visits. Finally, Phoenix is more geographically isolated than any other major league city. With about the same population density as Colorado, Arizona is surrounded by some of the most sparsely inhabited states in the country. Once you exhaust the Phoenix and Tucson metropolitan areas, you find no significant population bases within four hundred miles—unless, that is, you head west about 350 miles to San Diego. We wonder if people in Yuma, Arizona, about halfway between these two large cities, would travel to Phoenix or San Diego to see a major league baseball game in mid-July.

Economic Development or Community Self-Esteem?

As in Denver, justifications for spending public dollars on Phoenix's new baseball stadium generally stressed the economic windfalls that would benefit area residents. There were occasional arguments about "not being another Tucson," but this strategy was far less common. The economic approach makes perfect sense when we compared it to the situation in cities such as Cincinnati: Phoenix, like Denver and San Diego, is growing rather than shrinking. Each year, hundreds of thousands of people migrate to or near these cities without considering whether or not it has a new sports stadium. With anti-tax resistance so strong in Phoenix, supporters knew it was important to create the impression that using public dollars for private stadiums did more than just subsidize the bank accounts of professional athletes and powerful individuals such as Jerry Colangelo.

Because the county commissioners' special stadium-tax vote largely neutralized all public discussion before BOB's construction, economic impact studies did not appear until after the stadium was finished. The primary study, commissioned by the Downtown Phoenix Partnership (Pollack Study 1998), is worthy of a detailed analysis. The study begins by stating that BOB's final cost was $354 million, meaning that the team's $100 million contribution came to about 28 percent. This cost was not significantly different from that of most new stadiums, although the fact that the Diamondbacks agreed to be responsible for cost overruns kept the public share from soaring as it did in other cities. The bottom line may be inaccurate, however, due to additional public spending not directly associated with BOB. For example, parking problems during BOB's first year led the city to finance a new $43 million parking garage. The city carefully said that the garage was not intended for the baseball stadium, even though it is located within walking distance (*Arizona Republic*, February 11, 1997). Instead, they publicly pronounced that the parking garage was intended for the downtown science center and the Civic Plaza retail facility. It's pretty clear why the local government framed the garage that way. If they had said that the garage were being built for the team, they would have violated the referendum that requires a public vote on any spending in excess of $3 million for sports or entertainment. Moreover, the garage was not included in BOB's bottom line. If it had been, total construction costs would have reached $397.5 million, making the team's contribution only 25.2 percent of the total. Although this cost is still not far from the new stadium norm, it is more than 10 percent above the official price tag.

Besides possibly underreporting total costs, the study relies on methodology typical of the impact studies done by consulting firms, some of which is problematic. Most important, the study was conducted halfway through the Diamondback's first season, with the data extrapolated to a full season. This time frame is the so-called honeymoon period of a new stadium, in which attendance and spending may be exaggerated due to the novelty of the park and the first-time rush to buy team paraphernalia.

The study claimed that the stadium's two-year construction created more than 4,500 jobs, whose tax revenues contributed an extra $9.3 million to county coffers. Of course, these jobs were temporary and disappeared at the end of construction. More important were the 4,000 permanent jobs supposedly created by the stadium. Here, the study extrapolated half-year data to the full year of 1998, estimating that the stadium and the team would generate $129 million in spending within the stadium (ticket sales, concessions, and so on) and $38 million outside the stadium (such as restaurants, parking, and retail). The city would receive about $2.3 million in tax revenue from this stadium economy, while the county would receive $5.7 million.

In addition to its problematic "honeymoon" extrapolations, the study, like most similar documents, fails to consider the substitution effect of consumer spending: the money spent at or near the ballpark may substitute for money spent elsewhere in the city or the county. Failure to account for the substitution effect at the county level is especially egregious because more than 60 percent of Arizona's total population resides in Maricopa County. Chances are great that entertainment money not spent at BOB would be spent on entertainment somewhere else in the county. Even if consumers were moving money into their entertainment budgets from, let's say, their food budgets, that transfer still amounts to moving the money from one place to another in Maricopa County. The only way the county treasury can show a net increase is if stadium-related spending comes from people who normally spend their money outside of the county.

It is quite possible that BOB may be helping the city of Phoenix capture consumer spending that might otherwise take place in other Maricopa County municipalities. In fact, Phoenix proper is the slowest-growing city in the region, trailing behind East Valley towns such as Scottsdale, Tempe, and Mesa. But this particular manifestation of the substitution effect was not studied, which is not surprising: BOB was financed with a countywide tax, and people in Scottsdale (and its political leaders) might be upset to learn that county money is disproportionately subsidizing the city of Phoenix. In any case, failure to consider the substitution effect is not treated as a significant shortcoming and, of course, is often ignored by those who extol the wonders of spending public dollars on private stadiums.

The New Phoenix

When we visited Phoenix a year after BOB opened, it showed some signs of downtown rejuvenation. There is new construction near the ballpark, but that's also true in other parts of Maricopa County. What struck us, however, was an extreme contrast between the downtown business district and the barrios only a few blocks away, just across the tracks (see figs. 8 and 9). Presumably residents of those barrios should benefit most from BOB, which is only fair because sales-tax burdens are disproportionately borne by the poor.

Economic development on the wealthier side of the tracks is equally unimpressive. In addition to our observations, some data support that lack of development. Licenses for new businesses in the area of the ballpark went up from 248 before the park opened to 277 in 1998 but then dropped back to 252 by the end of 1999, for a net increase of only four (*Phoenix New Times*, March 9, 2000, 1). Certainly, there are fun sports-themed restaurants close to the ballpark, and they appear to be crowded on game days. Otherwise, however, they struggle to find a niche. When people leave their offices for lunch, they tend to look for a bite to eat within a block or two and don't regularly walk six or more blocks just to be near an empty stadium, especially when the temperature is 110 degrees in the shade. One business leader told us,

Fig. 8. This is the view of Bank One Ballpark from the barrio located behind the stadium.

Fig. 9. Immediately behind Bank One Ballpark, this neighborhood has not been the re-cipient of much ancillary economic development.

> Some of the existing restaurants: during game time there seem to be enough [patrons] to go around. We are having trouble keeping people here after games, particularly day games, weekday games. And the office crowd hasn't gotten bigger. So you have all these restaurants that have popped up, and they do well with events, but they are sharing the same lunchtime crowd that used to be shared by a lot fewer restaurants.

There has been only secondary (albeit noticeable) talk about BOB's effect on Phoenix's community self-esteem and community collective conscience. But even that minimal amount of talk is couched in terms of population growth, such as "We need a team in rapidly growing Phoenix to give people a shared identity." That argument may be somewhat effective in a city with a transient population. In this case, however, people are streaming into the Phoenix area; and it is doubtful that BOB's presence has much to do with their decision. For them, moving to Phoenix seems unrelated to BOB's supposed role in demonstrating that Phoenix is a world-class city. If Maricopa County were actually losing residents, then we would predict a substantial increase in arguments about community self-esteem. If Phoenix had a strong, corporate-led, local growth coalition that needed to draw executive talent, we might also see more talk about how Phoenix is better than Tucson because it has major league baseball. But for now, advocates of the prior and future use of public dollars for private stadiums in Phoenix focus mainly on problematic arguments about economic windfall.

SAN DIEGO: POWER VACUUM WITH A CALIFORNIA TWIST

On November 4, 1998, the same day that Denver voters approved public financing for the Broncos' new football stadium, San Diego residents voted 60 to 40 percent in favor of Proposition C, which directed a joint public-private effort to redevelop the downtown's East Village area. The centerpiece of this planned redevelopment was a new baseball stadium for the San Diego Padres, who currently share suburban Qualcomm Stadium (née Jack Murphy Stadium) with the NFL San Diego Chargers. Although the Broncos began playing in the second version of Mile High Stadium (also known as Invesco Field) in August 2001, by late 2002 construction had barely begun on San Diego's new baseball stadium. Its original proposed completion date was April 2002. There is talk today of finishing the stadium for opening day in 2004, but even that may be wishful thinking. What has caused this significant delay, even with strong public support for Proposition C? Why is San Diego having a much more difficult time with stadiums compared to the experiences of other frontier cities, such as Denver?

The simple answer, of course, is that San Diego is different because it is San Diego. Despite many similarities with Denver and Phoenix, it has its own sociological peculiarities, which have created a less hospitable climate for the successful public funding of private stadiums. San Diego shares with Denver and Phoenix a nonexistent corporate community (with a correspondingly weak local growth coalition) and a political machine that has not matured commensurately with a quickly expanding population. As in Phoenix, this situation has set the stage for a powerful, charismatic team owner (or, in this case, owners) to fill the vacuum and lead the charge to a new publicly financed ballpark. Unlike the other two cities, however, San Diego has an existing business community that very much wants to be a corporate community and believes a new downtown ballpark is the key to that plan. This desire has inadvertently led to a number of problems related to the downtown site, which was not the first choice of the Padres or the general community.

Other distinguishing factors in San Diego have added obstacles to the prompt public funding of a new baseball stadium. First, the composition of the city's growing population is much different from

Phoenix's (although fairly similar to Denver's) because it is significantly younger. Second, and perhaps related to demographics, original opposition to Proposition C and current opposition to the ballpark were not completely dominated by an anti-tax philosophy. Instead, opponents also challenged the conception of growth and economic development embodied in the proposition. Third, the proposed location of the new ballpark encroaches on existing residences and businesses. Although there aren't a lot of people living and working in this part of downtown, the area certainly has more residents than did the ballpark footprints of Phoenix and Denver. Finally, unlike the football teams in the other two frontier cities, the NFL Chargers are seriously entangled in the public funding of the new baseball stadium.

How to Win an Election

In August 1998, the San Diego City Council approved placing Proposition C on the November ballot. The proposition was purposefully worded so that it did not concern only a new stadium. Since 1996, California law has required that public spending on specific projects (such as stadiums) be approved by a two-thirds vote, whereas general redevelopment tax increases need only a simple majority. Proposition C itself referred vaguely to the new baseball stadium. Instead, the details of the redevelopment project were explained in a memorandum of understanding (MOU) between the Padres and the city council. The voting public had access to the final MOU but did not vote directly on its specifics.

The details in San Diego are very different from the details surrounding other stadium deals because they are enmeshed with an allegedly tangible plan for economic development. The new $270 million ballpark would anchor an overall $411 plan for downtown redevelopment, referred to in the MOU as phase I. The bulk of this $411 million would be publicly financed from a city-sponsored $225 million bond sale, $50 million from the Center City Development Corporation (the city's economic development agency), and $21 million from the San Diego Port Authority. The Padres would contribute $115 million and be responsible for all cost overruns for the ballpark itself. But this was just part of phase I. The other part directed the Padres to arrange for approximately $400 million of investments in new hotel, retail, and office development near the ballpark. The MOU also mentioned phase II, which vaguely referred to the Padres arrangement for future development in the twenty-six-square-block redevelopment district. This is by far the most wide-ranging, ballpark-centered, redevelopment scheme ever conceived. It is even more unusual because team owners will be responsible for driving the entire project. The MOU stipulated that "by April 1, 1999 the city must receive sufficient assurances, from the Padres and/or Developer, that Phase I . . . will proceed and have the potential to generate the . . . revenue necessary to help finance the City and Agency Investments."

For the public portion of this financing, the city would need about $26 million per year to pay off its thirty-year $225 million bond. The primary source of the $26 million would be the city's transient occupancy tax (TOT), a fancy way to refer to the tax on hotel rooms. In 1998, the total TOT pool was about $100 million, which funded a variety of social and cultural programs. The city claimed that no money would be diverted from existing programs; the ballpark redevelopment project would surely generate enough new TOT money to pay off the bonds. The city was also counting on increased revenues from tax-increment financing: the assumption that a ballpark or redevelopment will increase the property values of the area (and maybe the whole city), leading to more public revenues. If all worked out as planned, the increase in taxes (that is, the tax increment) would be enough to fund a portion of the project. The important point here is that these public dollars were supposed to come from *potential* revenues rather than *existing* revenues. We will scrutinize this financing scheme later in the chapter.

Despite serious questions about public money, Proposition C was rarely in jeopardy of failing. Two months before the election, it received close to 60 percent of voter support in most polls. That support continued on election day. The demographic breakdown of the vote was very much like the split in the other referendums studied in this book. Men were more supportive than women (67 versus 52 percent), the rich were more supportive than the non-rich (who still favored it), and party affiliation was irrelevant. The only group that clearly opposed Proposition C was composed of retirees (44 percent in favor). Interestingly, public awareness of Proposition C was extraordinarily high, with about 95 percent of voters claiming knowledge about the referendum (*San Diego Union-Tribune*, October 23, 1998, A1).

Such awareness is not surprising, given the huge war chest of Proposition C's supporters. A group known as Citizens for Revitalized Neighborhoods and a Ballpark for San Diego spent a whopping $2.9 million, almost three times more than Cincinnati's pro-stadium alliance spent. This amount included both cash and in-kind goods and services such as donated labor, space, parking, and air time. Significant spending took place in the weeks just before the election. Filings with the election board indicate that less than a million dollars had been spent by the end of September. That figure skyrocketed to $2.2 million in mid-October and then to the final $2.9 million by election day, of which almost $1 million went strictly for TV and radio ads. Opponents to Proposition C raised about $26,000, meaning they were outspent 111 to 1. (A month before the election, the ratio was 708 to 1.) We spoke with a leader of the Stop C Campaign, who said she felt the groups were reenacting the David and Goliath story. The Citizens for Revitalized Neighborhoods and a New Ballpark for San Diego was pretty much an extension of the Padres, who footed most of the group's bills. As of late October, the Padres had contributed almost 80 percent of the $2.2 million total. No other person or organization contributed more than $25,000 either in cash or donated space and services. In contrast, the largest contributor to the opposition gave $500. At the late September filing period, the Stop C Campaign had $773 in its account.

Luck was also on the side of Proposition C's supporters. In 1998, the Padres had a Cinderella year, beating all odds and making it to the World Series for the first time since 1984 (their only other appearance). True, they were shellacked by the New York Yankees (and by the Detroit Tigers in 1984); but up to that point, their playoff victories were dramatic and entertaining. Qualcomm Stadium became known as the loudest major league ballpark, packed with fans contradicting the stereotypical mellow southern Californian. Most of the people we spoke with, including opponents of the referendum, agreed that the Padres' championship season was great fun. We don't think a more typical Padres' season would have doomed Proposition C, but it probably would have made the vote a lot closer. As we saw with the stadium referendum in Cincinnati, timing is sometimes significant.

The Power Vacuum

The Padres' leading role in the Proposition C campaign speaks worlds about San Diego's nonexistent local growth coalition. As we have shown, cities with strong local growth coalitions do not need to rely on sports teams to finance electoral campaigns. Indeed, it is often strategically advantageous to avoid team influence, which decreases the opposition's opportunity to frame public dollars for private stadiums as a giveaway to rich team owners. Instead, large local corporations have made publicly funded stadiums part of their executive recruitment efforts while portraying their self-interest as an enhancement of community self-esteem. San Diego, however, has no real corporate community to devise this sort of strategy. A business leader said,

> We are not a corporate town. That's what makes San Diego different. You take a Cleveland, which has a lot of Fortune 500 compa-

nies, and [the stadium dynamic] is completely different because there they can sell all those luxury boxes. There used to be a small group of big business leaders who ran San Diego for twenty to thirty years. That's history. In the last five to ten years those businesses disappeared. There was Gordon Luce, who ran Great American and some larger banks. So that corporate presence is somewhat diminished now, and you now have a smaller downtown business establishment, which has a pretty cozy relationship with the city council.

Like Phoenix and Denver, San Diego does not have the equivalent of the Cincinnati Business Committee or Cleveland Tomorrow. The local Chamber of Commerce is well established but reflects the traditional chamber philosophy of business services and networking. We spoke with the chamber's director, who said the organization strongly favored both Proposition C and the proposed downtown location. But in no way was the chamber a major player in the Proposition C campaign, although it did donate $20,000 worth of meeting space. The San Diego Taxpayers Association (SDTA) is another business group that tries to influence public policy in the city. Like the chamber, it doesn't seem to be terribly powerful, although it does hold the attention of city and county policymakers by claiming to represent positions of fiscal responsibility.

The offshoot of a taxpayer subcommittee formed at the chamber in 1925, SDTA really came into its own after World War II. After examining the history of the group and speaking with its executive director, we have concluded that the group is difficult to label ideologically. It is not strictly anti-tax, although it certainly does not advocate for a large public sector. It has little minority or labor-oriented representation on its governing board but does not unilaterally condemn social programs that predominantly help workers and minorities. The organization almost disappeared during San Diego's late-1980s recession but has recently gained strength with a membership increase in the more robust late-1990s economy.

SDTA's position on Proposition C was also hard to pin down. Officially, it supported the referendum. Less officially, it was extremely concerned about the MOU's April 1 deadline for the Padres' master plan. This concern was rooted in the many assumptions and loose ends that surrounded the entire redevelopment scheme, especially assumptions about TOT revenues. SDTA executive director Scott Barnett said he was worried that it would be impossible to withdraw public money after April 1 (assuming council approval), even if all these assumptions turned out wrong. He explained,

> Obviously you would like to get a shovel in the ground and start construction, but there are still all [these unanswered questions].

> We want to point out the risk to taxpayers surrounding this April 1 deadline, not criticize the entire idea. I would say the key is, you wait until after the environmental impact report is finished because no bank will commit to funding before that. If the financing never comes through [after April 1], we think the city will still have to put up its money. We raised concern about this last year [during the Proposition C campaign]. We can't figure out why this sort of deadline is needed.

The SDTA's concerns did not influence city council very much, which unanimously accepted the Padres assurances in March 1999.

As in Denver and Phoenix, San Diego's invisible local growth coalition (and nearly nonexistent corporate community) does not seem to have affected regional growth. Even as large military contractors left town or were gobbled up in mergers, the city and the surrounding county continued to grow. The economic emphasis on the military evolved into an emphasis on tourism and quality of life. Nevertheless, the downtown business community wants very much to be a corporate community. This creates an interesting spin on the relationship between community self-esteem and using public dollars for private sports stadiums. San Diego's business leaders wanted a new ballpark—not to attract and retain corporate talent but to attract corporations in the first place. Yet the socially constructed inferiority complex so evident in Cincinnati and Cleveland seemed to be concentrated solely in San Diego's downtown business community. A business leader explained,

> There has always been a certain inferiority complex among the downtown business community that we are a cul-de-sac of Los Angeles. L.A. is the big road. We used to be a sleepy little navy town. The railroad bypassed us originally because we were a cul-de-sac. And [the downtown business community] doesn't want to be this sleepy little navy town, so [they] want to make sure they have the world trade and the big teams and the corporations and the convention center and the airport. That underlying inferiority complex is [very strong] within the business community. It has been the underpinning of a lot of San Diego's elite: that we want to be a first-rate, world-class city and not just a stepchild of California's other cultural centers.

This inferiority complex has also affected the mayor and the city council, who constantly mimic downtown business leaders in their call for a world-class city. But a lack of community self-esteem has not spread to the general population, as evidenced by San Diego's rapid growth over the past thirty years. As we have mentioned, this growth has been dominated not by retirees but by individuals and families drawn to the fabulous weather. When we asked about resistance to the model for turning San Diego into a corporate town, a business executive joked,

> Just [from] the people. But nobody who matters. People *like* cul-de-sacs; they *like* to live on them. Most of the residents here *like* that we are not Los Angeles. We are buffered from them by the Marines at Camp Pendleton. We haven't paved over all of our canyons and have freeway nightmares. We are more environmentally sensitive with the beaches and bays and lagoons. The quality of life is important.

Because of the public's overall satisfaction (reflected by continued growth), it would have been almost impossible to turn the ballpark into an issue of community self-esteem and community collective conscience. Even a strong local growth coalition would have had trouble constructing this image, although declining communities such as Cincinnati, Cleveland, and Pittsburgh found that strategy useful. Unfertile ground for manipulating community self-esteem limited new ballpark advocates to promising grand economic windfalls or at least an economic payback from a very large public investment. That, combined with statutory constraints, turned the Padres' initial vision into much more than a new ballpark. Instead, the stadium was forced, almost literally, to become the linchpin of a huge downtown redevelopment project.

Several local community group leaders told us they had alternate ideas for local economic development, particularly in the area of the proposed ballpark; but their ideas did not resonate with city leaders. Opponents' strategic challenges were inexorably linked with the problematic East Village location of the new stadium. The Padres were initially opposed to the site. Ball club leaders were savvy enough (even though city council was not) to recognize the problems associated with building in a neighborhood with existing (if limited) businesses and residences. The team also cited fan preference for easy highway access at the Padres' current suburban location in Mission Valley. California certainly epitomizes the automobile society, and team owners saw no need to mess with that cultural phenomenon.

Most early opinion polls revealed a general public preference against a downtown location (see fig. 10). Many of the people who lived and worked in the East Village also did not favor the site (although some did). The area was already showing real revitalization as older warehouses were rehabbed into loft-style apartments. But the business community and the local government were convinced that a new downtown stadium would be a catalyst for turning San Diego into

Fig. 10. This type of existing development will likely be demolished to make way for A Ballpark for San Diego.

a major league corporate town. And it was impossible for the Padres to secure public money without agreeing to the downtown location. So although the site continues to create post-referendum nightmares, there could have been no referendum without it.

Taking the Town by Storm

In Denver, state government filled the growth vacuum left by a diminishing corporate community. In Phoenix, the Diamondbacks' owner filled the void. And in San Diego, successful Texas businessman John Moores rode into town in 1994 with dreams like Don Quixote. Moores started out as an IBM salesman and struck it rich after starting his own software company in the late 1970s. Through his real estate company, JMI, he has also successfully developed motels and other mid-priced projects. Interestingly, although San Diego is a traditionally Republican town (albeit a moderate one), Moores was a player in the Democratic party. But as one businessperson told us, Moores's money was green; and within two years he became arguably the most powerful individual in town, with visions of radical change:

> So [Moores] comes to town; he buys the Padres; he spends money. That doesn't mean that John Moores isn't genuinely philanthropic; he does care about things. He agreed to the [new lease between the city and the Chargers,] even though it reduced revenues because he was quietly promised a new ballpark. So he comes in, invests this money, joins boards, joins institutions, builds Little League parks. He builds all this goodwill and puts real money into the team. So you come in and give money to the arts and donate funds, and you are man of the year.[8]

If Moores was Don Quixote, then long-time baseball executive Larry Lucchino was Sancho Panza. Lucchino arrived with Moores and became the club's president and CEO, leaving the Baltimore Orioles' organization, where he had been more or less responsible for orchestrating the public funding of Camden Yards. Together, Moores and Lucchino poured money and energy into a floundering franchise. Central to their long-term vision was a brand-new stadium that would increase attendance, profits, and team value. Lucchino, who apparently saw many similarities between San Diego and Baltimore, began calling his ballpark vision "Camden West."

Moores and Lucchino hatched Proposition C as a strategic move to gain public financing for the new Padres' ballpark. Surveying the cultural landscape, they may have thought it would be easier to convince the public than city council directly, even though there was no legal requirement for any public referendum. One businessperson close to the action thought it was a clever strategy:

> Larry Lucchino is a cross between Elmer Gantry, P. T. Barnum, and Clarence Darrow. The man is highly sophisticated and brilliant to the level you don't see around here. Larry Lucchino sits down with politicians, and they are completely overmatched. . . . At one meeting Larry was a little upset because [somebody] had been raising a lot of questions about the [whole redevelopment scheme]. At one point he slams the table, gets up, points his finger at [this person,] and says, "If this referendum loses and the Padres leave town, it's all your fault." It turns out he had that same theatrical display with council members. Of course, he would never act this way in public. He's extremely charming.

In addition to pouring millions of dollars into the Proposition C campaign, Moores and Lucchino took advantage of San Diego's immature political apparatus. As in Phoenix, the Padres' new leaders found little resistance from the official government. A Proposition C supporter said,

> The mayor and city council are basically weak to start with, personalities aside. But [this council] seems to be a bunch of

lemmings. They *do* have some discretion [over the terms of the MOU]. But when the Chargers' deal blew up, the political dynamics changed. The city council was afraid to make a decision. It's not like those other [east-coast] cities with all that old wealth and old political muscle.

The Padres' power and persuasion were evident when they assured city council that the development plan would generate the tax revenues needed to finance the project.[9] The team had commissioned a preeminent local architectural firm (in which Moores had become a part owner) to put on a dazzling, state-of-the-art, multimedia presentation showing hotels, restaurants, and residences springing up around A Ballpark for San Diego (now its official name), which itself offered not just a great view of the game but "the park at the park." Basically, this would be a grassy knoll beyond center field where fans could pay five dollars, spread a blanket, enjoy a picnic, and watch the national pastime. The park at the park would also be available to the public on nongame days (presumably for free). The presentation regularly mentioned that ticket prices would be kept to a bare minimum so that the average San Diegan family could enjoy the new ballpark.

And in This Corner . . .

Even after taking advantage of San Diego's growth vacuum, John Moores and Larry Lucchino did not simply waltz to a Proposition C victory. Despite the quasi-landslide vote, issues raised during the campaign hung around like bad L.A. smog and continue to delay construction. They include criticism of the public revenue stream, the Padres' finances, and the ballpark location. Successful completion of the ballpark has also been hampered by problems within the Padres organization, a political scandal leading to a city council member's resignation, and the ill-timed shenanigans of the Chargers' football team. In many ways, opposition to the ballpark (specifically) and the redevelopment plan (generally) has grown exponentially since the approval of Proposition C, even without a single unifying issue. Still, there have been few official setbacks. The current mayor and the city council completely support the project, although it has changed somewhat since the original referendum. Nevertheless, the opposition has effectively managed to delay and stall the process so that the ballpark *might* open five-and-a-half years after the passage of Proposition C.

It is amazing how effective this opposition has been, considering its modest roots. When visiting San Diego in 1999, we met with people involved with the Stop C Campaign. Months after the election, the group was still trying to pressure city council into reconsidering the redevelopment project before the important April 1 deadline. We spent time with about fifteen members of the group; and according to one of the lead organizers, this was just about all of them. Their brief presentations before city council were impressive and often entertaining, although their simplicity was a vivid contrast to the Padres' multimedia technology. One person offered a clear and concise critique of the public financing plan using a visual aid that seemed to have been drawn in crayon. Another Stop C member seemed upset that city council was not being open-minded enough and suggested they all go out for a cup of coffee to talk things over. Some East Village dwellers demanded to know why new residences, hotel rooms, and stores were more important than existing apartments and businesses.

A number of individuals and neighborhood groups also spoke out against Proposition C and continue today to critique the ballpark redevelopment plan (see fig. 11). Relatively powerful individuals, such as former council members and lawyers, have weighed in against one or many parts of the project. Numerous lawsuits have been filed since 1999, and some are still pending. These lawsuits tackle a plethora of issues, from environmental impact to the question of what constitutes the fair market value of a publicly condemned property. Perhaps the

Fig. 11. Opponents in San Diego tried to connect the use of public money for stadiums to the underfunding of other crucial needs in the city.

most interesting issue has been whether or not the original referendum and MOU were illegal because they misled voters about the true
public cost of the project. The city's proposed $225 million bond sale
reflected only the principle, not the total cost including interest. The
courts have not agreed with this argument, but it is raising public
awareness of the discrepancy in numbers. When the identical issue
was brought up in Cincinnati, it had no practical impact on ballpark
construction, although it may have made it harder for the Reds to get
a deal as sweet as the Bengals' lease. But in San Diego, the issue has
fueled a strong public backlash that may indirectly be delaying the new
baseball stadium. Certainly, it will remain an issue as the Chargers
crank up their new stadium demands.

The Padres like to point out that these lawsuits have always been
decided in favor of the team or the city. But ballpark advocates still
have to spend time and money dealing with them, and they often force
construction halts while critical issues are debated and adjudicated.
Recently, the Padres sued lawyer and former council member Bruce
Henderson, who has initiated many of the suits. The team claims that
the rising cost of the project is due to Henderson's malicious and ha-
bitual filing of frivolous lawsuits that have no chance of being upheld.

Mostly Unforeseen Circumstances

A number of factors unrelated to the opposition have also delayed
building A Ballpark for San Diego. Construction ground to a halt in
October 2000 amid allegations that Moores and council member Va-
lerie Stallings were involved in unethical and perhaps illegal activities.
According to news accounts (see San Diego Union-Tribune, January 30,
2001, A1), an FBI investigation was launched to examine the propriety
of gifts that Stallings had received from Moores and the Padres. One
gift gave Stallings a special opportunity to buy stock in Moores's Texas
software company during its initial public offering in March 1999.
Stallings allegedly sold the stock later that month at a substantial
profit. Suspicions were aroused when she cast a deciding vote in June
1998 on whether or not the MOU should require a larger contribution
from the Padres. Stallings voted no. There were also several other gifts
from the Padres, albeit minor, that Stallings failed to report. Allegedly,
Moores lent her a vehicle so she could drive to and use his vacation
home in Monterey and gave her family free passage on the team's plane
(San Diego Union-Tribune, January 30, 2001, A1).

The federal investigation, which did not conclude until early 2001,
eventually exonerated Moores, claiming that giving gifts or special
opportunities to politicians is not illegal. Stallings was less fortunate.

With felony charges for mail fraud under consideration, she resigned her council seat in January 2001 and pleaded guilty to two misdemeanors, including failure to report a gift (www.TheSanDiego Channel.com, January 30, 2001).

The scandal cast a cloud over the council's objectivity on anything having to do with the team or the ballpark, and a plethora of lawsuits were filed or considered regarding this conflict of interest (as we will discuss). To blunt criticism and increasing calls for a new public referendum, the council decided in March 2001 to reconsider twenty-eight different ballpark-related issues. According to the council, the revote was a response to the Stallings's scandal as well as a large turnover within the council (only two people remained from the 1999 vote). The council also acknowledged that the new mayor, Dick Murphy, had shown significant skepticism about the stadium project during his campaign. Supporters and opponents of the project weighed in at public meetings, and the council gave unanimous support to all twenty-eight issues. Ironically, some wavering council members said that Mayor Murphy's new financing plan was central to their support. Apparently, the once-critical mayoral candidate was now a very supportive mayor.

Anger about this unanimous approval sparked a series of lawsuits that sought to negate the entire project, with claims that the city had violated California's municipal conflict-of-interest laws. The lawsuit argued that the recent vote merely reaffirmed actions taken by a Stallings-tainted council. The state superior court sided with the city, ruling that Moores's gifts to Stallings did not represent a conflict of interest under either state or local law and that all council decisions were legal. In July 2002, a state appeals court disagreed somewhat with the lower-court ruling. The appellate decision ruled that there was a clear quid pro quo relationship between Moores and Stallings but also concluded that the council's reaffirmation vote was perfectly legal and rendered moot Stallings's previous illegal activities.

This political scandal was paralleled by a breakdown in the John Moores–Larry Lucchino partnership. The details of their spat are unclear but seem generally related to the ballpark delays and the Stallings affair. One often-advanced theory shows Larry Lucchino growing increasingly upset with the legal delays and the resulting negative public opinion, which made his job as stadium pitchman much harder. Although Lucchino publicly denied any acrimony between himself and Moores, he eventually agreed to a partnership dissolution. In 2002, Lucchino became president and CEO of the Boston Red Sox, where he promised to deliver a World Series championship to Beantown, even if it meant building a new stadium. As we have discussed, Lucchino was an excellent salesperson; and his departure from San Diego will not expedite completion of the stadium.

The final obstacle to completing the ballpark quickly was its proposed location, which, as mentioned, opened a Pandora's box of problems. While the Padres' first choice (and supposedly the first choice of polled patrons) was to build a new suburban stadium next to Qualcomm Stadium, the fledgling downtown corporate community and the city government insisted that the new stadium be located somewhat near the central business district—in particular, the convention center. This insistence stemmed from the legal necessity requiring a two-thirds vote to raise taxes if the revenue is to go to a single specific project rather than larger redevelopment. Politicians also realized that the stadium would have to be framed as a large economic development effort rather than a public subsidy for team owners.

Two important factors contributed to this political realization. First, the city was being lambasted for its 1996 renegotiation of the Chargers' lease (which we will discuss later in the chapter). Second, the strategic impossibility of manipulating community self-esteem forced new stadium advocates, including the team, to insist that the ballpark was part of an overall design to reinvigorate what John Moores referred to as the "needle exchange district" of downtown San Diego. The redevelopment plan was framed as an extension of the trendy Gaslamp District located a few blocks from the business district and the convention center. The district is a smaller version of Denver's LoDo—somewhat vibrant but, in the words of one national food writer, "riddled with mediocre Italian restaurants" (Carreno 2002). Public money helped redevelop the Gaslamp District, and its success came on the heels of an expanded and publicly financed convention center.

As we have shown throughout the book, such economic arguments are increasingly hard to sell. Among other things, critics are beginning to better understand issues such as the substitution effect. Many challengers of the redevelopment plan correctly wonder if the new retail outlets in the Ballpark District won't just siphon business from the Gaslamp District or other parts of the city. This question is especially relevant in San Diego because the entire public financing scheme has been tied to increased tourist visits. Spending by local residents will not increase TOT revenues unless they decide to try out some of the new downtown hotel rooms or unless the TOT tax rate is increased. Somehow, the ballpark and its ancillary development will have to draw new outside tourists or conventioneers who want to stay downtown. Otherwise, there will be not be enough of an increase in TOT revenues to pay for the city's share of the Padres' new stadium. If this happens, presumably the city will have to pay for the bonds from some other pocket.

Fantasy Documents Galore

The TOT revenue scheme was the centerpiece of a series of fantasy documents used to justify spending San Diego's public dollars for a private baseball stadium. These documents included the Padres' assertion of poor financial health; the memorandum of understanding between the Padres and the city (providing details of Proposition C); and the team's city council presentation before the important April 1, 1999 reassurance deadline. The claims of fact in these documents were so problematic that they almost asked to be discredited. Challenged almost immediately after Proposition C's passage, those claims continue to be questioned today and have created much trouble for San Diego's new stadium supporters.

Almost immediately after buying the Padres in 1994 (for $83 million), Moores claimed he was losing money. While simultaneously spending more than $2 million campaigning for Proposition C in 1998, he said he had lost more than $41 million during his three-year ownership and projected another $20 million loss for 1998. To give this position some legitimacy as well as influence the Proposition C vote, the Padres released an audited financial report from Price Waterhouse a few weeks before the election. The report showed operational losses in 1997 of $8.2 million and total losses (including amortization and depreciation of "intangible assets") of $18 million.

As we have shown with similar "objective" documents, the devil is in the details. In truth, a company's bottom line is subjective. First, the team's financial status in 1997 may or may not have been typical of other years, making generalization somewhat dangerous. Indeed, attendance soared during the 1998 season as the Padres played their way to the World Series, even in an outdated ballpark. Second, "intangible assets" include players' salaries. For example, if Tony Gwynn signs a $15 million, three-year contract from 1996 to 1998, the team can say that his value depreciates by $5 million per year and claim that depreciation as an organizational loss.

This may be consistent with accounting practices in major league sports, but it is misleading to present it as an absolute financial loss. Because the Padres are not a publicly traded company, there is no issue here of misleading investors. Instead, it's a matter of misleading the local community. Moreover, focusing on operating losses diverts public attention from the increasing value of the team. By the end of 1998, *Forbes Magazine* estimated that the Padres were worth about

$160 million, about double the 1994 purchase price (*San Diego Union-Tribune*, January 16, 1999, B11). If precedents in other cities hold true, a new stadium could increase the Padres value by another $50 million or more.

We consider the Padres' March 1999 city council presentation (and accompanying written report) to be another fantasy document. It was extremely impressive and probably very convincing to people unfamiliar with municipal finance. The Padres' production was much more sophisticated than a similar presentation later that summer by the Philadelphia Phillies, which didn't seem to convince anybody of anything (see chapter 7). The animated video showed beautiful new hotels, offices, and residences springing up around the centerpiece Ballpark for San Diego. The team claimed to have identified fifty new tenants for this office space but gave no names. One of the office complexes, Park Place, was heralded as an urban campus teeming with high-tech companies that normally prefer the suburbs. Amerisuites had supposedly committed to developing one of the district's central hotels, which presenters said would be the perfect place for the visiting team to stay when playing the Padres.

We were struck by two things during this presentation. First, apart from the dazzling graphics, it reminded us of a school project in which a student comes up with a futuristic community without considering the social costs associated with that vision. Maybe a major league ballpark is just a bigger version of the playground that is always central to those school projects. Second, the mayor and the city council acted as if they were completely impressed by this presentation and had no significant questions or challenges.[10] Many people in the audience, however, asked the council some tough questions that night, including a request for more details about the commitments for all this proposed development. Several suggested that the city government reconsider public funding for a private stadium. Mayor Susan Golding usually replied that such questions and concerns were moot because the community's vote on Proposition C had provided a mandate that could not be reversed. According to the mayor, this council session was designed to reassure city government that the Padres' plan was viable; and they were, in fact, reassured.

A final element of the Padres' alleged need for a new stadium was the claim that San Diego is a small-market city that can't compete with large-market teams without a revenue-enhancing, new publicly funded stadium. This claim was repeated to us dozens of times during our interviews and appeared so regularly in newspaper stories that it became an unchallenged explanation of why San Diego should spend public dollars on a private stadium. We were taken aback by the frequency and apparent sincerity of new stadium supporters who were making this assertion. After all, San Diego is the seventh-largest city in the country, part of the fifth-largest county and the seventeenth-largest metropolitan area. Although it is somewhat constrained by Los Angeles up the road, the city is clearly a significant media market as well as a population center. It is one of the fastest-growing regions of the country. So if San Diego is a small-market city, then what constitutes a large-market city? Apparently, only the six-largest cities in the United States count as large markets, and everyone else uses the small-market argument for justifying a publicly subsidized stadium. Subsidy supporters in San Diego constantly mentioned Los Angeles' big market and how hard it was to compete with. But on the field, anyway, that may not matter. Since 1984, the Padres have appeared in twice as many World Series as the Dodgers have (two versus one).

The city council created its own complementary fantasy document to rationalize spending public dollars on a new private ballpark. A few weeks before the election, the city released a report from Deloitte and Touche claiming that the redevelopment project has the potential to generate tremendous economic rewards. These windfalls include $1.1 billion in community spending and 12,000 new full-time jobs during construction alone. Subsequent phases could spawn 5,000 more jobs, pump another $600 million annually into the local economy, and provide the city with almost $2 million more in tax revenues each year. Our criticisms of this report sound just like our criticisms of similar fantasy documents in other cities: it assumes steady growth, especially among tourists; it assumes that the project will actually develop as the Padres have laid it out in their own fantasy document; it does not consider the substitution effect; it does not include the public share money spent by the Center City Development Corporation (CCDC).

The single largest problem with this document, and the whole public financing scheme, is the assumption of tourist growth and the corresponding growth of the TOT. The centerpiece of Proposition C, as encased in the memorandum of understanding, was that all public financing (excluding CCDC and Port Authority) would come from TOT revenue increases. This means that existing TOT money would not have to be diverted from the more than two hundred cultural and civic projects depending on it. Crafters of the original MOU insisted that the TOT would grow 8 percent annually. Applying that growth to all the new projected hotel rooms yields enough money for ballpark financing and plenty left over for other things. But as one business leader told us, this plan depends on a complex choreography that requires perfect timing:

> The problem is that [in] the city's proposal . . . there must be 2,400 new rooms built in the downtown core, they must all have a certain occupancy level and daily rate, and they have to open by a certain date. In addition to all of [this new supply], demand must increase by 8 percent each year. If [anything] goes wrong with this plan, then you will have less TOT money, which means you have to take it from other places to pay the ballpark financing.

This business leader insisted that these new rooms will get used, but not by ballpark patrons. Instead, there seems to be a need for more hotel space close to the convention center. Unfortunately for San Diego, however, the worst-case scenario seems to be unfolding. First, there has not been a rush to build new hotels in the ballpark district, which is somewhat near the convention center (but separated by a multilane highway). Second, despite its traditionally strong tourist economy, tourism in San Diego slumped in 2002, presumably due to the recession and the reduction in business and personal travel; and tourism officials were pessimistic about tourist growth in the coming years (*San Diego Union-Tribune*, October 25, 2001, B5). Nevertheless, the 2002 city budget still assumed a 6 to 8 percent increase in hotel tax revenues alone, not to mention associated non-TOT revenue increases (that is, sales-tax increases on other spending). These two factors are clearly related to one another because declining tourist visits give hotel developers little reason to build new rooms.

Another related (although minor) piece of this fantasy funding has to do with tax-increment financing, a very speculative way to "assure" enough revenue growth to pay for the ballpark without dipping into existing pools. The speculation here is that the redevelopment project will also generate new taxes (sales, property, business, and so on) that will go into the city's general fund. As with the TOT speculation, tax-increment financing is a house of cards just waiting for a stiff ocean breeze to blow it down. While the Padres have assured the city of ancillary development, nothing is guaranteed. Nor is the value of existing properties guaranteed to rise. When we informally asked a city council member why San Diego would fare differently from other cities, the reply was that *this* plan really was different from any other public dollars for private stadium plan.

The Chargers Play Tackle

In 1996, the Chargers renegotiated their lease with San Diego, claiming the team could not stay competitive without some ability to increase its revenues. As usual, this meant building additional luxury and club-level seating at Jack Murphy Stadium (as it was then called), bringing the total number of seats to 71,000. Mayor Susan Golding seems to have initiated these discussions because she was told that San Diego could not host a Super Bowl without a 70,000-seat stadium, and she thought a San Diego Super Bowl would be a good thing. At that point, a new football stadium was not being considered. The Chargers claimed (then and now) that the mayor was more interested in building a new stadium for the Padres because that team's lease expired first.

When the Chargers made veiled threats of leaving, the city government responded with a fabulous deal for the team, even without a new stadium. The city agreed to sell $78 million in bonds to pay for renovations, $18 million of which came from the Qualcomm Company for naming rights to the stadium. The new lease nominally kept the Chargers in town until 2020 but included a five-year escape clause if the team could show economic duress. Finally, the city guaranteed the team revenue equivalent to the sale of 60,000 general admission (not luxury or club) seats per game. If that many tickets were not sold, the city would have to pick up the tab. By the end of the 2001 season, the city had spent $25 million on this seat guarantee. Most important, the new lease negatively affected the Padres and sparked their new stadium demands. The Chargers would now keep a higher percentage of shared advertising revenues from Qualcomm and receive all revenue from luxury and club seats, even at the eighty-one baseball games each year. Several observers we talked with believed that the mayor told Padres' officials to be patient because they would get their deal after the Chargers were taken care of.

As this lopsided deal became public, the fallout influenced the plan to use public dollars for a new baseball stadium. As mentioned, this was one reason why the baseball stadium had to be framed as part of a larger economic development strategy, not just another windfall for a local sports team. Feeling the political heat, Mayor Golding spearheaded an initiative for a public referendum on what would be known as Proposition E. This referendum, which appeared on the same 1998 ballot as Proposition C, required voter approval for building projects that provide "significant private benefit" and cost more than 10 percent of the city's general fund. In 1998, this 10 percent was approximately $57 million. Proposition E was approved even more overwhelmingly than Proposition C was. The mayor frequently tried to enhance the legitimacy of Proposition C, claiming that it complied with this new law and therefore could not possibly turn out like the Chargers' debacle.

As of this writing, five years have passed since the renegotiated lease; and the Chargers are claiming economic duress. The team has decided that the renovations and lease enhancements were not enough: they must have a new stadium to stay competitive in an NFL teeming with new stadiums. The Chargers say that some Los Angeles investors are very interested in luring the team up Interstate 5. They would, of course, prefer to stay in San Diego, but they have to do what's best for the team. That means gaining a competitive advantage over the other NFL teams with a source of revenue that is not shared with them: premium-seating fees.

A negative reaction to the Chargers' power sweep is spilling over onto the Padres and their dreams of a 2004 opening date. As a result, the Padres have recently made some concessions to assuage the increased official (city council) and unofficial (public) hostility toward all local sports teams, especially toward the public funding of private stadiums. For example, the Padres have agreed to spend $25 million on a parking garage that was initially supposed to be constructed by CCDC. This sort of unexpected backlash from another professional sports team was irrelevant in Denver, somewhat relevant in Phoenix, and mostly unexpected in San Diego. But there has been some precedent for it, so maybe San Diego's new stadium advocates should not be totally surprised. For example, similar things happened in Cincinnati (see chapter 4), where the arrogance of the Bengals forced the Reds to scale back their demands on Hamilton County. In Cincinnati, the local growth coalition was so strong that this sort of impediment never jeopardized or slowed construction of the city's new stadiums. But in San Diego, with no corporate-driven local growth coalition, the Chargers fiasco may leave a long-term legacy of problems for the new baseball stadium.

GROWTH WITHOUT GROWTH COALITIONS

The frontier cities of Denver, Phoenix, and San Diego differ from all other cities examined in this book because they are among the fastest-growing in the entire United States. Their phenomenal growth creates an entirely different logic for obtaining public dollars for private stadiums. In cities such as Cincinnati, Cleveland, and Pittsburgh, the structure and strategy of the local growth coalition are the most important parts of this logic. But on the frontier, the structure and strategy of the local growth coalitions are only one piece of a complex calculus of sociological factors that have combined in a multitude of ways to produce a myriad of outcomes. Cincinnati, Cleveland, and Pittsburgh are very similar to each other because they are contracting. Denver, Phoenix, and San Diego are very dissimilar to each other because they are expanding in disparate ways.

Other than growth, the primary similarity of these frontier cities is that they have weak local growth coalitions. In fact, as we explored in chapter 1, there is a fascinating inverse relationship between actual local economic growth and the prowess of local growth coalitions. Still, the cities are not uniform in terms of their nascent growth coalitions, which has had a predictable impact on the ease of building private sports stadiums with public dollars. Denver's growth coalition was certainly the strongest and seemed to reach its peak in the late 1980s, which was good timing for the successful building of Coors Field. The city's relatively strong growth coalition is not surprising because it is the most historically established region of these three. In contrast, very young Phoenix in very young Arizona has no trace of a local growth coalition. Bank One Ballpark was built, but not as easily as Denver's two stadiums. San Diego is more complex than either Denver or Phoenix. It has no powerful, corporate-driven, local growth coalition; but many economic and political actors want very much to develop one. This tension between present and future reflects San Diego's different historical personalities. Even though the city is older than Denver, and California is older than Colorado, San Diego has always been a sleepy little Navy town. Only in the past thirty years has the city become a more eclectic economic and cultural area. Today it is the seventh-largest city in the country, no longer just a retirement community for naval officers and home of the country's greatest zoo and (arguably) its greatest weather.

The absence of powerful local growth coalitions creates a power vacuum. In the three frontier cities, the genesis of new stadium movements was not a corporate-centered alliance looking to maintain and expand its pool of executive talent. Other social entities had to fill the vacuum and lead the way to obtaining public dollars for private stadiums. In Denver, the adolescent growth coalition got things rolling on Coors Field; but it was mostly the state government (coincidentally located in Denver) that filled the power vacuum. In Phoenix, powerful businessman and NBA team owner Jerry Colangelo acted in place of a local growth coalition to orchestrate the financing and construction of Bank One Ballpark. Local and state politicians were involved but seemed to follow rather than lead. John Moores and Larry Lucchino rode into San Diego, where the business community and local government longed to be treated like leaders of a first-class city on par with San Francisco (which has only half of San Diego's population). This need helped form a symbiotic relationship in which the Padres exploited the elites' inferiority complex while the elites viewed Moores and his vision of A Ballpark for San Diego as their ticket out of Palookaville. Alas, this marriage, like most, was bumpy at times; and the ballpark is still unfinished.

Ironically, the people or organizations that filled the power vacuum were partly frustrated in their stadium quests by the very social
force that had created the vacuum in the first place: economic and
population growth. Because the population of the cities and their surrounding regions was growing, people were immune to contemporary
arguments linking new stadiums with community self-esteem and
community collective conscience. Such arguments were by no means
absent, but they did not take center stage as they did in Cincinnati.
This situation forced advocates to stress ways in which a publicly financed stadium would transform the local economy. But even here
there was room for skepticism: the local economies were already
pretty healthy without new stadiums. That skepticism forced new stadium proponents to conjure up even more spectacular schemes to justify spending public money: Coors Field will rejuvenate all of Denver,
even beyond LoDo; A Ballpark for San Diego will anchor a complete
overhaul of San Diego's downtown; Bank One Ballpark will transform
Phoenix's downtown from a commuter destination to a thriving residential community. But as we have seen in other cities, attempts to link
new stadiums with economic development are often problematic, especially when the promises become grandiose.

New stadium opposition was also quite different in the frontier
cities. Denver had little organized opposition to Coors Field or Invesco
Field at Mile High, which is one reason why the parks opened relatively quickly. There was more organized opposition in Phoenix, but it
suffered from narrowly focusing on tax increases rather than challenging the whole premise of stadium-centered economic growth. That
focus prevented alliances from forming among people and organizations who were not necessarily opposed to taxes but didn't think Bank
One Ballpark was the best way to spend them. In contrast, an increasingly organized opposition in San Diego rallied around many different
issues, including (but not limited to) tax increases. Indeed, one of the
rallying cries of the San Diego opposition, reflected on this book's
cover, was that public money could be better spent on libraries and
schools for the growing local population. The city's eclectic opposition
has built a formidable barrier to completion of San Diego's baseball
stadium and will probably make a mess of the Chargers' plan for a new
football stadium.

Different opposition tactics in different cities were not merely a result of the idiosyncrasies of stadium opponents. Structural forces were
also at work. As table 2 shows, Phoenix is a somewhat elderly community in a somewhat elderly state, which is likely to oppose taxes because many residents live on fixed incomes and do not use social
services such as public education. Denver and San Diego have much

Table 2. Percentage of Population Greater Than Age Sixty

State and County	Percent
Colorado	9.7
Denver	11.3
Adams	7.8
Douglas	4.2
Arapahoe	8.6
Jefferson	9.6
Arizona	13.0
Maricopa	16.0
California	10.6
San Diego	13.0
United States	12.0

Source: Authors' analysis of U.S. Census Bureau data.

younger populations that are less likely to live on fixed incomes and more likely to covet excellent public schools, libraries, and even mass transit. Although this difference did not translate into any formidable opposition in Denver, it was a powerful force in San Diego.

We believe the road to ballparks was so smooth in Denver because the power vacuum was filled by an almost de facto local growth coalition that was missing only a central corporate component. There was a very strong alliance among downtown business leaders, the five regional county governments, and the state government. An enormous benefit was the lack of friction between the city of Denver and the county of Denver. Such city-county friction caused many problems in Cincinnati, Cleveland, and Pittsburgh and also proved troublesome to stadium proponents in Phoenix and San Diego. In Arizona there was constant tension within Maricopa County between Phoenix and other municipalities such as Scottsdale and Mesa. Each city wanted more of the county's formidable resources. There was also some tension between the city of San Diego and the county of San Diego. San Diego County has a much larger budget than the city does, but its responsibility for primary social services within a huge jurisdiction leaves little money to spare. The county commissioners often appeared to be offended that they weren't included in the ballpark discussions, but this offense never rose to hostility. Nevertheless, it's possible that the road to A Ballpark for San Diego might have been smoother if the county had been an ally rather than just a bystander.

Serendipitous factors also contributed to the relative ease or trouble that cities had in opening their new publicly financed stadiums.

Although Denver went through its share of scandals, it saw nothing like the special legislation in Arizona (and resulting shootout) and the Moores-Stallings wrangles in San Diego. The football team in Denver posed no problems during the building of Coors Field, and the Broncos eventually got their own new stadium. Previous (and possibly future) public subsidies for the Arizona Cardinals were certainly blips on the community's radar during the sometimes contentious battle to build Phoenix's new ballpark. No doubt those issues will continue to be contentious, given the uneasy relationship between Phoenix and other parts of Maricopa County. And in San Diego, the fate of the Padres' new ballpark has always been linked with the circumstances of the Chargers. Sharing a single stadium has only exacerbated this tension.

These three cities show that securing public dollars for private stadiums is possible without a strong local growth coalition that emphasizes less tangible rewards (such as community self-esteem) rather than more tangible ones. But in the absence of powerful coalitions, the speed of building stadiums depends on a plethora of other sociological forces. Those factors are sometimes rooted in the conscious decisions of individuals but may also be embedded in a larger cultural reality beyond the control of any individual. If these forces line up in certain ways, building a publicly funded stadium becomes easier. But if they line up otherwise, it becomes much more difficult.

7

Pittsburgh and Philadelphia

STRONG VERSUS WEAK
LOCAL GROWTH COALITIONS

In March 1999, the government of Pennsylvania approved spending $320 million on four new professional sports stadiums, two each in Pittsburgh and Philadelphia.[1] Two years later, the Pirates and the Steelers were playing baseball and football in brand-new PNC Park and Heinz Stadium. Meanwhile, the Philadelphia Eagles did not start playing in their new stadium until August 2003, and the Phillies' new ballpark won't be ready until April 2004. The contrasting stories of Pittsburgh and Philadelphia drive home the three important factors we have been stressing throughout this book. First, a unified and powerful local growth coalition is crucial for swiftly securing public dollars for private stadiums, even in the face of staunch opposition. Second, notions of community self-esteem and community collective conscience are more effective arguments for stadium supporters than are promises of economic nirvana, although in certain cities the former arguments may be unconvincing. Third, many serendipitous sociological factors can create or eliminate the opportunities available to the actors involved in new stadium initiatives.

PITTSBURGH: HOW NO STADIUMS
BECAME TWO STADIUMS

In November 1997, voters throughout the eleven-county Pittsburgh metropolitan region overwhelmingly defeated a referendum to raise the region's sales tax from 6 to 6.5%.[2] Every county voted against the referendum, although the margin of defeat was smallest in Allegheny

County, which includes the city itself. The tax increase was officially known as the Regional Renaissance Initiative (RRI); its public champion was officially known as the Regional Renaissance Partnership (RRP). According to the RRP, the RRI would fund a slew of economic development projects throughout the metropolitan area. The most expensive of these projects were new ballparks for the Pirates and the Steelers and an expanded convention center in downtown Pittsburgh. Despite heartfelt disclaimers from members of the RRP, the RRI quickly became known as "the stadium tax."

As with some other cases in this book, the tax initiative was precipitated by hints or threats from the professional teams that they might leave town for financial reasons. One of those reasons, of course, was an outdated stadium that did not generate enough revenue for the teams to stay competitive. Pittsburgh's Three Rivers Stadium had opened in 1971 and was part of the highway-accessible, multipurpose stadium trend that included Cincinnati's Cinergy Field (née Riverfront Stadium), Qualcomm Field (née Jack Murphy Stadium), and Philadelphia's Veterans Stadium. Owners of the Pirates and the Steelers felt that Three Rivers was a horrible place to play and watch professional sports, even though the Steelers had sold out every game for decades.

We were shocked when the RRI, sometimes referred to as plan A, went down in flames. But we were less surprised when plan B rose from its ashes to finance the stadiums *without* public approval. Initially, we had speculated that the RRI would pass because the city's demographic, political, and economic reality was similar to Cleveland's and Cincinnati's, both of which had developed successful initiatives. Pittsburgh was another midsized northeastern city ravaged by industrial decline, a declining population, and a strictly nine-to-five downtown. It nevertheless maintained a powerful corporate community and was the headquarters of many large firms, including Westinghouse, Alcoa, Heinz, and Mellon Bank. Thus, there are two components to Pittsburgh's journey to secure public dollars for private stadiums. The first part is Pittsburgh-area voters' surprisingly harsh treatment of plan A. The second is how new stadium advocates overcame this unequivocal rebuff with a new strategy (plan B) that circumvented the voters.

The Local Growth Coalition Gets Hammered

Historically speaking, Pittsburgh's local growth coalition is even more powerful and unified than Cincinnati's. While many corporations no longer maintain a large productive presence in Pittsburgh, their administrative presence still generates a lot of clout. The local corporate community took the reins in designing and implementing plan A. One executive noted,

> The corporate community here is very supportive, very supportive. That's the one thing we have going for us here. We don't have the population base, but we have a very strong corporate community: [companies like] Mellon Bank, PNC Bank, Alcoa, USX, Heinz. We've taken some hits, losing Rockwell and Westinghouse, [but] it's still a significant corporate community. They were very supportive of [plan A]. We spent $6 million on the initiative. They put money up for it. [Thus], when it comes to selling the suites, club seats, and naming rights, you have a built-in reservoir [and] don't have to go outside the city.

The local growth coalition is spearheaded by a group called the Allegheny Conference. Like the Cincinnati Business Committee and Cleveland Tomorrow, it is a powerful CEO-only group that tries to influence public policy in ways that benefit corporate investments and profits (while publicly professing more egalitarian goals). Local banker Richard King Mellon started the Allegheny Conference in the early 1940s to try to change Pittsburgh's image as a nineteenth-century industrial town covered in soot and smoke. In the mid-fifties, the conference believed that a new stadium—in this case, Three Rivers—should be part of Pittsburgh's makeover, although it took fifteen years to actually accomplish this goal (*Pittsburgh Post-Gazette*, April 7, 1999, B1). A business leader explained,

> The Allegheny Conference was the driving force behind the [plan A] initiative. There are, I believe, thirty members. Their goal is to create educational and economic investment in the community. They work to make Pittsburgh a better place to live.

Backed by this powerful corporate group and a whopping $6 million war chest, plan A seemed like a shoo-in. For months, residents of the eleven-county metropolitan region were bludgeoned with messages that the area's survival and growth were inexorably entwined with plan A's passage. Supporters unleashed an avalanche of advertising, the largest local paper (the *Post-Gazette*) became a constant editorial champion, and local golf legend Arnold Palmer drove home the initiative's importance. Almost every local business leader, including the owners of the sports teams, took a crack at championing the RRI. Still, despite all these financial and organizational advantages, plan A never stood a chance.

The Wrong Messenger

Plan A's defeat was rooted in two strategic errors. First, the corporate community was a little too prominent in supporting the tax increase, which could easily be construed as self-serving. Many citizens concluded that the Allegheny Conference was trying to make Pittsburgh a better place to live and work only for the corporate elite, not for the average citizen. These were, after all, the same corporations that had been moving high-paying manufacturing jobs out of Pittsburgh for decades. Second, the campaign was never consistent in its justification for why public dollars should be spent on private stadiums. Sometimes advocates promised that the tax would stimulate economic development and create great new jobs; at other times they focused on fostering community self-esteem and community collective conscience. On balance, they placed relatively more emphasis on the problematic economic-benefit approach.

The powerful Allegheny Conference was extremely ineffective in building public support for plan A. Its members did not seem particularly attuned to the trials and tribulations of local politics. One executive reflected,

> Corporations and political processes are two different things. The [conference] wasn't used to dealing with an electorate. Just not their sphere of reference. They needed to involve the community at large [in] putting such an initiative together before presenting a referendum. They didn't.

Unlike the case in Cincinnati, where business leaders stayed behind the scenes, Pittsburgh's corporate community was on the front lines, which did not always resonate well with the community. According to a member of the plan B working group,

> Were [regular people] relevant to the Regional Renaissance Initiative? I think the answer is no. It was a bunch of folks cloistered with the Allegheny Conference who found out these guys don't know anything about anything, which is scary but true when you think about corporate leaders. Talk about being out of touch. The Allegheny Conference really ran the Regional Renaissance Partnership and only brought the politicians in after outlining the specifics of the initiative.

The RRP did not anticipate such resistance to a sales-tax increase, even though the tax had been raised only a few years earlier. This unintentional insensitivity to the real experiences of middle- and working-class folks fueled public condemnation of plan A as another form of corporate welfare, much as Cincinnati residents had reacted to the corporate community's overt attempt to change the city charter. An opponent of plan A said,

> The . . . initiative foundered because these were projects the corporate community wanted very badly but did not want to pay for. If they had stepped forward and said they would accept a tax from themselves and from upper-income people, there would have been little opposition. You can't put [Steelers' owner Dan Rooney], who will most benefit materially, up there on TV saying, "Please vote for this."

The Wrong Message

We think there also would have been less opposition if the RRP had placed less emphasis on economic development and more emphasis on community self-esteem and community collective conscience. The RRP reframed itself as the Community Alliance for Economic Development and Jobs, hoping to convince people that the RRI was not just a stadium tax. It assured residents that the tax would generate all sorts of infrastructural improvements to local sewers, roads, bridges, and tunnels as well as two new stadiums and an expanded convention center. In addition to the jobs directly created by these projects, the local economy would certainly flourish as existing businesses expanded and new businesses moved in to take advantage of these infrastructural improvements. A sports team representative said,

> [You must] create a destination point. You create a ballpark here that is so unique that people want to see it. If it is part of a development on the river, I think that people will come from three hundred to five hundred miles away to see it all. If they can go to an aquarium, visit a museum, eat, stay over a night, and drive home. The rivers are underdeveloped here. We have a lot of advantages. People are very friendly; it's a safe city. People will feel comfortable staying here.

These same economic promises are proving very hard to support in other cities, and insisting that visitors will travel five hundred miles to Pittsburgh may be wishful thinking. Such a radius includes Chicago, Cleveland, and Baltimore (which already have relatively new stadiums), not to mention far-off places such as Charlotte, North Carolina. Ironically, before the Regional Renaissance Initiative, new stadium supporters had not been promising economic panaceas. But those involved with the RRI told us that, as the corporate community assumed more control, there were fewer promises of enhanced community self-esteem and more promises of economic payoff.

Referendum supporters had sown the seeds of their own destruction. One executive reflected,

> Sports: . . . you can argue over the numbers, but they are just not economic generators. If you had $100 million to spend in the region and wanted to get the most impact, sports wouldn't do it. It's not like it's creating a lot of jobs. You know, the Steelers won all those Super Bowls when the steel mills were pulling out of town.

An opponent of plan A thought it might have been more successful if supporters had focused on quality-of-life issues rather than making financial promises:

> I was at [Three Rivers] last week, and the place is completely dead. There is nothing happening there. If anyone calls [sports stadiums] economic development, they should be slapped in the face. It's a stupid statement to make. It [may be] a quality-of-life issue, but it has nothing to do with our future as a region.

As Luck Would Have It

While plan A's failure might have been averted by a different strategy, available alternatives to the RRP were greatly constrained by somewhat random structural factors. One was the political and economic dynamic between the city of Pittsburgh and its surrounding counties. As in Cincinnati and Cleveland, Pittsburgh's core urban population has been migrating to the suburbs. As a result, Allegheny County, which includes Pittsburgh, is a much more powerful player in local policy than is the city itself. A generation ago, only the mayor and the city council would have been politically relevant to initiatives such as the RRI. These days, however, the three Allegheny County commissioners (and their constituents) are also included in the political mix. And given the overall financial scope of the RRI, it was necessary to involve political institutions from the ten counties surrounding Allegheny. The farther you go from a city, the less effective arguments about both urban economic development and community self-esteem become. This was clearly reflected in the referendum vote: the percentage of people opposing the RRI increased as you move away from Pittsburgh.

A second structural constraint on the RRI came from the nature of Pittsburgh's downtown. Like the downtown areas of Cleveland, Cincinnati, and Phoenix, Pittsburgh's Golden Triangle becomes a ghost town after 5 P.M. This makes it harder to justify linking new stadiums with downtown development because there really isn't anything to develop in the first place. If Pittsburgh's downtown had been more like Denver's or, especially, Philadelphia's, promises of ballpark-influenced economic development might have been more convincing to local residents.

But the most pervasive structural impediment was the Allegheny Institute for Public Policy's organized opposition to plan A. The institute is a libertarian think tank well connected to Richard Mellon-Scaife. Scaife publishes the *Pittsburgh Tribune* and has supported many visible conservative causes such as investigating and publicizing the alleged Bill Clinton–Paula Jones tryst. While not as widely read as the *Post-Gazette*, the *Tribune* is part of the community's mainstream media; and its coverage of the RRI was as critical as the *Gazette's* was fawning. Such unabashed opposition from the mainstream media was practically unheard of in other cities we have studied. In addition to its unprecedented media access, the Allegheny Institute generated dozens of position papers that were distributed to community leaders and made available on its user-friendly web site. Thus, even though Pittsburgh has a very strong local growth coalition (led by the Allegheny Conference), the Allegheny Institute (no relationship) emerged as a wild card that challenged the ability of stadium supporters to completely dominate public discussion of the RRI. An initiative supporter said,

> The day [we received state approval for the tax referendum], the opposition framed this as a stadium tax, and that's all you heard. For *x* number of days or weeks all you heard was that this was a stadium tax and the [other infrastructural items] were just a cover. A stadium tax, a stadium tax—they beat you over the head with it. It's a conspiracy. It's Richard Scaife, it's the *Trib*, it's the Allegheny Institute. It's [so easy] to just be negative. The *Trib* beat us up *every single day*. We were on every talk show; the talk shows beat us up. Even [the Pirates'] own flagship station beat us up.

Had stadium supporters in other cities faced such a well-financed and visible opposition, their referendums might have fared much differently. Contrast the power of the *Tribune* and the Allegheny Institute to the self-published *Point of View* newsletter (in Cleveland) and San Diego's atomized coffee house and Internet-based opposition. In the rare instances when local growth coalitions are unexpectedly confronted by formidable challenges, they seem inclined to focus on personalities and conspiracies rather than reexamine their central arguments. An executive in Pittsburgh said,

> I think it's a personal vendetta [by Scaife]. It's a combination of his politics and a personal vendetta. Because the *Post-Gazette* was for it, he was against it. There had to be three editorials a week against it. Letters to the editor three against for every one for it."

This unusual opposition to a stadium referendum was an important influence on the "wrong message" discussed previously. When the Allegheny Institute and the *Tribune* hammered away at specious economic development claims, RRI supporters were compelled to counter them. The situation is like spitting into the wind because economic development claims are so flimsy to start with: the more you talk about them, the more ridiculous they sound—and the wetter you get. Therefore, even if plan A supporters had wanted to stress intangible rewards such as community self-esteem, the Allegheny Institute's pressure constrained that possibility.

A Phoenix in Pittsburgh

In a last-ditch effort to build election-day support for the RRI, Mayor Tom Murphy unequivocally announced: if the referendum fails, there will be no plan B, and community members had better prepare for the inevitable departure of their beloved sports teams. The ultimatum failed to stir local voters; and on election day, RRI supporters mourned their devastating loss. Within hours, however, Mayor Murphy had a change of heart; the plan B working group hit the ground running. Rather than raising taxes, plan B would merely find ways to redirect existing taxes (often called revenue streams) to fund the new stadiums and the expanded convention center. Without new or increased taxes, plan B would not require voter approval.

In the eyes of stadium supporters, plan B was simple. The state of Pennsylvania had already pledged to pay roughly one-third of the costs of each new stadium (approximately $86 million for each $250 million stadium). The Pirates and the Steelers had agreed to contribute $35 million and $50 million respectively. This left approximately $209 million of needed local funding. The city of Pittsburgh and Allegheny County would issue bonds to cover this amount and make regular payments on them (about $26 million per year) by cleverly manipulating existing revenue streams, which included a ticket surcharge and a tax on stadium parking.[3] Most important, the plan B financing scheme called for redirecting a regional pool of tax revenues collected as part of the county sales tax. This tax/revenue stream is called the Regional Asset District (RAD) and, at the time plan B was being formulated, amounted to about $65 million per year. The money was directed toward local parks, museums, libraries, community cultural events, and a $10 million subsidy to Three Rivers Stadium.

Plan B called for diverting this $10 million subsidy and adding $3 million to $5 million of "new" RAD money each year to reach the targeted $26 million. Supporters insisted that the approach would not divert money from other regional assets because the RAD pool had been growing steadily over the past several years, reflecting a generally robust local economy. Therefore, they argued, there would be more money for everything, including the new stadiums and the convention center. Opponents of the financing scheme, however, refused to believe the robust local economy would last permanently:

> This is an old story. I think once the commitment [for the $3 million to $5 million] is made, if there isn't an increase in the pot, it will have to come from somewhere. And it will come from the smaller arts and cultural organizations right here in the communities, which help to operate community facilities that are accessible to people from grass-roots places. This plan will just move [RAD] resources out of the communities and into the downtown; to enjoy these monies, you will have to go to the stadiums or convention center.

When we asked plan B supporters what would happen if the RAD pool were to shrink during an economic slowdown, we never received a concrete answer. In fact, today the pool *is* shrinking; and some plan B critics are saying, "I told you so!" But the stadiums are open, and the words are falling on deaf ears.

New Messenger, New Message

Much of plan B's eventual success, whether intentional or not, was linked with substantive strategic changes (in addition to avoiding another referendum). There was a noticeable shift in the espoused justifications for the new stadiums as well as new public espousers. Plan B supporters started emphasizing community self-esteem and community collective conscience while downplaying promises of economic nirvana. These supporters were no longer corporate chieftains but local politicians and community dignitaries such as professional athletes. Promises of economic spin-off and corporate advocacy did not completely disappear, but Pittsburgh's powerful local growth coalition underwent a serious public makeover between plan A and plan B.

The less tangible justifications offered in Pittsburgh were no different from those offered in other cities that have used public dollars for private stadiums. One political advocate asserted,

> The teams are the city's identity. The Japanese know who Jaramir Jagr is; they don't know who Tom O'Brien is from PNC Bank. For better or for worse, [teams are] a national identity. When the Steelers are in the championship game, it is broadcast all over the world.

Mayor Murphy became one of the most visible spokespersons for the new emphasis on community self-esteem and community collective conscience (*Pittsburgh Post-Gazette*, April 7, 1999, A1; April 8, 1999, B1):

> These teams are a symbol of Pittsburgh. They're a symbol of moving forward or moving backward. Something is at stake far bigger than what they're worth financially. The larger value is being a major league city. It becomes a defining element. Pittsburgh is thought of as a major league town because of our sports teams even though we are the same size as Oklahoma City, Dayton, and Birmingham. Baseball is timeless. It can cut across economic, ethnic, and racial boundaries. It's a reflection of how society ought to work.

Representatives of the sports teams also began moving away from promises of stadium-generated economic development and toward stadium-generated community self-esteem:

> This [ballpark] represents a city that's moving forward. It's time that the rest of America knows that Pittsburgh is alive and well. When you have 113 years of tradition on your side, you can't quit. Look out—here comes Pittsburgh! (*Pittsburgh Post-Gazette*, April 7, 1999, A1)

This tactical shift in no way indicates a weakened local growth coalition; it was simply a strategic move designed to thwart opposition to plan B and increase the likelihood of securing public dollars for private stadiums. A Pirates' executive said,

> [The business community] just transferred the lead over to the mayor and county commissioners. Now we work behind the scenes. We meet to keep working out all the details. [The Allegheny Conference is] not as active in plan B as they were in the RRI; but I had breakfast with Rick Stafford last week, and I keep him apprised. And we will go back to them again, believe me.[4]

As a result of a shift in message and messenger, power politics became a more important element of ensuring plan B's success. One political supporter made it clear that much thinking had gone into designing a scheme in which meaningful opposition would be minimal. Obviously, the general public would not have a direct say over plan B. Neither would city council because none of the proposed revenue streams were under city jurisdiction. The RAD board members, who had to approve the revenue stream changes, were appointed by the mayor and the county commissioners. The commissioners were not initially a lock, but they eventually (although not unanimously) sup-

ported the plan. Other agencies, such as the local auditorium authority, were also led by people appointed by plan B supporters. As a team
executive told us, "we only need three signatures to get plan B done."
In his mind, this was much better than depending on the hundreds of
thousands of necessary supporters needed to pass plan A.

In both expected and unexpected ways, this strategic shift made
the Allegheny Institute for Public Policy irrelevant and ineffective. The
institute's ability to help shape public opinion (at least via voting) was
moot because plan B had circumvented public opinion. But even without this procedural issue, the Allegheny Institute's efforts to ridicule
plan B became more challenging after the theme shifted from economic development to community self-esteem. Even with a lot of
money and your own daily newspaper, it's hard to challenge notions
like community self-esteem, which are, after all, impossible to prove in
the first place.

The Twenty-sixth Pirate

Plan B's shift in message and messenger was embodied in one person:
Steve Leeper. Leeper was Mayor Murphy's director of economic development and the primary architect and catalyst of plan B. Unlike Bob
Bedinghaus in Cincinnati, who we argued was little more than a corporate front man, Leeper was acting somewhat independently of Pittsburgh's corporate community, although it clearly had the same goals.
After talking with him directly as well as hearing what others said about
him, we were convinced that Steve Leeper took this issue personally:
he's a Pirates' fan. A team executive recognized this stroke of luck:

> Leeper is a big [sports] fan, and that is a big advantage. You are not
> negotiating with an adversary. He really cares. When you go in to
> negotiate, and all you see on the walls is pictures of the Pirates, you
> feel better. If I had any choice who to deal with, it would be him.

A government official told us that he once joked at a meeting that
the community would be upset if the Steelers left, but nobody would
care if the Pirates left. Apparently, Leeper emphatically responded,
"Are you crazy?" An opponent of plan B also recognized Leeper's
contribution:

> This guy Leeper is a hugely talented person—Pittsburgh born,
> bred, and raised. He actually cares about the city. They are relying
> on him to pull this thing off. If he does pull this off, the city and
> county should name both stadiums after him. He's the genius. He's
> the one telling the mayor they can do [this creative financing], and
> then the mayor comes in front of [various community groups].[5]

It would be less than sociological of us to suggest that plan B's eventual success was rooted in one person. Our experiences in other cities indicate clearly that structural forces, regardless of the individuals involved, are generally amenable to using public dollars for private stadiums. But we do believe that plan B's road to success was less problematic because of Leeper's tireless and possibly brilliant advocacy.

Pittsburgh Revisited

Pittsburgh is a great place to live in the twenty-first century if you are a fan of using public dollars for private stadiums. As of this writing, the Pirates and the Steelers have both completed their first two seasons in PNC Park and Heinz Field. It would be pretty hard to conclude, however, that the stadiums had any consistent impact on the teams' performance. The Steelers made the playoffs in both those years, but they were also successful during the 1990s in antiquated Three Rivers Stadium. The Pirates, on the other hand, had two horrible seasons in their new ballpark, which is typical of their decline since the early 1990s.

The Steelers continue to sell out all their games. During their first year in PNC Park, the Pirates established a single-season attendance record (barely), averaging a little more than 30,000 fans per game; but the number of fans diminished in the course of the year as the team continued losing. Second-year attendance was disappointing, averaging just 22,600 fans per game for a 25 percent decline from the inaugural season. So far there seems to be little economic spin-off from the new stadiums, downtown or otherwise. In fact, downtown restaurant owners (including some in half-empty hotels) have asked the Pirates to move their night games from 7:00 to 7:30 to generate some dining business; but the team and Steve Leeper have refused to consider this request.[6] Perhaps now that the stadiums are finished, proponents are less worried about putting peoples' heads in beds—or in this case, seats in seats.

Despite complaints from restaurant owners, the teams are having no trouble cashing in on the new stadiums. Although Pittsburgh's public-private deals were not the most lucrative of those we've studied, the teams should not be complaining. Most of the "contributions" from the teams were covered without requiring the owners to dip into their savings accounts. For instance, the Pirates will collect $20 million from PNC Bank for naming rights, about $5.2 million from luxury-box sales, and almost $10 million from club-level seat-license fees. The Steelers will receive $57 million from Heinz for naming rights and at least $37 million for seat-licensing fees. In a sense, the team owners are paying nothing out of pocket and will accrue all stadium revenues.

They only have to provide regular upkeep and maintenance to the facilities, which are owned by the sports and exhibition authority (controlled jointly by the city and the county).

The regular revenues accruing to the teams also illustrate the subsidy of private bankrolls with public dollars. In 2001, the Pirates' gross revenues were significantly higher compared to the year before and almost five times higher than they were when current owner Kevin McClatchy bought the team in 1996. McClatchy gives PNC Park complete credit for this revenue explosion: "The fact is that for the first time we control the building" and all revenues generated by the ballpark (*Pittsburgh Post-Gazette*, September 21, 2001, B1).

For its part, the city also boasts of increased revenues from parking and ticket surcharges; but at last look, those revenues fell short of the predictions made when plan B was being sold. Even if this shortfall is true, however, advocates of public dollars for private stadiums in Pittsburgh will no doubt try to shift the focus to less tangible issues. So what if public revenues fall short of what was promised? Pittsburgh is exploding with community self-esteem and community collective conscience!

We don't doubt that the city was in a frenzied state of unity as the Steelers marched toward the Super Bowl. But this community collective conscience would have been the same if the games had been played in Three Rivers Stadium or an abandoned coal mine. It will be interesting to keep an eye on Pittsburgh over the next few years. The city, like many in the United States, has been suffering from an economic recession and a decrease in tourism both before and after the events of September 11, 2001. As this situation chips away at the RAD revenues, some groups or individuals may have to take it on the chin for the "successful" implementation of plan B.

PHILADELPHIA: GROWTH COALITION WANTED

There are really two stories in Philadelphia. One is about victory, the other about defeat—at least from the perspective of those favoring the use of public dollars for private stadiums. The victory is that there will soon be two new stadiums in Philadelphia largely financed with public dollars. The defeat is that there will be no *downtown* baseball field in Philadelphia, although that was clearly the first choice of many new stadium proponents, especially the Phillies themselves.[7] Instead, both new stadiums will be built at the site of the old Veterans Stadium, about four miles south of Center City near the other professional sports arenas. As of late 2002, the Eagles' football stadium was under construction, and the Phillies' baseball stadium was just breaking ground. An offshoot of this defeat is that the Philadelphia stadiums will take much longer to complete, and the teams will make a comparatively larger contribution. Indeed, almost two years passed between the time when Pennsylvania approved financing to when the city itself agreed on a funding plan, even without fully working out the lease details. And there wasn't even a public referendum to deal with!

Nuts and Bolts

Because the stadiums are unfinished, it's probably wise to treat their cost figures as highly volatile. Officially, the total project will cost $1.01 billion. The Phillies' stadium will supposedly open in April 2004 and cost about $350 million, while the Eagles' stadium will cost about $400 million. The remaining $250 million is for site development and capital reserves. The Eagles will also receive a new practice facility near the stadium, but it is unclear if that is included in these costs. The $1.01 billion total will be paid for using a mixture of private and public money. The plan, as approved in December 2000, was for the Eagles to contribute $310 million, the Phillies $172 million, the state of Pennsylvania $170 million, and the city $300 million plus another $90 million that will go specifically toward operating and maintaining the Eagles' stadium. The Eagles have already offset their share by selling the naming rights to Lincoln Financial Group for $139.6 million over twenty years. They will also offset their share by selling personal seat licenses. The teams will lease the stadiums for thirty years from the Philadelphia Industrial Development Corporation (PIDC), the city's economic development agency, and keep all revenues while the city and, to a lesser extent, the state only collect taxes on admission and concessions, as they have done at Veterans Stadium. Compared to Pittsburgh, then, Philadelphia's teams are being asked to cover a greater burden of the expense. For example, if costs remain constant, the Phillies are responsible for about half of their stadium's costs while the Pirates are responsible for only 20 percent.

The city was banking on increases in tax revenues (that is, tax-increment financing) to pay for its share of the stadium, much as Pittsburgh's stadium proponents were assuming that RAD tax revenues would increase. Estimates ranged from $159 million to $199 million more during the thirty-year lease. Philadelphia also raised the local rental-car tax (which includes airport rentals) with the hope of generating about $105 million during the same period. Even with these assumptions, however, when the plan was first approved by the mayor and city council in late 2000, it contained an acknowledged $54 million shortfall. The director of PIDC said there was no way the city would pay for any of this $54 million and claimed that, if nobody came up with the money, the parties would just walk away from the proposal. Just over a year later (March 2002), there was still an approximately $30 million shortfall, even with Pennsylvania throwing in another $10 million (citing balance between the cities) and the Delaware River Port Authority donating $14 million (claiming that its revenues would sky-rocket as people crossed the bridges from New Jersey to the new stadi-ums). The city did not walk away.

This $30 million shortage is very conservative because it takes the revenue projections at face value. A more critical assessment might challenge the validity of these soft economic predictions. What hap-pens if the revenue streams deliver less money than predicted? The most problematic stream is the tax-increment financing plan, which assumes increases in net stadium-tax revenues. In making this projec-tion, the city is assuming, among other things, that 3.3 million people per year will buy tickets to the new Phillies ballpark. That would reflect a 50 percent increase from the 2.2 million who have attended in an av-erage recent year. But attendance in Baltimore only increased 31 per-cent after Camden Yards opened, and that ballpark was the first of its kind (*Philadelphia Inquirer*, January 1, 2000, C1). Stadium proponents within city government have offered few answers; and several lawsuits have been filed or contemplated, including one by a member of city council.

There are many complex reasons explaining why the nuts and bolts of the Philadelphia deal are far less generous to the teams and took far longer to work out compared to the deal in Pittsburgh. First, there was a lot of arguing in Philadelphia about where the baseball sta-dium should be built. The Phillies' decision to pursue a downtown ball-park opened a Pandora's box of problems, which added significantly to the delays. Second, despite being five times more populous than Pitts-burgh, Philadelphia has a very weak local growth coalition rooted in a very weak corporate community. Third, political players and political arenas were much more central in Philadelphia than in Pittsburgh, even without a public referendum. Finally, unlike Pittsburgh, Philadel-phia does not readily lend itself to arguments about low community self-esteem and how new stadiums might assuage feelings of collective inferiority.

These four general factors are greatly interconnected. For exam-ple, the absence of a strong local growth coalition creates an environ-ment in which political processes play a much more prominent role in forging stadium deals. In this case, many city-sponsored forums dealt with the downtown ballpark. The very existence of those hearings, in addition to their substance, made it clear that downtown Philadelphia was far different from downtown Pittsburgh (not to mention other downtowns studied in this book). The Phillies' proposed ballpark was going to affect an upwardly mobile residential neighborhood, not a warehouse district or a sea of parking lots. Philadelphia is not just a nine-to-five city but a place where people live full time, and many things besides ballparks contribute to community self-esteem and community collective conscience. The new stadium-building process took longer in Philadelphia and was less generous to the team owners in Philadelphia because it *took place* in Philadelphia.

Location, Location, Location

In early 1998, before Pennsylvania's final decision to allocate money, the Phillies had already decided on a desirable downtown location for their new ballpark. Their preferred spot was at the intersection of Broad and Spring Garden streets on the northern fringe of the central business district. The team had even started developing architectural models and pictures of the new stadium at this location. The Phillies believed that a downtown ballpark would be best not just for the team but also for the city as a whole. The alleged benefits would be both economic and psychological (that is, community self-esteem). A team official told us,

> One study shows there would be a great benefit to building in Center City because of all the increased spending at restaurants. Hotels see their occupancy rates go up with a stadium. And the psychological impact: . . . if you look at Cleveland and Baltimore ten years ago, they were dying industrial Rust Belts, and now they are hot spots. People feel good.

But it quickly became clear that the path to Philadelphia's new stadiums (especially the baseball stadium) was going to be much different from the paths in Pittsburgh and most other cities. Beside the Phillies themselves, there were few other outspoken champions of the Spring Garden site. Indeed, one powerful local developer was publicly advocating building the stadium in another section of town. Other relatively powerful voices believed that it would be best for the stadium to stay in South Philadelphia. At times the Phillies seemed to be trying to convince the public *and* the politicians *and* the business community that the Spring Garden location was truly superior. San Diego was the only other city in this study in which location was a major issue, and we saw in chapter 6 how important that issue can be.[8]

Not only did the Phillies have an unusually solitary voice in supporting their downtown location, but also the location they selected was unusual in itself. All but one of the stadiums examined in this book have been built in mostly vacant, undeveloped urban areas. This was certainly the case in Pittsburgh. The Spring Garden neighborhood, however, was much different. Within just a few blocks of the proposed ballpark was a vibrant, middle-class neighborhood that had become slowly gentrified over the past decade. Many of the residents were professionals and decidedly not members of racial or ethnic minorities, quite unlike the citizens in the barrio near Bank One Ballpark in Phoenix.

With parking as the key issue, the composition of the grass-roots opposition became clear. Nothing could be more middle class, even in the city. Neighborhood groups commissioned expert studies showing that game-day parking would be a nightmare for residents. Others argued that emergency vehicles could not get to a local nursing home with 10,000 extra cars in the area. The Phillies spent countless hours and resources refining plans to ensure that most people would not drive to games (there was a subway stop adjacent to the site) and claiming that the few drivers would park in lots outside the neighborhood, where the team identified many thousands of spots (within 1.5 miles) available for night games.

Two public meetings were organized by the city council member whose district included Spring Garden. The turnout was enormous. Demographically, the audience was not representative of the city as a whole (which is 55 percent nonwhite), but it may have been representative of the Spring Garden neighborhood and other adjacent neighborhoods. The most tumultuous meeting was in August 1999—after Pennsylvania approved the money but more than a year before the city decided on a plan.

Phillies president David Montgomery offered the team's plan for protecting the neighborhood's parking integrity. Joining him was Bill Hankowsky, director of PIDC, who said that the city would help out in any way possible if the stadium were built at this location. The Phillies offered a video presentation highlighting all the advantages of the Spring Garden location and addressing the opposition's concerns. This presentation was in stark contrast to the San Diego Padres' city council production discussed in chapter 6. The Padres' show was very slick, teeming with the latest audiovisual doodads and promising that the new downtown stadium would change the course of humankind. The Phillies' show was like watching slides from a neighbor's European vacation. The presentation also offered a surprising show of support (although tempered) from representatives of the city government—surprising since we had been told by a local official that the city had reservations about the Spring Garden site because of potential costs and saw some advantages in building a new stadium in South Philadelphia. Possibly the city's apparent support reflected a change in position. But it may also have been Mayor Ed Rendell's way of gauging public opinion about the Spring Garden site.

Nevertheless, grass-roots resistance to the site continued to mount. In early 2000, just after John Street replaced Ed Rendell as mayor, the city suggested that the team should consider a different spot about a half-mile away, near Tenth and Vine streets. The area was mostly a warehouse district but also abutted the northern edge of Chinatown, yet another vibrant, nonpoor, residential, and commercial neighborhood. Within minutes of the announced plans, groups and individuals representing Chinatown residents and businesses spoke out against the idea. Once again, parking was a key issue. The neighborhood already has a shortage of available spots, so who needs another 10,000 cars around on game nights? Restaurant owners did not believe business would increase on game nights, only that spectators would take the spaces of regular customers. In addition, civic leaders cited the steady growth of the neighborhood and said that the proposed ballpark was located in the middle of where the neighborhood might expand.

There was also some official opposition to the downtown locations. First, several members of city council were not enamored with this or any downtown stadium plan. Some were reluctant to discuss a stadium-financing deal at all because the teams' current leases ran through 2011. Second, a powerful state senator, Vince Fumo, promised to oppose the Spring Garden location because building a stadium there might require eliminating the local state office building. Some analysts believed Fumo's position was rooted in his personal problems with Ed Rendell and later John Street. Others speculated that the senator was simply unconvinced of the need for a new downtown ballpark. In any case, his opinion had to be dealt with, which took up time.

The Phillies decided to cut their losses and head back to South Philadelphia. Clearly, the city had all but abandoned its support for the Spring Garden location, and the team was not particularly fond of the Chinatown plan. Much time had already been chewed up discussing location; and meanwhile, across the state, plan B had been implemented, with construction commencing. In Philadelphia, financing arrangements were barely on the table because so many of the monetary issues were site-specific. But even if the city and the team had formed a more unified alliance to promote either of these locations, it is doubtful they would have succeeded in building the stadium—partly due to the relatively more powerful residents of the desired location; partly because Center City Philadelphia, unlike Pittsburgh's central district, actually has residents. But problems went beyond the nature of the target neighborhood. Philadelphia's political economic landscape is much different from Pittsburgh's. Businesses work differently, politics work differently, and they interact differently with each other.

A Weak Local Growth Coalition

In relation to Pittsburgh, the financing and location delays in Philadelphia were greatly exacerbated by a weak local growth coalition. Unlike Pittsburgh, not to mention Cincinnati and Cleveland, Philadelphia is not a headquarters town. Even though it is the fifth-largest city in the United States, it is home to very few large corporations. The lack of corporate roots is especially true in the financial sector. There are currently no large commercial banks based in Philadelphia. As we mentioned in chapter 1, such banks are often the driving force within the corporate segment of the growth coalition. When First Union bought out Core States in the mid-1990s, it eliminated Philadelphia's last large, locally based commercial bank. But by then, Philadelphia's financial community was already moribund. A business leader explained,

> Pittsburgh is not run by steel [but] by large banks. Was Core States really a player in Philadelphia? Not really. You have to go back to the 1970s to find a strong banking presence in Philadelphia; all the way back to First Pennsylvania or [the Philadelphia Savings Fund Society]. To what extent does the [corporate community] still have dominant market share? In Philadelphia it does not.

Even though First Union quickly became the dominant bank in southeastern Pennsylvania (and put its name on the two local arenas), it did not dominate the local corporate community. Its headquarters and corporate soul remained in Charlotte, North Carolina. First Union recently merged with Wachovia Bank, which will soon put *its* name on the arenas. But Wachovia is based in Winston-Salem, North Carolina; and its presence will not affect the weak local growth coalition. The only local corporation that could lead and strengthen Philadelphia's growth coalition is Comcast, which has recently grown to be a cable-TV giant and is trying to become a digital subscriber line (DSL) power. In addition, it controls most of the parking at the current professional sports venues. Charles Pizzi, head of the local Chamber of Commerce told us,

> Frankly, the business community here is fragmented—geographi-
> cally, industry-wide, their interests. This is partly because 85 per-
> cent of the chamber members are family-owned businesses that
> play a much greater role in local business affairs than in other big
> cities. Cleveland and Cincinnati are all corporate towns, not family
> business towns. And the banks: . . . you can have one bank that is
> the financier of the Phillies and another that is the financier of the
> Eagles; you can have different law firms representing each team.
> It's only at certain rare times when [the business community] lines
> up properly and you can actually say, "Get it done."

The leader of a downtown business group agreed that Philadelphia has a less well organized and weaker corporate community spear-
heading the local growth coalition:

> Pittsburgh's [corporate leadership] dominates the city and the re-
> gion in a way that Philadelphia's does not. Many other cities are
> also driven by these downtown interests. . . . You can look at Char-
> lotte, which is a one-man town with Hugh McCall from Nations-
> Bank. In Phoenix, it's one man, this guy Jerry Colangelo, who runs
> the downtown. In Philadelphia, when there's a divisive issue, the
> [corporate community] kind of ducks down because they can't really
> do that much.

This assessment highlights many of the ideas we have been emphasizing throughout the book. The local growth coalitions in many cities
(such as Pittsburgh and Cincinnati) are spearheaded by large companies headquartered in that city. In Charlotte, Hugh McCall's power is
rooted in his affiliation with a large commercial bank, while Jerry
Colangelo's power in Phoenix is not anchored in his corporate membership.

Philadelphia's weak local growth coalition is reflected by its local
CEO-only group. Greater Philadelphia First (GPF) is the organizational equivalent to Pittsburgh's Allegheny Conference. They share a
basic group structure: twenty-five to thirty corporate executives pay a
significant fee to join each business roundtable. Their similarity, however, ends here. Unlike the Allegheny Conference, GPF does not pow-
erfully shape local public policy, although it does have an influence.
The executive director of GPF did not apologize for this difference:

> I'm prepared to say there is a difference in [corporate] cultures in
> the different cities. In Pittsburgh, the [corporate community] is dif-
> ferent. There are all sorts of ways that unfolds: culturally, politi-
> cally, and in the nature of business leadership. Or if you go to
> Detroit and look at the [CEO-only group] there, the third-largest
> company in that organization, Chrysler, has about $80 billion in
> revenues. Forget GM and Ford. If you total up *all* the GPF mem-

bers in terms of revenues, you're between $80 billion and $100 billion. So if Detroit needs $50 million, those three companies put it up to do something. Can it happen here? Not a chance. You want to beat up on these companies for that? Well, go ahead, but so what. They are what they are.

We are not implying that Philadelphia's business roundtable is better or worse than Pittsburgh's Allegheny Conference, only that the absence of a powerful CEO-only group greatly affects the dynamics of securing public dollars for private stadiums. A city official also noted this crucial difference:

> There is no parallel to the Allegheny Conference in Philadelphia. There is a history in Pittsburgh of the business community as a cluster of [large corporations]. The key is that these companies are active; and there's this entity, the Allegheny Conference, which gets them to the table to execute an agenda. Philadelphia does not have something comparable. The Chamber of Commerce has been around a long time, and ours is very good; but they are meant to cover the wide array of businesses. Greater Philadelphia First is only fifteen to twenty years old, and many of its large members are really not city-based but regionally-based.

Thus, Philadelphia's corporate community is not particularly powerful. Its almost nonexistent local growth coalition was unable to expedite the stadium deal and perhaps make it more beneficial to the Phillies and Eagles, nor could it influence support for a downtown baseball stadium.[9]

Who Needs Stadiums Anyway?

In addition to being organizationally weak, the corporate community did not include securing public dollars for private stadiums on its primary agenda. It turns out that other policy issues were more important to the business community. Its lack of interest was especially apparent in the Phillies' quest to build a new stadium in Center City. Businesses in Philadelphia, and the groups that represented them, had other priorities. The director of GPF acknowledged,

> [Stadium funding] is on our radar screen, but it is not seen as a priority. Our judgment is that it is an important public policy question; and when its time has come, it may be one of those issues we select to focus on. But our judgment is that its time has not come in this city. This doesn't mean that there aren't people interested and concerned. Certainly [the owners of the Phillies and Eagles] are very concerned.

Instead, Philadelphia's business community and its representative groups were much more concerned with improving public education in city schools. This concern went far beyond the rhetoric we heard from business and political leaders in other cities. In the late 1990s GPF's main public policy priority was improving public education in the Philadelphia public schools. The organization felt that improving public education, not building new sports stadiums, would have the greatest positive impact on the quality of life in the city.

This concern with public education was by no means rooted in pure humanitarianism but reflected the unique reality of the Philadelphia business community. In Pittsburgh, as in other headquarters cities such as Cleveland and Cincinnati, corporate leaders were clear that their most important business concern was recruiting the so-called A players of the corporate world. New stadiums were part of the social construction of community self-esteem, which would help these companies attract qualified mid- and upper-level executives. But Philadelphia is not a headquarters town, so its labor market needs are very different. Rather than requiring executives to staff the company headquarters, the Philadelphia business community needs lower-level workers who can perform nonmanagerial tasks. According to the chamber director,

> Public education. Business people in Philadelphia care about this because of their work force. The quality of the work force. We have a great work force here if you need college graduates. But if you have to get a high school graduate here, you're in a world of hurt. High-tech firms are feeling it to the extreme, but everybody is looking for qualified people today.

Clearly, the business community in Philadelphia is less interested in attracting the A-level executives and more interested in cultivating its own nonexecutive work force right in the city. GPF's director concurred:

> This region is increasingly dependent on the skills and knowledge of its work force. We will not succeed as a region if we don't have a more highly capable work force. Some businesses have said they have to move a major part of their company to another part of the country because they reject 98 percent of high school graduates here. And that's not just urban graduates. Boeing almost took 6,400 jobs from the city because they couldn't get adequate machinists. Our [labor market] is particularly deficient in postsecondary technical skills.

These are not the sorts of workers who will be buying luxury boxes at brand-new sports stadiums. In Pittsburgh, none of the business or political leaders we spoke with seemed very interested in these sorts of jobs. The only other city that raised a similar concern was Hartford, which also has a very weak local growth coalition. It seems, then, that the Philadelphia business community's concern with public education reflects the particular nature of that community. Who needs new stadiums if your labor force can't read or do simple math? A team executive recognized the dilemma of trying to build a new publicly funded stadium in center city:

> In other cities there have been leaders of the business community heading up the effort to build a new downtown stadium, speaking for how great this will be for the city. In Houston it was Enron, a power company. I'm not really sure why Enron, but usually some business leader steps up and champions the effort. But we have not had that yet. We have a zillion people saying they are behind it but no one has stepped up to say, "We have to make this happen for the city of Philadelphia."

The director of the chamber believed that business support for a new downtown stadium was maybe fifty-fifty, and at least one business leader thought it was ludicrous to even think about spending public dollars on private stadiums while the schools deteriorated:

> Why are [stadiums] being publicly subsidized? Why? There has never been any evidence that there is a financial payoff from stadiums. Perhaps it could be worth it after taking into account emotion, the self-worth of a city, but that has never been quantified. In so many places it seems to be [an important issue,] especially with the sports blabbermouths on radio. I mean if the value of these teams is so important to a community, then the league should not prohibit the public from buying the teams. I mean, if [the sports teams] have a right to extort public funds, then the public should have the same right as any other citizen to buy the teams.

This opinion would probably never emerge from a businessperson in a city with a powerful local growth coalition, either because he or she doesn't agree with it or because there would be severe ramifications for saying something like this out loud.

Filling the Power Vacuum

Philadelphia's weak corporate community never championed the two new stadiums that are now being built with much public money. Perhaps a stronger local growth coalition, anchored by a stronger corporate community, would have received a better deal (from the teams' perspective) and a quicker one—especially because no public referendum seemed to be needed. In the absence of corporate champions, the path to new stadiums in Philadelphia was blazed almost completely by political actors. The main ramification of the politically rooted pro-stadium movement is that it moves much more deliberately than a corporate-rooted movement does. The processes of representative democracy, even if they are not particularly democratic, are slower than the processes of the boardroom.

Many of the business and political leaders we spoke with agreed on one thing: Philadelphia has a very centralized, strong mayoral form of local government and usually has a personally strong mayor in the position. This was certainly true of Ed Rendell, who was mayor from 1992 to 2000. In terms of new stadiums, Rendell called the shots. There was little doubt that he personally championed a new downtown baseball stadium. He was as much a Phillies' fan as Steve Leeper was a Pirates' fan. Clearly, the Phillies were banking on the mayor's leadership because they knew it would not come from the business community. But as mayor, Rendell seemed hesitant to go to bat for such a problematic project. A local official said,

> This was on the radar screen in the third or fourth year of [Rendell's] first term. At the beginning of his second term he basically thought he could decide to ignore this. The teams' leases did not expire under his term. The leases are enforceable. But he also thought it was a tough question and that the next mayor will have a tough time facing this and might be in a relatively weak bargaining position. So the mayor wanted to think about this without necessarily knowing what the answers would be.

This was bad news for the Phillies. Ed Rendell called the shots in Philadelphia, but he wasn't calling this one. One political official in Philadelphia told us,

> Mayor Rendell is a totally different story. [Mayor] Murphy is not that strong in Pittsburgh. Everything goes through Rendell; no one goes around him. He's the leader. If I say a downtown stadium is a good thing, he might pick up the phone and tell me to shut my mouth. Nobody could put this mayor in a box and force him to do something. It is the mayor's agenda under whatever formula he comes up with. The only person to establish the priorities is Ed Rendell. If there's going to be a downtown ballpark, it's going to be Ed Rendell who pushes it.

The combination of a weak business community and a strong mayoral system with a reluctant mayor was not conducive to rapidly securing public dollars for private stadiums, especially not one in Center City. In fact, not until John Street became mayor in 2000 did the stadium deals really start to pick up steam.

John Street is another strong mayor in a strong mayoral city government. He was the powerful president of Philadelphia's city council from 1992 to 2000 and was a council member for twelve years before that. Except for Rendell, he is by far the most powerful politician in Philadelphia (although Vince Fumo might disagree). Under Street's leadership, the financing bill began its successful, if bumpy, journey through city council. Ultimately, there may be political ramifications because of the stadium deal, but so far Mayor Street doesn't seem to care very much:

> Mayors don't always get what they want. . . . I'm going to see what we need, and then we'll go get what we need. You hear me? We go get what we need. People scoff at me. I say I walk by faith and not by sight. (*Philadelphia Inquirer,* November 14, 2001, 5; *Philadelphia Inquirer,* November 14, 2000, A1)

It would have been interesting to watch Mayor Street (or Mayor Rendell) advocate for the stadium deal if it had required some general public approval. What strategy would he have taken? We believe that either mayor would have emphasized economic development rather than community self-esteem and community collective conscience. Indeed, we heard pieces of this argument from the new stadiums' political supporters and from the teams. This, as we have seen throughout the book, is an increasingly ineffective strategy for convincing people to support the idea of using public dollars for private stadiums. It proved to be *very* ineffective when the Phillies were pushing their preferred downtown locations. Why didn't Philadelphia's stadium advocates follow the lead of other cities and stress noneconomic advantages?

Yo, We Got Your Esteem

As we argued in chapter 2, Philadelphia is one of those cities in which it's hard to link community self-esteem with new sports stadiums. Philadelphia already has community self-esteem. People who live and work there are not susceptible to arguments that the city is about to become another Harrisburg or another Wilmington. One local official who did support the downtown stadium recognized the challenge of such an argument:

> If [the team owners] stand on a street corner and threaten to move the teams from Philadelphia, the people of Philadelphia

will say, "Fuck you, move the teams. Move." Whether they mean it or not.

This made it very difficult to link the new stadiums, especially a new downtown stadium, with enhanced community self-esteem. Most of the political and business leaders we spoke with agreed that Philadelphia was a vibrant urban area that was not on the brink of becoming a second-class city, even if it lost a professional team:

> We have so many things going on but without the concentration of New York and Los Angeles. We have so many different things, such [a great] quality of life. Philadelphia is fundamentally a more healthy city than Pittsburgh. It has a more vibrant downtown than Pittsburgh. This is considered one of the top restaurant cities in America. We don't need a stadium to have restaurants in downtown Philadelphia.

Unable to make convincing arguments about how new stadiums would save Philadelphia from, well, becoming another Pittsburgh, supporters had little recourse but to stress the tangible economic benefits that would be generated by spending public dollars on private stadiums. Not only was that argument problematic to start with, but the local growth coalition—such that it was—had no party line on the issue. In fact, most (but not all) business and political leaders we spoke with were at least somewhat skeptical about these alleged economic benefits:

> I believe there is an incremental additional expense to a downtown site. It will be more expensive, *and* you will have to build parking, *and* it has to be garages. Two thousand spaces is $20 million; 4,000 is $40 million. I don't agree with the Arthur Anderson study that [a downtown ballpark] would be better. . . .[10] [Stadium-like] projects are not going to create tons of money for everybody. People who think they are, it's not true. Go back to the convention center. There's not a ton of money there. We still have the debt service, so dollar-for-dollar it still loses money. . . . If I was trading off-limited [public] dollars, I would love to have a stadium in Center City; but it's not the end of the universe if it stays in South Philadelphia. It's cheaper and easier to put cafés and restaurants on the Benjamin Franklin Parkway and capture those visitors and those dollars than by moving the baseball team there.

These are remarkable statements coming from people who are at least nominal members of the local growth coalition. In Pittsburgh, it was much less likely for people in those positions to have said those things—just one more important reason why Philadelphia's path to publicly funded stadiums was very different from Pittsburgh's.

ONE STATE, TWO CITIES

While Pennsylvania gave the same support to new stadiums in both Pittsburgh and Philadelphia, the cities' paths to those stadiums could not have been more different. Despite a population of about 350,000, Pittsburgh has a very powerful local growth coalition anchored by a commanding corporate presence. This coalition was heavily involved in conceptualizing and orchestrating the city's stadium initiative, with local politicians basically along for the ride. The coalition seemed to learn, albeit through some serious setbacks, that it should keep a modest profile (allowing room for political champions) so it would not be easily accused of using public money for its own private gain. The coalition also learned from its plan A defeat to stress the nontangible benefits of new stadiums rather than the promise of an economic windfall. The social characteristics of Pittsburgh lent themselves beautifully to this strategy. For example, the city's rapid deindustrialization, the resulting population decline, and the lack of a vibrant residential downtown created an atmosphere in which the growth coalition could easily manipulate community self-esteem. By strategically emphasizing the links between new stadiums and community self-esteem, the growth coalition managed to overcome the unusual opposition of one of the city's mainstream newspapers.

On the other hand, Philadelphia, with more than 1 million residents, has an almost nonexistent local growth coalition that basically left the Phillies all alone in supporting their downtown stadium plan and greatly slowed the procurement of public dollars. As we have shown, when the sports teams are forced to be out front promoting public dollars for private stadiums, they are easily portrayed as rich owners asking for a handout.

The strategic shift from promoting new stadiums as economic generators to promoting them as enhancers of community self-esteem did not work in Philadelphia as it did in Pittsburgh. With a vibrant downtown, filled with both residences and businesses, Philadelphia's social character did not lend itself to this manipulation. When the team advocated for a new downtown stadium, it fomented local residents' beliefs that their middle-class quality of life would be hurt, not helped, by the team's presence. The battle over the site, irrelevant in Pittsburgh, led to enormous delays.

The weak corporate community in Philadelphia, combined with the inability to manipulate community self-esteem, increased the importance of the political arena in the stadium battle. And once the battle moved to a public venue, the process slowed down as the trappings of procedural democracy took hold. In this more open arena, residents at least had a voice; and even if it was eventually ignored, it still had to be listened to. This took time. The lesson here is that a more open process to securing public dollars for private stadiums may mean that subsidy advocates don't get everything they want as quickly as they want. But they still get the core of what they want: a private stadium built largely with public dollars.

8

Public Dollars, Private Stadiums, and Democracy

The processes by which local growth coalitions and their proxies have secured public dollars for stadiums raise important questions about our democratic institutions. We believe we have made a strong case for the fact that, when it comes to using public dollars for private stadiums, there isn't much democracy going on in U.S. cities. As we mentioned in the introduction of this book, such threats to nominally democratic institutions are what interested us in this topic in the first place. The recent trend of publicly subsidized sports stadiums may exacerbate the already exorbitant and unjustifiable social inequalities in the United States, especially in its cities. In this concluding chapter, we will discuss how and why these new stadium battles are emblematic of larger political and social issues in our society and why we should all take these battles (and their ramifications) seriously.

WHERE'S THE DEMOCRACY?

Overall, the process of building private stadiums with public dollars in the United States is more akin to plutocracy and oligarchy than to democracy. Here, we include both a procedural definition of democracy (in which everyone affected by policy decisions has a meaningful say in making them) and a substantive definition (in which policy decisions reflect the real interests of affected parties without those interests being manipulated).[1] Sometimes the anti-democratic processes are blatant and unmistakable, sometimes they are more subtle, and sometimes they are obfuscated by the workings of normal politics. Residents in and around Pittsburgh and Phoenix were crystal clear about not wanting to spend public dollars on private stadiums. But in both cases, powerful stadium advocates simply trampled on public sentiment and built the stadiums anyway. When a city official in Pittsburgh told us that, given the fate of plan A, there would be no vote on plan B because "we thought this through long and hard," we were amazed: less that this could happen but more that he was clearly so comfortable with the idea. We were equally shocked to learn that the Arizona state government and the Maricopa County board of supervisors deliberately ignored local residents and established a sales tax to fund Bank One Ballpark. We were shocked less by these events themselves than by how easy it seemed to pull them off and how people in and around Phoenix continued to believe that they lived in a democratic society.

Sometimes the threats to democracy are more subtle, although still obvious if you look in the right places. In Philadelphia, for instance, there was no need to blatantly trample on popular sentiment because the public was never given any say on the matter except indirectly through city council and state representatives. When a Pennsylvania state representative explained to us the inner workings of the legislature, it seemed to have little in common with democracy as we conventionally define it. He explained exactly how Pennsylvania decided to put up two-thirds of the money for the four new stadiums in Pittsburgh and Philadelphia:

> Ninety-five percent of the calls we get on this issue are against it.
> . . . For dynamic issues like these that are wildly unpopular, the legislative leaders decide it will happen; and then they decide how many votes each side [Republican and Democratic] will give up and which representatives are least vulnerable—so they don't get taken out [for voting for something so unpopular].

This representative was clear that, even though Pennsylvania residents were overwhelmingly opposed to using public dollars for the four new stadiums, the legislative leadership did it anyway. The leaders selected which representatives would vote for the "wildly unpopular" issue by determining who was in a safe district and would thus be insulated from voter backlash. So, for example, a Democrat in a district that is 90 percent Democratic is cajoled into voting for the unpopular issue because she or he will be unlikely to lose reelection. Of course, that Democrat will not vote "correctly" without some serious horse trading. When we interviewed the representative just quoted a few months before the final vote, he predicted, "I would bet this [funding for new stadiums] will happen because most members have their price" in terms of pet projects (such as, acquiring park land or resurfacing bridges), which others will vote for in exchange for supporting the stadium issue. It turns out he was correct.

In fact, we were told that one of the big inside fights on this issue concerned the fact that Republicans wanted to provide fewer than half of the total *yes* votes needed to pass the stadium bill. The Democratic leadership, however, argued that because Republican governor Tom Ridge wanted the bill so badly, the Republicans should give up more than half of the votes. The Republican leadership countered that because the stadiums would benefit the two largest cities in Pennsylvania, which are largely Democratic, the Democrats should give up more than half of the votes. All of this finagling may not surprise a cynical observer, but it is not exactly what you read about democracy in a high school civics text.

While such blatant and clandestine power plays pose clear threats to democratic institutions, we think there are even more sinister threats within the everyday political process. Here, the trappings of democratic procedure often mask very undemocratic social policies. The best ongoing examples are the referendums that seem to indicate community support for new publicly subsidized stadiums, apparently demonstrating that policies allocating public dollars for private stadiums reflect popular sentiment. But this belief assumes that the referendum process is balanced and fair—that all interested parties have an equal opportunity to influence public policy.

As we have shown throughout this book, referendum campaigns are anything but fair arenas for hashing out the advantages and disadvantages of using public dollars for new stadiums. Subsidy advocates have much more power in the referendum process than do stadium opponents. At the most basic level, advocates directly outspend opponents by at least ten to one and sometimes, as in San Diego, by much more. These powerful individuals and organizations also have far superior "unofficial access" to decision makers than do average citizens—access that often occurs in stadium luxury boxes! We heard a story in Pittsburgh about a city council member who spent Sundays at Three Rivers Stadium, not watching the Steelers but keeping track of who was meeting whom in the corporate boxes. In this way, the council member knew what was going on behind the scenes when certain people or companies tried to influence city policy.

In addition to these obvious advantages in the referendum process, stadium advocates also have a third-dimensional advantage: citizens grant more legitimacy to powerful people (the so-called experts) than to average people such as themselves, especially when it come to complex issues like stimulating economic growth. This advantage is paralleled by a political system that also grants much more legitimacy to the opinions of powerful individuals and organizations than to more ordinary ones. In a sense, then, stadium supporters rarely have to fight city hall to achieve their goals. With important exceptions, the default position among many political elites is to equate new stadiums with economic growth or heightened community self-esteem. Subsidy opponents have to convince politicians *not* to believe what they have already been conditioned to believe.

WHY GROWTH COALITIONS?

We have argued throughout the book that unraveling these stadium battles is best accomplished by examining the structure of each city's local growth coalition (or its proxy) and the strategies these coalitions use to build private stadiums with public dollars. As we have shown, the strength and unity of the growth coalition shapes the stadium battles in American cities. Both the structure of growth coalitions and the decisions they make are deeply embedded in the unique social characteristics of each city. Some combinations of structure, decisions, and social characteristics carve out relatively uncomplicated paths to publicly subsidized stadiums, while other combinations create many more challenges. Either way, no route is a shining testament to democracy in action.

We have built our analytical framework around growth coalition theory because it allows us to identify some of the covert threats to democratic institutions. We believe these threats are not just sporadic and temporary breakdowns of a fair, self-regulating system but are embedded in the workings of the system itself. Most academic and nonacademic studies of new sports stadiums, good as they usually are, miss an important part of the story because they focus only on the most obvious public-policy players: the politicians and the sports teams. But guided by our search for local growth coalitions, we have discovered a world of less discernible players; and they have tremendous power over the policies allocating public dollars for private stadiums. Like more public players, these individuals and organizations stand to gain from new stadiums, but in less noticeable ways. Because growth coalitions can be so powerful, because they are largely invisible, and because they are mostly unaccountable to other social actors, we think it is imperative to understand how they are involved in the battles over new stadiums and how this involvement poses an especially insidious threat to a democratic society.

This point has not been emphasized enough, even in critical discussions of sports-stadium funding. Instead, conversations on the issue generally take a corporate welfare approach, castigating wealthy team owners who ask for handouts and local governments that universally grant these requests. But team owners are acting in the way that team owners are *supposed* to act; so the brunt of criticism, from the corporate-welfare perspective, ends up being aimed at the spineless politicians who sell out the rest of the community for a private seat in the owner's luxury box or a future campaign contribution. In contrast, our growth coalition approach insists that we must also look at the large nonsports corporations in a community (with multibillion-dollar gross revenues) rather than just the teams themselves (with gross revenues close to $100 million) in assessing who might benefit from the public financing of new stadiums.

These corporations are far more powerful than any local sports team; and their influence over the policymaking process may be ideological (that is, third-dimensional), not just a matter of throwing their money around or threatening to take their huge companies elsewhere. Local politicians "naturally" turn to the leaders of corporations for advice on important matters. Executives are invited to sit on economic development task forces and be part of municipal stadium authorities. If these successful business leaders, who are also involved with local philanthropic organizations, think that publicly financed stadiums are good for the local community, then why should policymakers (or the general community) think otherwise? Thus, corporations' particular parochial vision of suitable growth strategies comes to rule the day. Too often, however, this vision is not portrayed as particular, parochial, or self-interested but as civic-minded and altruistic. In this regard, nonsports corporations can more easily than sports teams conceal their organizational self-interest and maintain that community welfare is driving their interest in new publicly funded stadiums—if anyone even knows they are interested in the matter.[2]

The Corporate Arm of the Growth Coalition

Why do the corporate members of a growth coalition want new stadiums? We found that business leaders (sometimes including team owners) were more likely than politicians to promise social rewards from new stadiums, such as increased civic pride or a closer-knit community. While politicians talked more of economic activity to justify opening the public coffers, business leaders knew very well that there were better ways to create jobs than by subsidizing a huge stadium that operates either eighty-one days per year (baseball) or ten days per year (football). Thus, when we interviewed growth coalition leaders about their advocacy of public dollars for private stadiums, they talked about "wearing their civic hat" rather than stimulating economic growth. But this attitude only begs the question, Why promote sports stadiums rather than any other type of civic good? What underlies corporate executives' interest in advocating public dollars for private stadiums?

We think a number of factors have led corporate elites to favor building new stadiums. First, corporations want to be able to use stadiums—especially their luxury boxes—and the aura surrounding professional sports to attract new executive talent. Many of the corporate executives we talked with spoke about the challenges they faced recruiting top talent to their city. This is a particularly strong sentiment in small cities with little allure for graduates from top law schools and business schools. Business leaders in Cleveland and Cincinnati told us that, when competing with firms in New York and San Francisco, the new stadiums gave them something to show off. We can't help but wonder whether a gender bias exists here. Of course, women can be interested in professional sports. But in all our conversations with executives about recruiting A-level talent, they always seemed to be talking about men. Although we aren't even sure whether A-level talent cares all that much about stadium luxury boxes, clearly the "real truth" doesn't matter. As long as current executives believe that future executives will care, they continue to treat new stadiums as part of their recruitment effort. And why not have the local government subsidize this particular recruitment tool?

We speculate that the growth coalitions in larger, more exciting cities have less success in emphasizing new sports stadiums as an executive recruitment tool. Places such as New York, San Francisco, Boston, Philadelphia, and Los Angeles have so many other amenities that they don't really need (or think they need) new sports stadiums to attract the A players. This is one reason why there has been little, or only very deliberate, progress toward new publicly financed stadiums in these cities. Simply put, in the minds of the local growth coalitions of midsized cities, the consequences are severe if they don't get a new ballpark. Therefore, getting a stadium is high on their agendas.

The recruitment effort put forth by local growth coalitions is also linked with the larger notion of community self-esteem. Many corporate executives desire an image of a city on the move. Cities such as Cleveland and Hartford, for example, seem to radiate negative impressions to the surrounding world. They are looked upon as decaying urban holes with declining and increasingly impoverished populations. Again, these images may be exaggerated far beyond empirical reality. But as long as the local growth coalition *believes* this is the projected image, corporate leaders will do tangible things to address it. Thus, members may see a flurry of new stadium construction as a visible and relatively fast way to counter the image of a city in decline. In hindsight, it seems to have been at least a moderately effective strategy. Outsiders are now more inclined to talk about turnarounds in places such as Cleveland and Baltimore, having absolutely no evidence except the presence of new stadiums and the growth coalition's constant reiteration that things have turned around.

It is also important to note that some corporate executives are simply big sports fans. They enjoy professional sports and want to be associated with building a new sports palace. Wearing their civic hats, executives will find it a lot harder to improve the test scores of inner-city schools (although a few do gallantly try) than to build a new stadium. Most want a visible monument to their efforts, and the stadium can serve that purpose. If you are a big-time sports fan, what better way to show your civic pride than to help give the team a new place to play and the community a new place to watch games? It would be grander still if you could manage to have the new stadium named after your company.

Today, many postindustrial cities in the United States are filled with hollow corporations: companies that split their administration from their production, the former staying in the home city and the latter moving elsewhere in the United States or even offshore. Thus, when we say that a firm's headquarters are located in a city, often this simply means that the company employs several hundred, or at most a few thousand, top managerial and administrative staff who work in the city. The production workers have left town—or perhaps more accurately, their jobs have left town—leaving only very low-wage workers who provide support services for executives. The result is a polarized social-class dynamic: cities have very well paid and very poorly paid workers on either end, with fewer people in the middle. The two polarized groups have very different stakes in the city itself. For the high-paid members of the local growth coalition, the city is a transient station for work and play before returning home to suburbia or moving on to their next outpost in another city. Their urban priorities include good roads or commuter rails, decent restaurants, and cultural diversions, which might include new sports stadiums with plenty of available parking. For minimum-wage workers, the city is usually a permanent place to work and live. Their urban priorities are more likely to include good schools, reliable buses, safe neighborhoods, clean streets and playgrounds, and decent grocery stores. Given the recent wave of using public dollars for private stadiums, it seems clear that the needs of the growth coalition are winning out over the needs of poorer urban residents.

This disparity was illustrated for us by a Cleveland business leader, who said that, among many of the top corporations in the city, *no* employee had ever been directly exposed to the Cleveland public schools. This astounding statement would not have been made fifty years ago, when these companies still had relatively well paid production workers living in Cleveland. Gone are the Fisher Body Division workers from the Euclid plant (which closed for good in 1993) as well as members of the United Steel Workers, whose Cleveland-area membership dropped from 47,000 in 1980 to slightly more than 20,000 in 1990. Urban neighborhoods, which were built around such factories, increasingly face economic and social decay when the facility leaves town. This reduces the overall tax base and puts even more strain on the public sector to maintain services (such as schools) and deal with the fallout (such as crime) from deindustrialization. Unfortunately, in cities like Cleveland, the powerful local growth coalition and its political champions have been subsidizing new stadiums rather than decent housing, further exacerbating the metamorphosis of the city into a playground for suburbanites.

The frontier cities have very different development histories. Here, suburbanization was a major factor from the beginning rather than a threat to an older urban tradition. Thus, the frontier cities have a power structure with less entrenched political expertise and a wider field for stadium battles to play out. The population explosion in these cities sometimes mitigates the issue of fighting over a shrinking pie, which is so common in Rust Belt cities. At the same time, however, citizens in frontier cities opposed to the particular growth strategies of subsidized stadiums often find few political champions with either the will or the political acumen to take up their cause.

The Political Arm of the Growth Coalition

Clearly, the corporate arm of the local growth coalition has reasons to be interested in new publicly funded sports stadiums and has the power to help turn this interest into reality. Ultimately, however, local government is still responsible for the actual policies that will direct public dollars to private stadiums. As a result, local governments become important components of coalitions. In cities with weak or absent corporate communities, the local government often (but not always) takes the lead on new stadium projects. Why do some governors, mayors, and other political leaders want stadiums if they are increasingly unpopular? Why do they risk their political lives on this issue?

As we have suggested throughout the book, the coalition between local government and the corporate community can take different forms. One form, which we refer to as second-dimensional power, occurs when the corporations capture and control policymakers through campaign contributions, relocation threats, membership on key task forces, or other overt types of influence. The other form, which we call third-dimensional power, occurs when policymakers "naturally" see a convergence between corporate interests and the overall community's interests without the application of any overt influence. These two types of relationships are by no means mutually exclusive, and it is not particularly important which type of power prevails. We saw them overlap in Cleveland through the relationship between the mayor's office and Cleveland Tomorrow. The business group had produced an economic blueprint for the city, which the mayor completely supported. This alignment seemed predictable enough because the executive director of Cleveland Tomorrow at the time had previously been the mayor's chief assistant for economic development, illustrating what some have called a "circulation of elites." But the fact that the new mayoral assistant (who replaced the person now directing CT) also completely agreed with this blueprint suggests that the convergence of corporate and government interests is more than just a personal matter. Whatever the case, alternatives to the corporate vision of local economic growth are not seriously considered.

This more systemic bias is reflected by politicians who genuinely believe that, for their city to survive, they need to transform it into a tourist destination—and they are betting on stadiums to do the job. Particularly in cities that have experienced substantial decline, politicians may be understandably desperate to hold on to businesses and residents. Professional sports and, in particular, new stadiums are seen as a highly visible way to indicate that a city is still powerful and important. But when politicians make these choices and place huge monetary bets on them, they neglect other urban needs. Cleveland was once a well-known manufacturer of basic durable goods. In fact, its pattern of industry originally attracted many of the corporations that subsequently located their headquarters there. With this history in mind, Norman Krumholz, a professor of urban studies at Cleveland State University and a former planning official in the city, is critical of the new civic tourism strategy:

> We haven't spent money on tool-and-die, metal bending, or steel, or certainly not comparable to the money we are spending reforming our image. It's at least worth a guess whether if we spent this kind of money on less spectacular but basic things, whether we'd put more of our industries back to work in jobs that people of this city could do.

You could, of course, argue that less visible factors are more important to the vibrancy of a city. For example, we were told by business leaders in several cities that the office sector would benefit most from improvements that were not stadium-related: enhancing Internet infrastructure, nurturing small business development through seed money, improving education beyond the most basic skills, and developing reliable and affordable mass transit. These kinds of improvements, however, are far less sexy, far less visible, and therefore far less attractive to politicians. You often see politicians holding a shovel during a stadium groundbreaking or throwing out the first pitch on opening day. But how many politicians are photographed sitting in the driver's seat and opening the doors on one of the city's brand-new low-pollution buses? Perhaps it is naïve to ask them to choose bread over circuses, but the question is still worth asking.

Some politicians fear threats (direct, implied, or imagined) that a sports team might leave town on their watch. Professional sports truly are different from any other kind of business because much more attention and emotion are attached to the home team. If a nonsports business that employed 150 people left town, hardly anyone would notice. But if that business were a professional sports team, thousands of hours of talk radio, hundreds of pages of print media, and millions of e-mail messages would be devoted to the news. Some politicians must also believe that they can contain the anger of citizens who are opposed to publicly financed stadiums, although many mentioned that they tried to schedule tax referendums as far away as possible from their own reelections. Some, too, believe that they just know better than the opponents of public funding, dismissing them, during several of our interviews, as "naïve," "nay sayers," "CANEs" (Citizens against Nearly Everything), or "crazed Naderite types," among even unkinder names.

In cities with a strong local growth coalition, elected leaders are better able to take a low profile in stadium initiatives, although, like Bob Bedinghaus in Cincinnati, they may choose not to. Politicians offer to serve as watchdogs over the political process, while the local growth coalition exercises its power behind the scenes. Conversely, in cities with weak or fractured growth coalitions, the teams or the politicians are forced to take the lead. This is much more problematic: if the teams are taking the lead, they are accused of holding the city hostage for a handout; if local government takes the lead, the entire process assumes the messy trappings of procedural democracy such as public hearings and rancorous city council meetings. These situations can sometimes derail a stadium initiative or at least slow it down, as in San Diego, Philadelphia, and Minneapolis. They usually also result in making the teams pay for a larger share of the new stadium. We aren't claiming that some cities are more democratic than others. But in cities with weaker growth coalitions, politicians often have trouble avoiding grass-roots input.

The Media Arm of the Growth Coalition

In every city we studied, the main local newspaper editorially favored using public dollars for private stadiums. Fortunately, this editorial bias rarely interfered with a relatively fair reporting of the stadium initiatives, and journalists and columnists often wrote scathing and embarrassing stories about the stadium-building process. In Minneapolis, for example, local newspaper publishers have historically played a central role in coordinating the local growth coalition, bringing together its political and corporate arms around a vision of how the city should define and pursue economic growth. John Cowles, Jr., assumed this role for many years, and his absence today is one of the reasons that the Minneapolis growth coalition is so fractured. When John Schueler tried to take on the task, his reporters roundly attacked him; and he backed off. Schueler was relatively new to the city, coming from the McClatchey group of newspapers, and perhaps did not have enough local ties to fill the role vacated by the powerful Cowles. A similar skirmish took place between the publisher and the journalists at the *Cincinnati Enquirer*. The powerful local growth coalition made it clear to the paper's owners and editors that it did not appreciate frequent negative stories about the stadium initiative. One business leader in San Diego told us a story in which a media executive was demanding that the San Diego Taxpayers Association not go public with its reservations about Proposition C. Instead, he urged the group to keep its concerns inside a task force on which they both served. The person we spoke with found it ironic (and maybe a little scary) that a newspaper publisher was suggesting that information be kept from the public.

Publishers and high-level editors, then, often seem to share the same ideologies and visions as the local growth coalition. This may be due in part to their sense that they know better than the masses. It may also be due to the fact that, as newspaper companies come to be part of larger media conglomerates, they are increasingly indistinguishable from the corporate arm of the growth coalition. High-level editors frequently rub elbows with growth coalition members and come to share a vision of what is needed for correct growth. Only in Pittsburgh did we find a maverick newspaper publisher with a strong set of libertarian beliefs who promoted significant media criticism from the top of the company. As we discussed in chapter 7, the opposition of the *Tribune* (and the Allegheny Institute for Public Policy) was a significant irritant to the growth coalition's plans to acquire public dollars for private stadiums. If more cities had competing mainstream media voices, their stadium initiatives might have taken much different paths.

WHAT IS A MAJOR LEAGUE CITY ANYWAY?

During our interviews, we repeatedly encountered the socially constructed notion that professional sports teams are a necessary condition of being a major league city. The more teams you have (taking population into account), the more major league you are. In some ways, we understand that having sports teams gives a city the stamp of authenticity by providing publicity and media exposure. Stadium advocates have taken this idea, however, and manipulated it to extract maximum public financing. They argue that, without a new stadium like those popping up in other places, their city will quickly become second-rate. Its fall from grace will be even faster and more embarrassing if the sports team actually leaves town. Increasingly, however, there is no actual threat that a team will leave without a new stadium (although the threats are still occasionally verbalized). And often the team owners aren't even the ones making this argument; rather, the corporate and political arm of the local growth coalition is making the claim. Policymakers, it seems, have internalized the assumption that "a new stadium" equals "the team stays" (or "a new one comes") equals "our city is first-rate."

Ironically, those cities with other sources of community self-esteem are more immune to this kind of manipulation. Rarely do pro-subsidy advocates in New York, Los Angeles, Philadelphia, or San Francisco claim that the city will cease being major league without a new sports stadium. The reason is obvious: these cities do not need the imprimatur of a sports team to make them major league in their own eyes or the eyes of the world. They have a diverse economy, vibrant downtowns open after bankers' hours, and great restaurants. Can you imagine somebody saying, "Without new stadiums, New York will be just another Hoboken with tall buildings," or "San Francisco will only be Sacramento with a bay view"? Los Angeles lost its NFL team in the 1990s because the city refused to build a new publicly financed stadium. At last look, L.A. had not become second- or third-rate.[3]

San Francisco, in fact, is a great example of how the manipulation of community self-esteem is ineffective in cities that are already first-rate. The new Pacific Bell Ballpark opened in 2000 and has been touted as the only privately financed ballpark among the recent wave of new stadiums. While this claim is an exaggeration, as we will explain, it is true that the public share of the stadium is significantly below average.

Although some view the Giants as magnanimous in not asking for handouts, this perception misreads the history. The Giants got fewer public dollars to be sure, but not for lack of trying! The new stadium went to public votes four separate times and lost each referendum. The team wandered around the Bay Area looking for some municipality to pay for their new ballpark and failed each time. Finally, the team's most recent ownership group, headed by Peter Magowan, decided to build a stadium largely with private financing. The Giants raised about $65 million from the sale of personal seat licenses and another $121 million from naming rights and other corporate partnerships, with Chase Financing backing much of the remainder. The price of the stadium reached nearly $307 million, although, as in all of the cases in this book, ongoing debate continues about the true cost.

A certain amount of public money has gone into the project, despite proclamations to the contrary. San Francisco used a tax-increment financing plan to provide money for infrastructure and neighborhood improvements around the new ballpark. The Giants received some tax breaks; and the city agreed to fund the construction of all needed amenities outside the park, including a light-rail stop and street lighting, and provided all water, sewerage, and other public service connections. Nevertheless, the Giants are able to say that the park itself was built with 100 percent private financing and no public dollars.

Despite some linguistic maneuvers, the important point still holds: the Giants got fewer public dollars for their new stadium. The key to this difference is the chemistry between San Francisco's growth coalition and the potential efficacy of manipulating community self-esteem. San Francisco certainly has a corporate community far stronger and more cohesive than those in Hartford and Minneapolis and probably just as strong (or stronger) as those in Cincinnati, Cleveland, and Pittsburgh. But San Francisco's local growth coalition doesn't really need a stadium to attract executive talent or create the image of being first-rate. The rest of San Francisco can do that all by itself. Property values in the city are among the highest in the nation, and it would be laughable to argue that those values will decline if the Giants leave town.

Equally important, San Francisco has an affluent population and a large number of corporations willing to buy seat licenses (at least for now). Recognizing the unique features of the city, Jack Bair, the Giants' senior vice president and corporate counsel, said in an interview on Minnesota Public Radio (http://news.mpr.org/features/199911):

> I can't speak for other communities. We faced our unique problem here in San Francisco and tried to fashion a solution that would work here. We also are blessed with having a community that has

enjoyed great economic times and also is the home to many of the
most successful companies: . . . the gateway to Silicon Valley. We
have a very affluent population here. And so we have been successful where other communities might not be able to be successful.

Despite San Francisco's powerful local growth coalition, appeals
to community self-esteem would have fallen on deaf ears. Many residents seemed perfectly willing to let the team walk away: after all, they
voted down stadium deals over and over again. Eventually the Giants
chose to stay and build their own park, but that decision may not work
in cities without a strong demand for private seat licenses or enough
money to buy them. Clearly, midsized cities and those fighting population decline are more vulnerable to being manipulated by arguments
about major league status.

STADIUM BATTLES AND COMPETING VISIONS OF CITIES

Stadium battles are struggles over competing and contested views of
cities in the United States. Are cities meant to be tourist attractions?
Are they places to improve exchange value (that is, drive up real estate
costs for speculators, sometimes at the expense of poor and middle-
class residents)? Should they be designed to attract high-priced corporate talent—the A players of the world? Are they places where people
live and care about schools, parks, libraries, public safety, traffic con-
gestion, and transportation systems?

The desire to become a tourist destination often informs the ideology of local growth coalitions as they press for new stadiums. In the
postindustrial economy, many cities, desperate for new revenues, have
been chasing elusive tourist dollars, hoping to attract visitors to their
city. There is often a certain faddishness to these attempts. For a while,
many cities were trying to build festival markets in imitation of
Faneuil Hall in Boston (Ehrlich and Dreier 1999). Then cities began
closing streets to create pedestrian shopping malls, mimicking malls in
the suburbs. For the past ten years, building new sports stadiums has
seemed to be the way to get tourists.[4] What we have learned from these
experiences, however, is that the copy cats tend not to do as well as the
originals because the novelty quickly wears off.

Being a tourist destination also depends in large part on uncontrollable things like weather and location. Only the most die-hard football fan will visit Cleveland in early January just to see a football game
in the new lakefront stadium. Pittsburgh is also likely to have a difficult
time attracting tourists, despite two new stadiums and the grand dreams

of city politicians. Unlike Baltimore, Pittsburgh cannot count on a large population within easy driving distance that will come to the new stadium. For a time, Pittsburgh planners considered placing a major tourist attraction between the two new stadiums, but some joked that a steel industry museum might be too depressing. Others imagined a high-tech amusement park but had trouble articulating exactly what that might be. Perhaps they envisioned a very fast roller coaster, with cars shaped like ingots, careening through an abandoned steel plant.

There is also a clear downside to becoming a tourist city. Tourist economies are highly dependent on the health of the national economy; and in recessions, tourist spending lessens significantly. In addition, those economies provide a large number of low-wage service jobs, which can increase inequality in cities. For example, in Phoenix, several proposals are in the works for new single-room occupancy (SRO) housing in the downtown area near Bank One Ballpark. The demand for such housing is intimately related to the quality of jobs produced not just at ballparks but in the tourist economy as a whole. Hotel desk clerks, hot dog vendors, and ticket takers do not make high enough salaries to afford a place to live. Three developers have approached Phoenix Downtown Partnership with plans to build new, modern SROs. They are repackaged versions of the old flophouse hotel, only with amenities such as a security system and a fax machine for residents' use. Despite the high-tech wiring, however, the SRO illustrates a way to provide a very cheap, single room for someone who works in and around the ballpark, the hotel industry, or the restaurant industry and is simply not paid well enough to live anywhere else. A business leader who focuses his attention on downtown development described it this way:

> This is a step above homelessness, obviously. . . . [SROs] are meant to house hospitality workers, students, and others on fixed incomes. They are very small units, your typical SRO, but they have security at the front door, cable TV, a little refrigerator. They have "business centers" in them, a whole bunch of amenities that obviously aren't flophouse amenities. . . . Because our economy is built so much on the hospitality industry, I think there is a pretty good market for it here.

To be fair, some political leaders really do not know how to make their cities more vibrant. They are not sure if investment in schools or basic work force training will pay off in the long run. Dependent on being reelected, politicians tend to favor a more visible project over a less visible investment in job training or public schools that might pay off only gradually over several decades. Sadly, though, sports stadiums may not be our urban saviors. As we showed in chapter 2, a growing body of anecdotal experiences and systematic research show they stimulate little economic growth. They probably provide notoriety and good publicity in the short run as well as temporarily shoring up a city's reputation. Nevertheless, this advantage is surely waning as the stadium boom peaks. These days, people seem much less excited about the next new stadium. Baltimore can only happen once. Recent data show that the increase in attendance at new stadiums is declining and that the honeymoon effect is lasting for a shorter period. Nine major league baseball teams have established new lows for single-game attendance in their stadiums, and all nine built new stadiums in the 1990s or 2000s (*Philadelphia Inquirer*, April 28, 2002, D18).

Stadiums don't seem to promote the kind of mixed residential, retail, and business development that actually builds vibrant neighborhoods in the long run. When urban governments finance new stadiums, they are really spending hundreds of millions of dollars to entertain suburbanites. Unfortunately, the political relationship between city and suburb is often so contentious that there is little regional cooperation between poorer and wealthier municipalities in funding stadiums. In Philadelphia, for example, the city decided to put a rental-car tax in place to help fund the stadium. City leaders approached suburban leaders about the possibility of instituting this tax in all of the counties surrounding Philadelphia. Not surprisingly, the suburbs politely declined. (Some local officials, we were told, actually laughed out loud.) As a result, the rental surcharge applies only to renting a car *in the city*. So city residents, who are generally poorer, must pay an extra tax for a rental car. Granted, this particular tax was designed as a visitor tax, but it will still have a detrimental effect on city residents who need a rental car.

OPPOSITION AND THE GROWTH COALITION

It's tough being opposed to new sports stadiums, especially when you are up against a powerful local growth coalition that can obfuscate its vested interests in such social policies. Although we have described the role of opposition groups in the cities we have studied, we now want to place this opposition into the larger context that frames our conclusions. That is, what does the plight of new stadium opponents have to say about the state of democracy in the United States? We have seen several well meaning and occasionally well organized opposition groups rolled over by pro-subsidy forces. Supposedly democratic venues like referendums are almost inherently unfair because opposition groups cannot raise anywhere near the money generated by stadium advocates. Indeed, in cities such as San Diego, new stadium advocates wanted very much to have a public referendum because they thought it would be easier to manipulate the general public than to get prompt action from the local government without a public mandate. And what are opponents to think when apparent referendum victories such as those in Pittsburgh and Phoenix are simply ignored by stadium advocates? Why even bother?

There is no monolithic pattern to these opposition groups. Like the growth coalitions they battle with, their existence, shape, and form are firmly tied to the social characteristics of a particular city. In Minneapolis, they coalesce around an anti-corporate welfare position that has roots in Minnesota's longstanding populist tradition. In Pittsburgh, one of the most effective opposition campaigns came from a wealthy newspaper owner with a libertarian streak, who just happened to live there. If Richard Scaife had lived in a different city, the opposition in Pittsburgh would have been far less effective; and plan A probably would have passed or at least been much closer. Of course, there is no guarantee that Scaife could have organized an effective opposition in another city because that city might have had social characteristics constraining his actions. Arizona's relatively elderly population generated a fairly formidable opposition in Phoenix that was rooted almost totally in an anti-tax philosophy. They were simply ignored, however; and their single-minded anti-tax focus prevented them from forming more sustainable alliances with smaller bands of opponents with different philosophies. Members of Philadelphia's relatively middle-class opposition were effective in preventing a downtown baseball stadium from being built in their neighborhood but were largely irrelevant to the more general issue of building the ballpark in the first place. Interestingly, Cincinnati's patchwork opposition, outspent more than ten to one by an extremely powerful local growth coalition, might have actually won its referendum if not for the Cleveland Browns' bad timing in leaving Ohio. We suspect, although we can't be sure, that with such an outcome in Cincinnati's election, the local growth coalition would have dealt with it like Pittsburgh's did.

How can citizens build more effective opposition to subsidizing private stadiums with public dollars? One reform might be to create spending limits on referendums that concern stadium funding. This would at least even the playing field. Our research shows that proponents typically outspend opponents by at least a ten-to-one margin and sometimes much more. At the same time, we are aware that such a reform might not make a difference in the long run. Stadium proponents have ways to manipulate the community even without a funding disparity. Newspapers can still run an avalanche of editorials and print home team press releases documenting the economic pain that the franchise is enduring. Corporate elites can still pressure politicians or more subtly influence the political discussion over "correct" forms of economic growth and development. The teams can continue to threaten that they will leave the city, and politicians can wring their hands over the tragedy of becoming a minor league city. We are also wary of campaign finance reform because ultimately the referendums only seem to matter if ballpark proponents win, not if they lose. With that in mind, opposition groups might decide not even to bother trying to influence the outcomes via a popular referendum.

Stadium opponents often try to pressure the local sports teams who seem to benefit most from these policies, arguing that using public money for private stadiums is a form of corporate welfare for wealthy team owners. Opponents might publicize the finances of the team and its owners (in hopes of embarrassing them) or organize a boycott. But based on what we have learned in our research, these tactics might not be very effective. For one thing, it is no surprise that teams are trying to use tax money to build their stadiums. They are forever trying to increase revenues through soaring ticket prices and six-dollar beers, so why not try to get the community as a whole to pay for a new stadium? Owners are lodged in an economic system (professional sports) that leads them to press for more than the other guy gets. So an obvious reform, suggested by other observers, involves pressing for reform of the economic structure of the leagues, which would benefit all teams and cities: for example, national legislation limiting the amount (or percent) that a municipality can spend on a sports stadium or laws mandating that leagues pay a substantial share of new stadium costs. Other possibilities include placing limits on teams' mobility (particularly after receiving a large public subsidy in the stadium), thereby undercutting any future threat to leave town.[5]

More important, however, our identification of the growth coalition's leading role in building publicly financed stadiums suggests a different tactic for any opposition. Opponents need to target these nonsports organizations and try to raise awareness about their manipulation of policymakers and their influence over dominant ideologies. So instead of pressuring sports teams, opponents might pressure local businesses that advocate using public dollars for private stadiums. In Cincinnati, this could mean boycotting Chiquita bananas. In Pittsburgh, this might mean pulling accounts from PNC Bank or refusing to buy Heinz ketchup. The strategy has actually been used in Denver, although in a twisted sort of way. As we mentioned in chapter 6, while there was no real opposition to the Broncos' new football stadium, there was intense opposition to Invesco's attempt to change the cherished Mile High name. Apparently, some Broncos' fans have been trying to organize a boycott against the company until it completely removes its name from the ballpark. The irony here is that this was the only naming rights deal we are aware of that went toward the public share of the ballpark instead of the private one. It is not clear if the tactic has been successful or if Denver residents should even want it to be successful: what if Invesco takes back its money and forces the city to come up with another $60 million?

A successful opposition should also adapt to the shifting strategies of local growth coalitions and other stadium advocates. While some attention still must be paid to critiquing the alleged economic benefits of new stadiums, even more should be paid to countering arguments that link new stadiums with community self-esteem and community collective conscience. In other words, opponents must have a good response to "Keep Cincinnati a Major League City" and "Keep Cleveland from Becoming Akron." They must articulate ways in which public dollars can be better spent to keep their city vibrant and remind people that the public coffers are not bottomless. A stronger connection must be made for community development, stronger neighborhoods, lower crime, a vibrant downtown, and better schools instead of new ballparks. It might be easiest for opponents to highlight these community trade-offs in cities where advocates have mostly abandoned strategies that justify new stadiums in economic terms. By admitting that stadiums will not expand the public till, advocates can no longer make arguments that there will soon be enough money for new stadiums *and* new libraries *and* new public schools.

Thus, opponents must force a public realization that there are actual choices to be made about which of these amenities contributes most to enhancing community self-esteem and community collective conscience. At the moment, sports stadiums have been cornering the market on what makes a city first-class. But this perception is not inevitable, even though it will be hard to change. Perhaps political representatives and corporate leaders can be educated about the possible consequences of "wearing their civic hats" or "leaving their marks" through new stadiums rather than in less visible ways. For example, in 2001, racial unrest erupted in Cincinnati just as the city built two new sports stadiums that were supposed to enhance community collective conscience. We think that unfortunate situation in Cincinnati may foreshadow events in other cities where good stadiums have been defined as more socially important than good jobs, good libraries, and good schools.

THE FUTURE OF DEMOCRACY

We began the book by saying how surprised we were when Pittsburgh's plan A was overwhelmingly defeated. Beyond this surprise were some very mixed feelings. As sociologists beginning a long research project, we were disheartened that our very first case study was unfolding in the exact opposite direction from the way we had predicted. But as sociologists opposed to increased inequalities of wealth and power, we were delighted and fascinated to see that Pittsburgh residents had successfully derailed a policy that we believed would intensify the city's inequalities. Of course, our sadness and glee reversed themselves as plan B worked its way through Pittsburgh's power structure. What's the point, we thought, in even trying to explore and address the community dangers of spending public dollars on private stadiums?

We soon discovered the point. After finishing our interviews in Pittsburgh, we stopped at a neighborhood bar for a couple of Iron City draughts. We chatted with a pair of patrons to see what they thought about the new stadium plans. Both men were in their thirties, had families, rooted with great passion for their home teams, and had voted against plan A. When we told them it looked like plan B was almost a done deal and that it would require no public vote, we expected they would be angry. Instead, they just shrugged their shoulders in resignation. They talked about how nobody downtown really listened to the people in the neighborhoods, said that the team owners wanted to suck as much money out of the city as possible, and told us there was nothing regular people could really do about it. When we asked if their feelings would lead them to stop rooting for the Pirates and the Steelers, they looked at us like we had six heads. Let's not be silly, they implied.

But then we talked with them about what we had learned regarding plan B and how it was being influenced by the Allegheny Conference (which they had never heard of) to serve corporate interests well beyond the sports teams. We told them that a mayoral assistant was quietly orchestrating much of plan B while Mayor Murphy remained a figurehead. They were genuinely interested, and we detected that some of their resignation was turning into anger. We don't think they were going to run home and burn their team paraphernalia or throw out their Westinghouse appliances, but they seemed to realize that professional sports was about much more than the game on the field or even the team owners' bank accounts. At that point, we decided our project was worthwhile.

We really had two goals in writing this book. The first was to provide a behind-the-scenes look at the social policies that allocate public dollars for private stadiums, why these policies get implemented despite increasing opposition to them, and why it is relatively easier to implement these policies in certain cities. Our second goal was to examine the almost hypnotic effect of professional sports and argue that publicly subsidized stadiums may be more harmful than helpful to the vast majority of people living in American cities, despite a lot of rhetoric insisting that they are beneficial. To make this more critical argument, we have tried to show how funding private stadiums with public dollars is not just about sports and sports teams. Instead, it reflects much larger issues about social power, inequality, and the nature of democratic societies. We believe that using public dollars for private stadiums is another mechanism for transferring social resources from the not-so-powerful to the already powerful and that it is likely to further polarize social inequality in the United States. Urban schools will continue to deteriorate, high-quality jobs will continue to leave town, and basic health care will continue to be inaccessible to an increasing percentage of city residents. Meanwhile, billions of dollars of public money continue to be spent on ostentatious sports palaces that cater to the whims of rich, powerful individuals and organizations at the expense of more important community needs.

This trade-off between the needs of the many and the needs of the few was played out recently in our home city of Philadelphia. The local growth coalition, weak though it is, has been pushing for years to lower the city wage tax that is levied on all working city residents (4.5 percent) and nonresidents (3.9 percent) who are employed in Philadelphia. Many believe that the high wage tax leads many businesses and residents to leave the city for the suburbs. Former mayor Ed Rendell, along with city council, started to reduce the tax in hopes that his move would draw new businesses to Philadelphia and keep existing ones from leaving. But in 2002, current mayor John Street announced he wanted to slow down or stop these tax reductions because the city could no longer afford them. Halting the planned reductions would add $120 million to the city treasury, which Street said was sorely needed. The mayor warned that the city would have to close fire stations, recreation centers, and libraries if the wage tax continued to be reduced.

The ensuing dialogue about the wage cut was more interesting for what it failed to mention than for what it did. Not a single councilperson, a single business leader, a single newspaper, a single TV news show, or a single DJ on sports radio brought up the several hundred million dollars the city was spending on the two new stadiums. It was as if public funding for these stadiums had no relationship to any real or perceived fiscal problems in Philadelphia. Meanwhile, Pennsylvania has threatened to take over public education in Philadelphia and has already started privatizing some schools, leaving many of the poorest city children's education in the hands of for-profit companies such as Edison Inc., which has never been able to make a profit. Philadelphia had to legally threaten the state government to release $75 million of promised funds for the city schools. This was the same government that had practically begged its professional baseball and football teams to accept hundreds of millions of dollars for four new stadiums and whose leaders worked behind the scenes to line up the necessary votes for passage.

We waited for a member of the business community, which had never been thrilled with the new stadiums anyway, to point out these hypocrisies. We know from our interviews that Philadelphia's business community was more interested in education than in new stadiums. But the inevitability of spending public dollars on stadiums rather than education had become completely embedded in the city's dominant ideology. Indeed, the case is a shining example of third-dimensional power at work, in which members of the community have been conditioned to ignore certain policy options. Policies that exacerbate social inequalities have become almost automatic. Our hope, then, in writing this book is to expose these seemingly natural and automatic policies as real choices made by real people that could have been decided differently. So long as cities keep spending lots of public dollars on new sports stadiums rather than on public schools, affordable health care, and safe neighborhoods, social conditions will continue to deteriorate for a great number of urban residents. Perhaps we need an entirely new vision for what makes an American city a major league city.

Appendix: Methodology

We wish to say a few words about our methodological approach and some strategic choices that we made during the writing of this book. We include this statement in part because our methods are a bit different from those of traditional social science research and also because we hope to share some of the lessons we learned in writing the book. In other words, we wish to be as clear as possible about how we conducted our study, with the hope of offering some insights and ideas to others who might like to conduct research in a similar way or improve on some of the things we have tried to do.

We decided to study the public funding of professional sports stadiums because, as economic and political sociologists, we found it both fascinating and relevant to important social issues. Each of us had already written a book on economic and political processes in large public battles: one on the use of Chapter 11 corporate bankruptcy as a strategic weapon, the other on why some nuclear power plants open while others don't. In those books, we developed ideas related to growth coalitions, corporate strategies, growth ideologies, and fantasy documents. We were always dissatisfied with the simplistic explanation that greedy owners wanted corporate welfare in order to build new stadiums. The matter appeared to be more complicated; we suspected that there was a lot more going on in the construction of new stadiums than the naked eye could detect.

Our suspicion was quickly confirmed when we began studying Pittsburgh. As we've mentioned, we were quite surprised when the Pittsburgh referendum was defeated—and even more surprised that it was defeated so handily. Because we had predicted just the opposite result, we immediately set out to determine what was going on so we could use Pittsburgh as a counter-example of normally successful attempts to build private stadiums with public dollars. It turned out, of course, that our initial prediction was correct; and Pittsburgh was scratched from the counter-example list. Switching categories is messy for the methodologically rigid social scientist but is pure delight for a social scientist who loves trying to understand the puzzles of political process.

In addition to deciding what to do with Pittsburgh, we faced the larger problem of deciding which cities to actually study—a particular difficulty with cities that did not precisely fit into our growth coalition model. Because of the qualitative nature of our research as well as time and resource constraints, we couldn't possibly study every relevant city. We were discovering that every city had its own individual story, and we debated which needed to be represented. We knew we wanted some geographic diversity because we detected a difference between Rust Belt cities and Sun Belt cities, although we couldn't articulate that difference clearly at the time. In the end, we did include cities that have still not loosened the public purse strings (notably Minneapolis), although we argue this is true not so much because of the strength of any opposition group or missteps of a team owner but because of the vacuum left by a declining growth coalition. And we remain acutely aware that, by the time this book is published, things may have changed yet again!

Our interest in the process of building these stadiums also generated methodological challenges. Because many cities were in the middle of that process, our research sometimes felt comparable to throwing a ball at a moving target. We had to keep checking and updating what we had found and follow some of the stories right up to the point of publication. And we're sure things will happen in the ten-month production period that also need to be included. It would have been much easier to choose only cities with finished stadiums. But it also would have been much less interesting and exciting because the process itself would have been played out already. Several times we were in cities where the battle was literally unfolding around us. We mentioned in chapter 1 the e-mail barrage in Pittsburgh. We also got to talk to Hartford's new stadium advocates minutes after they got off the phone with a Patriots' representative. In San Diego, we were present at city council hearings that allowed us to meet many stadium opponents just after they had spoken out on the stadium issue. These opportunities gave us a great many impressionistic insights into how people felt about certain issues, not just what they said about them.

Once we chose a city, how did we actually conduct our study? We knew we wanted to interview people. Too much existing research relies only on aggregate macroeconomic data or only on secondary sources such as newspaper articles. There is nothing wrong with either of these approaches, but we wanted to go deeper into the stories. We wanted to talk with some of the actual people involved with these initiatives and ask specific questions about why they were involved. Because we are sociologists, we approach the whole story from a particular theoretical perspective, one that is different from the angle that might inform a newspaper reporter. Often, we seek out completely different people and ask completely different questions because we are framing the issue differently.

Like most other people interested in the topic, we spoke to the obvious people involved in stadium battles: team executives, politicians, and opposition leaders. But our overriding concern with the strength of growth coalitions and the strategic choices they make directed us to other people who are rarely interviewed: a city's corporate leaders. Because these people are not always in the spotlight, it was sometimes difficult to figure out whom we needed to interview. So before visiting each city, we read as much as we could about the stadium battles in that city. The Internet was a tremendous help because we were able to access at no cost the archives of newspapers across the country. Unfortunately, many newspapers have since begun charging for online access; it would have been much harder to start this book in 2002 instead of 1998.

After familiarizing ourselves with the nuts and bolts of the stadium story, we sometimes contacted local newspaper reporters for direction to the most important players. We found these reporters to be excellent resources and suggest they are vastly underused by academic researchers. Usually, one or two reporters in each city had covered the stadium battle closely. Because they knew so much, they could guide us to exactly the people who made for the best interviews, once we described the kinds of issues we wanted to understand. Many times, a reporter told us, "No, that isn't who you want to talk with. This is who you *really* want to talk to!" Reporters also made suggestions about what we should ask, with comments like "Because I am a reporter, I could never get anyone to really talk about x or y; so you guys should try asking about this."

Once we decided whom to interview, we usually sent introductory letters explaining our project, made multiple phone calls, and sent multiple faxes to arrange interviews for the few days we would be in town. Overall, these people were enormously cooperative. We received very few refusals; in fact, one initial refusal eventually turned into an interview. Most people gave up their time generously and talked at great length on the topic, sometimes during the business day but also after hours during dinner or drinks. We thank them all for their time and truthfulness. Our goal was always to understand the way in which each person saw the battle in his or her city, and everyone helped enormously in this regard.

We conducted formal interviews with about sixty-five people, including top corporate executives, team owners and executives, politicians, and opposition leaders. We talked more informally with dozens of others as we traveled around the cities. Most of our interviews were open-ended and wide-ranging. We usually had a general game plan going in, such as "Let's find out how the corporate community is structured." Sometimes we were armed with specific questions that only this person could answer, such as "Where did the county get the money to bail out the city?" We tried always to include questions about how the person viewed his or her city and the role of sports stadiums there. We transcribed all of the interviews ourselves, and we highly recommend that researchers undertake this painstaking process themselves rather than hire other people to do the work. If you are the one hitting that transcriber foot pedal every few seconds, you come to know your data very, very well. In addition, there are inflections on the recordings that would mean nothing to a third party but can change the whole meaning of a quotation. In every respect, these interviews were a priceless source of information.

Another source of primary data was our physical exploration of the city under study. We spent most of our free time walking around the stadium (if it was already built) or the areas contemplated for new stadiums (if it wasn't yet built). We visited the Flats in Cleveland to see what all the fuss was about. We toured the various sites being proposed by stadium advocates in Minneapolis. We visited restaurants and bars and chatted with people on the streets, especially in neighborhoods surrounding stadiums (or proposed stadiums). We took photographs whenever we could. Certainly, our casual conversations do not reflect a representative or random sample of city dwellers, but we did gain some strong impressions of people in each city. While we plead guilty to the charge of not being methodologically pure here, we think there is much to learn from the time we spent in the trenches as well as by analyzing aggregate data.

Once we were in the midst of the study, we wrestled continuously with the idea of how to organize the material into a book. There were two obvious choices. One was to organize the book as a series of case studies around each of our nine cities. That way we could retain the wonderful "city stories," as we came to call them. We became convinced that you cannot understand stadium battles without understanding how a battle fits within a city's unique social character. For example, you cannot understand the dynamics in Cleveland without gaining a handle on how the stadium battle fits into the historic development of the city's growth coalition, the tensions between those who favor spending on large downtown projects and those who favor spending in the neighborhoods, the impact when Art Modell moved the Browns, the community self-esteem of Clevelanders confronting the devastation of deindustrialization, and the county's SAFE crisis. Similarly, without understanding how politics are evolving in the growing city of Phoenix, the tension between the city and the county governments, the power vacuum that exists in the city, and the anti-tax sentiments of an older population, you cannot make sense of the antagonisms that played out over the funding of the BOB.

We soon discovered, however, that writing a book that handled each city as a separate case study and thus saving all comparative material for the end was probably not the wisest approach. While the cities are all different in many ways, they aren't always *completely* different. Nine stories in a row would become redundant; and readers might not make it to the end the book, where we would finally do some comparing and contrasting. Because we were totally committed to being comparative, we vetoed this particular format.

The other obvious choice was to organize the chapters around important analytic issues or themes such as local growth coalitions, city-county relations, demographic changes, strong mayoral–weak mayoral governments, referendums, and community self-esteem. This is the more common approach of academic researchers and is often used to isolate variables in order to test hypotheses and theories. We found several problems with the approach. First, our sample is not large enough to really think in terms more common to larger quantitative studies. Second, as soon as we tried to take this approach, we found ourselves delving into the city stories to explain why city-county relations mattered in, say, Phoenix but less so in San Diego; and as soon we started writing about this issue, we began saying, "And then this led to this, and then this was because of this, and then this happened because this had happened. . . ." We believed strongly that the substantive issues were all connected and that it was silly to try to control some of them to demonstrate the prowess of others.

We finally settled on a middle ground between the two approaches: striving to retain the distinctiveness of the city stories and all of the insights they provided, while being as comparative as possible within the city stories. We decided to organize each story around our two-part analytical framework: the strength and cohesiveness of growth coalitions, and the strategies they employ. This gives each chapter some common bond while maintaining the integrity of each city's story. We begin the city chapters with studies of single cities, then increase the comparative focus by beginning to pair cities in subsequent chapters, and then end with a contrast between two cities with very different growth coalitions. We purposefully finish with the Pittsburgh-Philadelphia chapter because it highlights, in a comparative fashion, some of the analytical points we make in the entire book. By organizing the chapters in this way, we hope to take the reader through the process we ourselves went through—starting with what we thought was a clear model, finding all sorts of variations on that model, and then realizing the model was solid yet far more complicated than we had originally suspected.

Finally, we would like to go on record as supporters of the marvels of collaborative research. There are so many ways in which this project is geometrically better than it would have been if either of us had worked alone. First, there was the sheer quantity of research, which benefited from a division of labor. Generally, each of us took charge of certain cities, learning about the stadium initiative and setting up the interviews after some consultation. Eight-hour car rides and five-hour plane flights would often be spent bringing the other person up to speed so we could both be knowledgeable when conducting interviews. This division of labor also helped when transcribing the interviews.

A second specific benefit of collaboration became clear during interviews. We developed a technique in which one of us would ask a series of questions while the other listened carefully to develop the next series. Then we would switch. When discussing very complicated issues, it is hard to ask questions and process answers at the same time; so our collaborative technique turned out to be helpful in making the most of our interview time.

Of course, both the hardest and most rewarding aspect of collaboration is actually writing up the material in some coherent fashion. Here, again, we divided the labor, with each taking primary responsibility for different chapters. When finishing an initial draft, we sent it to the other for serious editing and rewriting before the manuscript returned to the first person. A typical chapter bounced back and forth between us five to fifteen times before we "put that baby to bed." At the best of times, one person helped the other think or write more clearly until we had something that really sounded good. At the worst of times, we heatedly debated points where one of us felt completely disconnected from what the other was thinking. Fortunately, there were far more good moments than bad, and the collaborative process forced us to think more clearly about the issues. The result is a book that was worked and reworked more times than it would have been if we were writing alone. We hope our rewarding collaboration is reflected in the final product.

Notes

Chapter 1

1. The growth machine idea has been widely used by sociologists since it was first introduced by Molotch (1976). Other examples include Whitt (1982), Friedland and Palmer (1984), Logan and Molotch (1987), Eckstein (1997), and Lauria (1997).

2. Useem (1984) argues that this leadership from financial organizations provides a classwide rationality that subsumes conflicts among other competing capitalist firms. For a comprehensive examination of how banks influence the corporate community, see Mintz and Schwartz (1985).

3. Such CEO-only groups include the Cincinnati Business Committee, Cleveland Tomorrow, the Allegheny Conference (Pittsburgh), Greater Philadelphia First, the Bay Area Council (San Francisco) and the Greater Denver Corporation (now defunct).

4. Governments are always involved with these coalitions, but the form and content of this involvement varies greatly.

5. A similar typology is developed by Alford and Friedland (1985), who prefer the term *domains of power*.

6. Within political sociology and political science, this first-dimensional school of thought often goes by the name *pluralism*. This theory of power maintains that democracy is ensured when there is competition among political elites for the support of the masses. For pluralism's classical roots, see Dahl (1982), Polsby (1980), Huntington (1980), and Verba and Nie (1978).

7. See Euchner (1993) and Crenson (1971).

8. Gramsci (1971) might say that sports have a hegemonic place in the dominant ideology. For example, see Bissinger (2000) on the importance of high school football and Shulman and Bowen (2000) on college athletics. This exaggeration of the importance of sports is not limited to the United States but may express itself differently across cultures.

9. A cogent and readable presentation of corporate liberalism (and competing ideologies) can be found in Greenberg (1985). See also Goodman (1986).

10. This is the key difference between a local growth coalition perspective and what is sometimes called urban regime theory (see Stone 1989, 1993), which acknowledges that certain individuals and organizations have inordinate influence over public policy. Ultimately, however, local governments are *not* predisposed to being captured by these powerful parties and can resist this power and form a commercial republic that better meets overall community needs.

11. We thank Ed Royce (1993) for helping us think about this issue more clearly.

Chapter 2

1. The National Hockey League's Minnesota Wild actually play in neighboring St. Paul at the Xcel Energy Center. This is close enough to allow the Twin Cities to claim all four major professional sports teams.

2. See Euchner (1993, 55).

3. Besides, the gold rush analogy would work much better with the 49ers than with the Raiders.

4. Revenue sharing is complicated and differs by sport. Teams try to increase revenues that are not subject to sharing with other teams to gain a competitive advantage. In general, teams are usually able to keep most of ticket sales (in some leagues the visiting team gets a share) and all of the concession sales. This is one reason for the proliferation of club-style seating. The teams price the ticket in two parts. The first and smaller part is the actual price of the ticket, which is subject to revenue sharing. The second and larger piece is the fee for having access to premium seating. This is treated as a concession and is not subject to revenue sharing. See Noll and Zimbalist (1997) for more details on revenue-sharing rules. According to the new labor agreement in Major League Baseball, a modest revenue-sharing plan will require teams to contribute 34 percent of net local revenues, after ballpark expenses, to a pool to be redistributed among all teams. We predict that "ballpark expenses" will rise dramatically in the coming years.

5. In fact, Baade has updated his previous study and has concluded that the newer-generation stadiums are not very different (Baade 1994, Baade and Sanderson 1997). For a comprehensive look at the relationship between teams and cities, see Danielson (1997). For a complete listing of references on sports stadiums and economic issues, see http://garnet.acns.fsu.edu/~tchapin/stadia/stad-ref.html.

6. For more details, see Eckstein and Delaney (2002).

7. Some social scientists have criticized the notion of collective conscience on the grounds that it is condescending to preindustrial societies. We understand this criticism but employ the idea in a nonpejorative way. Our main point is that powerful actors are trying to convince citizens that collective conscience, or a sense of solidarity and belonging, is desirable, obtainable, and intimately linked with sports and sports stadiums.

Chapter 3

1. The Reds then objected to this agreement claiming that it violated the "equal treatment" provision of its lease.

2. Apparently, these fears did not apply to the price of tickets themselves, which were slated to be 14 percent higher in the new stadium than in the old one.

3. The county was spared this expense because the stadium opened just in time for the first exhibition game.

4. These companies are Proctor and Gamble (18), Kroger (28), Federated Department Stores (78), American Financial Group (331), Cinergy (415), and Mercantile Stores (447).

5. This is a smaller working group of company representatives who are interested specifically in downtown issues, much like Philadelphia's Center City District and Phoenix's Phoenix Downtown Partnership.

6. Lindner became majority owner in 1999. As mentioned, his company, Great American Insurance, a subsidiary of American Financial, purchased naming rights to the Reds' ballpark. The money goes to the team and is counted as part of the team's contribution toward stadium costs.

7. Detroit has recently built a new downtown baseball-only stadium. Although we have not studied the city in detail, early reports intimate that the stadium has not led to an economic miracle.

8. Marge Schott was serving a suspension at the time we conducted our research in Cincinnati.

9. We believe this happens for two main reasons. First, the city government's waning power decreases even the slight possibility that everyday political players might challenge the wisdom of publicly financed stadiums, which simultaneously makes cities more vulnerable to promises that link stadiums with direct and indirect economic payoffs. Second, a power shift to the suburbs reflects a juxtaposition between what might be called city ideology (relatively liberal) and suburban ideology (relatively conservative), with the latter more sympathetic to the activities of local growth coalitions.

10. We think it is ironic that the growth coalition was defeated when it tried to eliminate the city manager system, which might actually be more beneficial to its long-term interests.

Chapter 4

1. The title of this chapter plays off the fact that many have called Cleveland "the comeback city" since it has built sports stadiums (see Keating 1997). The story we tell, however, is more about the comeback of the local growth coalition in setting the city's urban agenda. For more on the Cleveland story, see also Austrian and Rosentraub (1997).

2. This book is not about indoor arenas, which have their own economics. But it is impossible to discuss Jacobs Field without also discussing Gund Arena, which was also part of the project called Gateway Development.

3. Ironically, Cincinnati's pro-stadium boosters couldn't have been happier (see chapter 3).

4. Kucinich's refusal to sell off the city's electric company, Muny Light, led to Cleveland Trust Bank's decision to put the city into default. This, among other things, was seen by many in Cleveland's corporate community as a national embarrassment.

5. We can't help but point out the hyperbole in these stadium tales. In the last chapter, Bedinghaus was like Winston Churchill; here, Chema is the Henry Kissinger of Cleveland.

6. The local teachers' union draws a direct link between tax abatements for businesses in Cleveland and the state of the public school system, arguing that generous tax-abatement policies have cost the school system on the order of $20 million per year (see Adams and Parr 1998).

7. As luck would have it, the referendum on extending the sin tax came one day after Art Modell announced he would be moving the Browns to Baltimore. The parking tax was not subject to voter approval.

Chapter 5

1. Weiner (2000) provides a comprehensive analysis of all these attempts. He generally concludes that the attempts failed for a confluence of reasons, including missteps by the Twins' ownership and supportive politicians, a declining civic leadership, and the often-fractious politics of the Twin Cities.

2. This was the first time this person had heard of Schueler's decision, so we were able to witness an unedited reaction. Schueler eventually resigned from the *Star-Tribune* in 2001. He was replaced by J. Keith Moyer, also from the McClatchey group and not from the Twin Cities.

3. While the city of Hartford itself has only about 120,000 residents, the Hartford metropolitan area has a population of 1.2 million, about the same as the Nashville metro area.

Chapter 6

1. Much of this information comes from random GDC minutes deposited in the Denver Public Library. They were not organized in any particular way. See also Hornby (1997).

2. These documents were accidentally found in a special collection of the Denver Public Library.

3. The somewhat long construction time was due to Denver's harsh winters.

4. We are not sure why Omaha was the comparison city of choice, and nobody we asked in Denver could offer an explanation. Some traditions are hard to explain.

5. Toronto's Skydome also has a retractable roof, but it takes hours to open or close and is extremely noisy.

6. For more details of these events and many others leading to the new Diamondbacks' franchise, see Colangelo (1999).

7. The mainstream press was very much in favor (editorially) of the new stadium, so we are confident this information is not based on journalistic exaggeration.

8. This deal between the city and the Chargers will be discussed later in the chapter.

9. This was the April 1, 1999, deadline discussed in the section "How to Win an Election."

10. For example, nobody even challenged the architects' assertion that it would be great if the visiting team could stay in this new hotel adjacent to the ballpark. The teams are already staying in some other San Diego hotel, so moving hotels would offer no real economic benefit to the city.

Chapter 7

1. The state had, for all intents and purposes, agreed to fund these stadiums a few years earlier. The 1999 vote finalized the commitment and established the numbers.

2. The Pennsylvania legislature had to approve the proposed increase before it was voted on locally.

3. There was also some talk of diverting to the stadiums certain revenue streams promised to the convention center.

4. Stafford was executive director of the Allegheny Conference.

5. Leeper was later appointed to head the newly created Sports and Exhibition Authority, which would oversee the new stadiums.

6. Apparently, Leeper has a veto as head of the Sports and Exhibition Authority (*Pittsburgh Post-Gazette*, September 2, 2001, B1).

7. The football Eagles did not desire a downtown location, so the defeat we discuss is almost entirely about the baseball Phillies.

8. There were some minor disagreements about where to put the Reds' ballpark in Cincinnati, but they never became a major issue that threatened to sidetrack the stadium.

9. In fact, in late 2002, Greater Philadelphia First and the Philadelphia Chamber of Commerce agreed to merge. This is much less likely to happen in Cleveland or Cincinnati, where the largest corporations obtain great benefits from having a lobbying group separate from the much broader business interests represented by the chamber.

10. This was the fantasy document we examined in chapter 2.

Chapter 8

1. The key to Lukes's (1974) third dimension of power is the distinction between perceived and real interests.

2. This is similar to our discussion of urban regime theory in chapter 1.

3. The population of Los Angeles increased by 6 percent between 1990 and 2000, despite losing the NFL Rams.

4. We thank Norman Krumholz for helping us think about stadiums in this way.

5. Several analysts have offered a host of suggestions for the reform of professional sports. See, for example, Costas (2000) and the final chapter of Weiner (2000).

Bibliography

Adams, B., and J. Parr. 1998. *Boundary Crossers*. College Park, Md.: Academy of Leadership.

Adriaen's Landing Preliminary Master Plan. 1998. Hartford, Conn.: Adriaen's Landing Team.

Alford, R., and R. Friedland. 1985. *Powers of Theory*. Cambridge: Cambridge University Press.

Anderson Study. 1997. "The Economic Impact of a Ballpark in Center City Philadelphia." Philadelphia: Arthur Anderson, LLP, commissioned by the Central Philadelphia Development Corporation.

Austrian, Z., and M. Rosentraub. 1997. "Cleveland's Gateway to the Future." In *Sports, Jobs, and Taxes*, edited by R. Noll and A. Zimbalist, 355–84. Washington, D.C.: Brookings Institute.

Baade, R. 1994. "Stadiums, Sports and Economic Development: Assessing the Reality." Heartland Policy Study, no. 62. Chicago: Heartland Institute.

———. 1996. "Sports As a Catalyst for Metropolitan Economic Development." *Journal of Urban Affairs* 18: 1–17.

Baade, R., and R. Dye. 1990. "The Impact of Stadiums and Professional Sports on Metropolitan Area Development." *Growth and Change* 22 (spring): 1–14.

Baade, R., and A. Sanderson. 1997. "The Employment Effect of Teams and Sports Facilities." In *Sports, Jobs, and Taxes*, edited by R. Noll and A. Zimbalist, 92–118. Washington, D.C.: Brookings Institute.

Bernstein, M. 1998. "Sports Stadium Boondoggle." *Public Interest* 132: 45–57.

Bissinger, H. 2000. *Friday Night Lights*. New York: Da Capo.

Blair, J., and D. Swindell. 1997. "Sports, Politics and Economics: The Cincinnati Story." In *Sports, Jobs and Taxes*, edited by R. Noll and A. Zimbalist, 282–323. Washington, D.C.: Brookings Institute.

Carreno, C. 2002. "San Diego in Season." *Food and Wine* (August): 44–50.

Clarke, L. 1999. *Mission Improbable: Using Fantasy Documents to Tame Disasters*. Chicago: University of Chicago Press.

Coates, D., and B. Humphreys. 2000. "The Stadium Gambit and Local Economic Development." *Regulation* 23: 15–20.

Colangelo, J. 1999. *How You Play the Game*. New York: American Management Association.

Costas, B. 2000. *Fair Ball: A Fan's Case for Baseball*. New York: Broadway Books.

Crenson, M. 1971. *The Un-Politics of Air Pollution*. Baltimore: Johns Hopkins University Press.

Dahl, R. 1982. *Dilemmas of Pluralist Democracy*. New Haven, Conn.: Yale University Press.

Danielson, M. 1997. *Home Team*. Princeton, N.J.: Princeton University Press.

Durkheim, Emile. 1933. *The Division of Labor in Society*. New York: Free Press.

Eckstein, R. 1997. *Nuclear Power and Social Power*. Philadelphia: Temple University Press.

Eckstein, R., and K. Delaney. 2002. "New Sports Stadiums, Community Self-Esteem, and Community Collective Conscience." *Journal of Sport and Social Issues* 26: 235–47.

Ehrlich, B., and P. Dreier. 1999. "The New Boston Discovers the Old: Tourism and the Struggle for a Livable City." In *The Tourist City*, edited by D. Judd and S. Fainstein, 155–78. New Haven, Conn.: Yale University Press.

Euchner, C. 1993. *Playing the Field: Why Sports Teams Move and Cities Fight to Keep Them*. Baltimore: Johns Hopkins University Press.

Friedland, R., and D. Palmer. 1984. "Park Place and Main Street: Business and the Urban Power Structure." *Annual Review of Sociology* 10: 395–416.

Gramsci, A. 1971. *Selections from the Prison Notebooks*. New York: International Publishers.

Greenberg, D. 1985. *Capitalism and the American Political Ideal*. Armonk, N.Y.: Sharpe.

Goodman, R. 1986. *The Last Entrepreneurs*. Boston: South End.

Huntington, S. 1980. *American Politics: The Promise of Disharmony*. Cambridge: Harvard University Press.

Hornby, W. 1997. *Eye on the Horizon: The GDC, 1987–1995*. Denver: Denver Metro Chamber of Commerce.

Keating, R. 1999. "Sports Pork: The Costly Relationship between Major League Sports and Government." Cato Policy Analysis, no. 339. Washington, D.C.: Cato Institute.

Keating, W. D. 1997. "Cleveland, the 'Comeback City': The Politics of Redevelopment and Sports Stadiums amidst Urban Decline." In *Reconstructing Urban Regime Theory: Regulating Urban Politics in a Global Economy*, edited by M. Lauria, 189–205. Thousand Oaks, Calif.: Sage.

Lauria, M., ed. 1997. *Reconstructing Urban Regime Theory*. Thousand Oaks, Calif.: Sage.

Logan, J., and Molotch, H. 1987. *Urban Fortunes*. Berkeley: University of California Press.

Lukes, S. 1974. *Power: A Radical View*. London: Macmillan.

Mills, C. Wright. 1959. *The Sociological Imagination*. New York: Oxford University Press.

Mintz, B., and Schwartz, M. 1985. *The Power Structure of American Business*. Chicago: University of Chicago Press

Molotch, H. 1976. "The City As a Growth Machine." *American Journal of Sociology* 82: 309–30.

Noll, R., and A. Zimbalist. 1997. "Build the Stadium—Create the Jobs!" In *Sports, Jobs, and Taxes*, edited by R. Noll and A. Zimbalist, 1–54. Washington, D.C.: Brookings Institute.

Pollack Study. 1998. "Economic and Fiscal Impact of Bank One Ballpark and Arizona Diamondbacks." Scottsdale, Ariz.: Pollack and Company, commissioned by Phoenix Downtown Partnership.

Polsby, N. 1980. *Community Power and Political Power* (2d ed.). New Haven, Conn.: Yale University Press.

Quirk, J., and R. Fort. 1992. *Pay Dirt: The Business of Professional Team Sports*. Princeton, N.J.: Princeton University Press.

Rosentraub, M. 1996. "Does the Emperor Have New Clothes? A Reply to Robert Baade." *Journal of Urban Affairs* 18: 23–31.

———. 1997. *Major League Losers: The Real Cost of Sports and Who's Paying It*. New York: Basic Books.

Rosentraub, M., D. Swindell, M. Przybylski, and D. Mullins. 1994. "Sport and Downtown Development Strategy: If You Build It, Will Jobs Come?" *Journal of Urban Affairs* 16: 221–39.

Royce, E. 1993. The *Origins of Southern Sharecropping*. Philadelphia: Temple University Press.

Shulman, L., and W. Bowen. 2000. *The Game of Life: College Sports and Educational Values*. Princeton, N.J.: Princeton University Press.

Silverstein, P. n.d. *Economic Impact of Major League Baseball in Denver* (call no. C338.477963). Denver: Denver Public Library, Special Collection on Local Economic History.

"The Stadium Game." 1996. *Economist* 339 (May): 26.

Stone, C. N. 1989. *Regime Politics: Governing Atlanta, 1946–1988*. Lawrence: University of Kansas Press.

———. 1993. "Urban Regimes and the Capacity to Govern: A Political Economy Approach." *Journal of Urban Affairs* 15: 1–28.

Useem, M. 1984. *The Inner Circle: Large Corporations and Business Politics in the U.S. and Great Britain*. New York: Oxford University Press.

Verba, S., and N. Nie 1978. *Participation and Political Equality: A Seven Nation Study*. Cambridge: Cambridge University Press.

Weiner, J. 2000. *Stadium Games: Fifty Years of Big League Greed and Bush League Boondoggles*. Minneapolis: University of Minnesota Press.

Whitt, J. A. 1982. *The Dialectics of Power: Urban Elites and Mass Transportation*. Princeton, N.J.: Princeton University Press.

Zimbalist, A. 1998. "The Economics of Stadiums, Teams and Cities." *Policy Studies Review* 15: 17–29.

Index

221

About the Authors

Kevin J. Delaney is a professor of sociology at Temple University and the author of *Strategic Bankruptcy*. Rick Eckstein is a professor of sociology at Villanova University and the author of *Nuclear Power and Social Power*.

CPSIA information can be obtained at www.ICGtesting.com
Printed in the USA
BVOW011705121011

273475BV00005B/1/P

9 780813 533438